Cities in a Time of Terror

Space, Territory, and Local Resilience

H.V. Savitch

CITIES AND
CONTEMPORARY
SOCIETY

M.E.Sharpe
Armonk, New York
London, England

Library of Congress Cataloging-in-Publication Data

Savitch, H.V.
  Cities in a time of terror : space, territory, and local resilience / by H.V. Savitch.
    p. cm.—(Cities and contemporary society)
  Includes bibliographical references and index.
  ISBN 978-0-7656-1683-8 (cloth : alk. paper) — ISBN 978-0-7656-1684-5 (pbk. : alk. paper)
  1. Terrorism. 2. Urban violence. 3. Cities and towns. I. Title.

HV6431.S29 2008
363.32509173′2—dc22   2007021957

Printed in the United States of America

The paper used in this publication meets the minimum requirements of
American National Standard for Information Sciences
Permanence of Paper for Printed Library Materials,
ANSI Z 39.48-1984.

∞

BM (c)   10   9   8   7   6   5   4   3   2   1
BM (p)   10   9   8   7   6   5   4   3   2   1

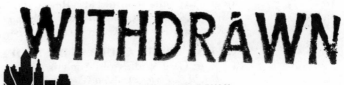

Cities and Contemporary Society

Series Editors: Richard D. Bingham and Larry C. Ledebur,
Cleveland State University

Sponsored by the
Maxine Goodman Levin College of Urban Affairs
Cleveland State University

This new series focuses on key topics and emerging trends in urban policy. Each volume is specially prepared for academic use, as well as for specialists in the field.

SUBURBAN SPRAWL
Private Decisions and Public Policy
Wim Wiewel and Joseph J. Persky, Editors

THE INFRASTRUCTURE OF PLAY
Building the Tourist City
Dennis R. Judd, Editor

THE ADAPTED CITY
Institutional Dynamics and Structural Change
H. George Frederickson, Gary A. Johnson, and Curtis H. Wood

CREDIT TO THE COMMUNITY
Community Reinvestment and Fair Lending Policy
in the United States
Dan Immergluck

PARTNERSHIPS FOR SMART GROWTH
University-Community Collaboration for Better Public Places
Wim Wiewel and Gerrit-Jan Knaap, Editors

REVITALIZING THE CITY
Strategies to Contain Sprawl and Revive the Core
*Fritz W. Wagner, Timothy E. Joder, Anthony J. Mumphrey, Jr.,
Krishna M. Akundi, and Alan F.J. Artibise*

THE UNIVERSITY AS URBAN DEVELOPER
Case Studies and Analysis
David C. Perry and Wim Wiewel, Editors

PEOPLE AND THE COMPETITIVE ADVANTAGE OF PLACE
Building a Workforce for the 21st Century
Shari Garmise

CITIES IN THE TECHNOLOGY ECONOMY
Darrene L. Hackler

CITIES IN A TIME OF TERROR
Space, Territory, and Local Resilience
H.V. Savitch

To the memory of my brother, Sy Savitch—
how dearly we miss him.

Contents

List of Illustrations

Tables

Figures

Photographs follow page 168.

Preface

A Thorny Subject

The experience and work for this book began before 9/11 changed our world. I first came upon what has come to be called urban terrorism back in 1981. At the time, I was spending a sabbatical year in Paris. My family found residence in a crowded inner-city neighborhood and all of us enjoyed its enormous diversity. One day, as we headed toward one of the neighborhood's landmarks—a Jewish restaurant noted for its superb corned beef sandwiches—we heard loud clapping sounds and saw crowds running in the direction of the noise. Within minutes the street was jammed and we discovered the restaurant had been machine-gunned by men firing from a speeding car. As is the case with so much of urban terrorism, the restaurant had been selected because it contained large crowds. The deathly charges were directed against anyone who happened to be in the vicinity. I later discovered that radicals from the French group Direct Action had targeted this predominantly Jewish area for mass carnage.

While the experience left a durable impression, I had not quite associated the violence with the city's built environment. The incident did, however, set off a keener awareness of terrorism, and as I read newspaper accounts, its unique city qualities gradually became evident. Not until later years when I spent time at the Woodrow Wilson International Center did the subject arise for me in any scholarly form. In the late 1990s a group of us were asked to write individual papers on cities and national security. Much to my surprise, I was the only one who had chosen to investigate urban terrorism.

My paper was short and attracted no unusual attention. The subject, however, sat with me—remotely because of the memory of Paris and more immediately because the data told me there was something to this phenomenon. Working with a graduate assistant, I continued reading about the subject and exploring data. By the spring of 2001, I had completed a paper for submission to *Urban Studies*. The paper was published just a few months later, in the weeks following directly in the wake of 9/11.

From that point onward I worked intermittently on the subject. Much of the subsequent research was prompted by stays in France and Israel, as well as by short-term travel elsewhere. The rash of terrorist attacks in Jerusalem between 2000 and 2003 was particularly unsettling. The experience did put me on the track of comparing Jerusalem's experience with those of other cities around the world. September 11 was pulled into a certain focus by seeing what was occurring in Istanbul, Madrid, and subsequently London.

The comparisons that seemed apparent to me and mainstream social science were not always appreciated in parts of the academy or the media. Terrorism is a thorny subject. It is all too easy to get pricked by those who see it in partisan terms. There are people who rationalize it, seek to explain it away, and even refuse to use the word "terror." Others insist that terrorism is impossible to define or too slippery to be put to scholarly use. Some academics see it as a "social construct" and too subjective to classify, though it is curious that for these skeptics "race" or "colonialism" have not posed the same conceptual impossibilities. The cliché that "one person's terrorist is another person's freedom fighter" says a great deal about its proclivity for subjective argument.

Having grown acutely aware to this problem, I devote the rest of this section to methodological issues of terrorism and I define urban terrorism in the next chapter. Spelling out these preambles has clarified my own thinking and was of great value in formulating the rest of the volume. I trust the reader will also see this as useful for the larger analysis.

Methodology and Data

How might we study urban terrorism? In attempting to answer this question, the first challenge for me was to carefully define and distinguish the concept and lay out the dimensions through which it transpires—space, territory, and logistics. The next challenge was to establish boundaries around which the analysis could be conducted. This was necessary in order to capture the essentials of urban terrorism without getting lost in peripheral experiences or becoming unwieldy. As often occurs in social science, what, how, and why certain choices are made involves personal judgment about how particular circumstances fit selected criteria. I have endeavored to make those choices within a sound framework and with consistency.

One of the more critical choices involved selecting a sizable number of nations and territories that might best represent general trends in urban terrorism. The challenge was to accomplish this while avoiding idiosyncratic cases that might distort the analysis. As I saw it, the most distorting factors involved areas beset by multiple kinds of warfare. These would be countries that were enmeshed in external wars, endemic civil wars, and internal upheavals where terrorism could too easily be mixed or confused with other types of warfare. For this reason I avoided the most extreme cases. Nations like Afghanistan, Iraq, and Lebanon were not part of this study, mostly because their situations were too cloudy and very difficult to ascertain. At the same time, it was important that the book capture "hot spots" of terrorism. These sites constitute an important part of the analysis because they tell us how terrorists behave, how cities are targeted, and how people respond to severe assaults. Some "hot spots" include Northern Ireland (Belfast), Israel (Jerusalem and Tel Aviv), Egypt (Cairo),

Turkey (Istanbul and Ankara), and Saudi Arabia (Riyadh and Jeddah). The selection process involved sorting nations or regions struck by terrorism as measured by incidents and casualties. Those nations and regions with the largest number of incidents and casualties were chosen. Listed below are twenty-five nations and regions selected by this process. A sample of their leading cities is listed in parentheses.

Algeria (Algiers, Oran)
Canada (Ottawa, Toronto, Montreal)
Chechnya (Grozny)
Colombia (Bogotá, Cali)
Egypt (Cairo, Alexandria)
France (Paris, Marseille, Lyon)
Germany (Berlin, Hamburg, Munich)
Greece (Athens, Thessalonica)
India (Mumbai, New Delhi)
Indonesia (Jakarta, Surabaya)
Israel (Jerusalem, Tel Aviv)
Italy (Rome, Milan, Naples)
Japan (Tokyo, Yokohama)

Kashmir (Srinagar)
Kenya (Nairobi, Mombassa)
Morocco (Casablanca, Rabat)
Northern Ireland (Belfast)
Pakistan (Islamabad, Karachi)
Peru (Lima)
Russia (Moscow, St. Petersburg)
Saudi Arabia (Riyadh, Jeddah)
Spain (Madrid, Barcelona)
Turkey (Istanbul, Ankara)
United Kingdom (London, Birmingham, Manchester)
United States (New York, Los Angeles, Washington, DC)

This study utilizes data from the Rand–Memorial Institute for the Prevention of Terrorism (Rand-MIPT) Terrorism Knowledge Base (TKB) database. The data have been sorted, edited, and adapted. Much of the adaptation involved examining and distinguishing urban-based terrorism from its nonurban variant.[1] The data encompass more than three decades of recorded events, beginning in 1968 and running through 2005; they include more than 1,100 cities or towns covering over 12,000 incidents. Because of the difficulties in collecting consistent longitudinal information, I have divided the data into three categories. These include Type 1 data (domestic and international incidents from 1968 to 2005); Type 2 data (international incidents from 1968 to 2005); and Type 3 data (international and domestic incidents from 1998 to 2005).[2]

Type 1 data are not uniform because they contain international incidents from one period mixed with international and domestic incidents from another period. Accordingly, Type 1 data are used sparingly, only for indicative purposes or to maximize the available information. Type 2 data have been uniformly compiled for over three decades, though only for international events. Type 3 data have also been uniformly compiled and are all inclusive, though for less than a decade. Naturally, different databases will shorten or lengthen time periods or constrict or expand information. Different types of data do hold certain advantages and disadvantages, and I have endeavored to use them as appropriate to a particular discussion.[3] Where I thought it useful, I employ both Type 2 and Type 3 data to verify certain propositions. This proved handy in Chapter 4, where I compared long-term trends (Type 2 data) with a shorter time interval (Type 3). All data types and sources are identified throughout the text, and supplementary information can be found in an appendix at the end of the volume.

A number of other techniques contributed to the narrative. I have relied on archival material, news reports, government documents, interviews, census counts, mapping, geographic information systems, and secondary literature. Especially important for a study of this kind is spatial analysis, and for this I have used maps and various graphic material.

Finally, I have tried to work within a framework of standard definitions of terrorism and have adapted them to the idea of urban terrorism. Chapter 1 goes through this in some detail, but it will be useful here to provide a definition derived from the Rand-MIPT TKB.[4] It reads:

> Terrorism is defined by the nature of the act, not by the identity of the perpetrators or the nature of the cause. Terrorism is violence, or the threat of violence calculated to create an atmosphere of fear and alarm. These acts are designed to coerce others into actions they would not otherwise undertake, or refrain from actions they desired to take. All terrorist acts are crimes. Many would also be violation of rules of war if a state of war existed. This violence or threat of violence is generally directed against civilian targets. The motives of all terrorists are political, and terrorist actions are generally carried out in a way that will achieve maximum publicity. Unlike other criminal acts, terrorists often claim credit for their acts. Finally, terrorist acts are intended to produce effects beyond the immediate physical damage of the cause, having long-term psychological repercussions on a particular target audience. The fear created by terrorists may be intended to cause people to exaggerate the strengths of the terrorist and the importance of the cause, to provoke governmental overreaction, to discourage dissent, or simply to intimidate and thereby enforce compliance with their demands.

The Rand-MIPT definition is important because it is the source for most of the data gathered. It is also consistent with the definition used by the United States and the European Union. A definition furnished by the U.S. Defense Department pays attention to the "calculated use of violence or the threat of violence to inculcate fear" and acts "intended to coerce or to intimidate," while the U.S. State Department points up the "deliberate targeting of noncombatants." The European Union stresses "seriously intimidating a population" and cites examples of "attacks upon a person's life," "kidnapping or hostage taking," or "seizure of aircraft, ships or other means of goods transportation."[5]

While the emphases may differ, the standard definitions contain certain common elements: (1) terror is defined by the nature of the act, (2) the act is centered on the application of violence, (3) the violence is deliberately used against civilians (noncombatants) to create fear, and (4) the fear is used for purposes of political intimidation. I have elaborated upon these definitions and adapted them to my own conceptualization of urban terror.

Organization by Theme

The organization of this volume is built on major themes. I suggest that urban terrorism is based on inculcating mass fear. The core of this fear consists of terrorists targeting high-density, mixed-use, high-value, and strategically located spaces. The book's themes unfold in three broad sections consisting of (1) background and theoretical perspectives, (2) geospatial features of urban terrorism, and (3) policy responses and city resilience. The opening section on background/theory contains chapters that explain the nature of urban terrorism, its practices, and its core components. Within this section, Chapter 1 explains how urban terrorism can be distinguished from other types of warfare and suggests how terrorism might be defined and applied as a basic concept. It also uses global, mega, and major cities to illustrate terrorism's key aspects and presents a broad picture of incidents and casualties within these cities. Chapter 2 continues the analysis by recounting the events of 9/11 in New York, 3/11 in Madrid, and 7/7 in London. It then puts these events in the context of terrorism's evolution. The chapter underscores that while the attacks in New York, Madrid, and London brought the world to a new awakening, this was but the tip of an iceberg whose formation was recorded many years before. That record is analyzed through different categories that measure *the scope, the frequency, and the severity* of urban terrorism. Chapter 3 moves to a theoretical treatment of how urban terror works through intimidation and fear. The chapter begins with mainstream accounts of urban terror as encapsulated by the news media's use of language. I suggest that language, particularly nouns, used to describe terrorism is often shaped by the proximity of individuals to acts of terror and their sense of fear. Characterizations of terror are a function of the fears it evokes. Another section deals with the potential use of weapons of mass destruction against cities and its connection to terrorist tactics. Also discussed is what has become known as post–traumatic stress disorder and its impact on city life. The chapter ends with an analysis of how mass anxiety is used by leaders and other elites to advance particular ends.

The next section, on geospatial features, contains chapters devoted to identifying terrorist organizations and how they utilize urban space to attack cities. Chapter 4 specifically discusses terrorist identity in terms of anarchistic, secular, and religiously motivated terrorism. It also describes the spaces used (city haunts) and how they sometimes connect with one another across the globe. Chapter 5 analyzes how urban terrorism exploits city vulnerability through tactics that include decontrolling territory, repetitive attacks, and, ultimately, shrinking urban space. Tactics of this kind are particularly effective in transmitting the shock of attack to other parts of the national and global social order. The experiences of London, New York, Paris, Istanbul, and Jerusalem are instructive for how cities cope with terrorism, how spaces change, and how urban life is altered.

The last section deals with policy responses and local resilience. Chapter 6 is dedicated to showing how cities attempt to conduct surveillance, broadly defined to include many types of public scrutiny in order to halt, deter, or mitigate terror-ism. Surveillance is far from new and began with the construction of walls around ancient and medieval cities. Its modern incarnation embraces "street watching," panoptic devices, technological detection, barriers, and fortress construction. While unintended, surveillance results in the shrinkage of urban space, and has the paradoxical effect of constricting the very freedoms it is supposed to ensure. New York, Washington, DC, London, Jerusalem, and Moscow serve as points of departure for examining its many applications. The chapter concludes by pointing up the tensions between surveillance and democratic freedoms.

Chapter 7 wraps up the analysis by looking at the issue of urban resilience, or how cities fare in the face of attack. This chapter opens with various prognoses about New York's future. A strain of intellectual opinion held to pessimistic forecasts about the city's future—which I subsume under the rubric of 9/11 dystopia. Most of these are shown to have been incorrect, and this leads me to discuss the city's capacity for resilience. As the chapter suggests, resilience is built into the nature of the city, though it will vary from locality to locality. In light of this, I return to broader questions of how public policy might be used to sustain resilience.

The very last section contains conclusions. Chapter 8 points to the premises of urban terrorism—that it tries to turn the strength of the city against itself—and then goes on to discuss the findings, showing the various ways in which terrorists exploit the urban terrain. In finishing, I review what has been discovered about urban terrorism, its tendency toward mega attacks and its targeting tactics. Emerg-ing from this chapter are two notions of urban vulnerability and local resilience, pitted against one another.

Acknowledgments

I owe a great deal to colleagues, friends, students and staff at the University of Louisville's School of Urban and Public Affairs. SUPA allowed me the resources, time, and good colleagueship to complete this work. It is a wonderful home that allows me to enjoy a wonderful profession. Steve Bourassa and Ron Vogel helped with friendship and assistance. Dave Simpson's experience with hazards research rubbed off on me (or at least some of it) and helped on the issue of local resilience. Bruce Gale continues to be a terrific office neighbor and gifted kibitzer. The staff at SUPA is exemplary. Thanks go to Juli Wagner, Patty Sarley, and Dionne Matthis for their help, efficiency and, most of all, their good nature. Over in philosophy Avery Kolers provided constructive advice on the Venn diagram.

As always, students are our greatest reward. In recent years Gregory Ardashev and Anar Valyev, both Russian speakers, were of immense assistance. I profoundly thank them for giving me the pleasure of being their mentor. Lin Ye also helped put together maps and analyze data. He was always an energetic, skillful, and careful researcher. The Brown & Williamson fund was invaluable in enabling me to travel, research, and write. I am appreciative for that gift.

It has been a pleasure working with the professionals and staff at M.E. Sharpe. Harry Briggs is a man of wonderful abilities and even greater patience. Rick Bingham encouraged the book, recruited me to M.E. Sharpe, and has been an able editor for the series on Cities and Contemporary Society. Ana Erlic came through with solid problem solving for which I am grateful. As with a previous book, Dianne O'Regan was true to form and did a wonderful job with the index.

The past is prologue, and I owe a great deal of gratitude to the Woodrow Wilson International Center for Scholars in Washington, DC. That organization enabled me to first write about urban terror back in the 1990s and provided me with support and a nurturing atmosphere. Blair Ruble and Joe Tulchin were instrumental in creating that atmosphere. Wilson gave me the opportunity to meet and work with people like Richard Stren, Gabi Sheffer, Maria Elena Ducci, and many others.

Farther away from home the Floersheimer Institute for Policy Studies (now at the Hebrew University) provided resources, time, access, and talent. Professors Amiram Gonen and Shlomo Hasson were instrumental in that endeavor. Eran Razin, Danny Felsenstein, and Noam Shoval were welcoming colleagues and introduced me to Jerusalem. The late Arie Shachar furnished his talents as a first-rate raconteur, and we all mourn his passing. Floersheimer also allowed me to gain the acquaintance of Yaacov Garb, and we later came to collaborate on issues of terror, barriers, and the re-topography of the city.

In 2002 I had the privilege of serving as a Fulbright Scholar at the Maison Méditerranéenne des Sciences de l'Homme (Aix-en-Provence, France). I remain grateful for that opportunity, which allowed me to ruminate about the subject and get started on subsequent work. I owe much to Andre Donzel, Alain Motte, and Daniel Pinson for a most productive and satisfying visit.

No acknowledgment would be complete without my expression of gratitude to Susan Clarke of the University of Colorado (Boulder) and Gabriel Sheffer of the Hebrew University of Jerusalem. Susan and Gabi read most of the manuscript, carefully and scrupulously. They told me where I had gone astray, made incisive comments, and offered sound advice. I remain in their debt. Naturally, the usual disclaimers are in order. Neither Susan nor Gabi are responsible for the faults that lie herein. That is solely my doing.

Last, I thank my family for their love and support. My wife, Susan, was always by my side—listening, cajoling, and enduring my idiosyncrasies. Adam, Jonathan, Jen, Luke, and Ethan had differing ideas on what I was up to and would have given their kindness no matter what I did. I am a fortunate man.

Ocean Grove, NJ

Cities in a Time of Terror

**MAXINE GOODMAN LEVIN
COLLEGE OF URBAN AFFAIRS**

Cleveland State University

Part 1

Background and Theory

Sketching Urban Terrorism

What the hammer? What the chain?
In what furnace was thy brain?
What the anvil? What dread grasp?
Dare it deadly terrors clasp?
—William Blake

What Terrorism Is and Is Not

Cities in a Time of Terror takes up the complex issue of how cities have fared in the midst of politically motivated violence against their citizenry and environment. I refer to the occurrence of this violence as urban terrorism, and explore its evolution, its meaning, and its ramifications for city life. In the last four decades, cities have been subject to more than 12,000 incidents of terrorism and incurred over 73,000 casualties. The proportion of urban to nonurban terrorism is staggering. Approximately three out of every four attacks and four out of five casualties occur in a city.[1] Urban terrorism has brought the equivalent of a major war to cities around the world. Its most conspicuous quality is that civilians are both the intended and the actual victims.

The questions behind these bare facts abound. Does urban terrorism differ from its more generalized version, and if so, in what ways? In what ways has urban terrorism changed? Who are the urban terrorists? How does urban terrorism affect citizens? And, are cities able to adopt protective policies without losing their openness, pluralism, and vibrancy? These questions lie at the core of the broad designation "urban terrorism." Before turning to these questions, some distinctions should be made between the general form of terrorism and urban terrorism.

In any enterprise of this sort, definitions are important.[2] They clarify what the writer is investigating, they lay out the scope of inquiry, they guide the collection of data, and they ultimately shape the analysis. Definitions are especially tricky in dealing with a controversial subject like terrorism, whose perpetrators have been variously described as "militants," "freedom fighters," "martyrs," "jihadists," and "fanatics." In an effort to follow good social science practice, I have tried to eschew euphemisms so often used by the popular media or characterizations used by those with an ideological axe to grind. No definition is perfect, and any definition of terrorism is bound to run into objections. This problem is compounded by the vast literature on terrorism with its very different perspectives on the subject.[3] To clarify the issue, I have adopted a definition of terrorism that best describes the act itself, that best fits patterns of terror across different chronological and national boundaries, and that most accurately describes terrorist behavior. The definition is also widely accepted in liberal democracies.

A commonly used legal definition of terrorism describes it as the *purposeful* and *deliberate* targeting of noncombatants through various forms of coercion.[4] Terrorism employs violence indiscriminately in order to threaten or intimidate people for political purposes.[5] To this I should add that intimidation can also be brought about by indiscriminate attacks on peoples' sources of sustenance (shelter, infrastructure, livelihoods). What distinguishes terrorism from other kinds of violence is its desire to strike a sample of a given population or their sources of support, so that out of sheer dread others will capitulate. Indiscriminate targeting is a key terrorist objective because it creates an atmosphere of mass vulnerability. Terrorists deliberately kill, cripple, or destroy that which pertains to a people (Israelis, Bosnians, Americans) or what those people constitute as a social group (bourgeoisie, Christians, kulaks, blacks). The inculcation of mass fear is inextricably linked to terror. Much of terrorism's effectiveness depends on the extent to which it can bring fear to a high pitch—so much so that terrorism can be described as leading to intense, sharp, overwhelming apprehension.

In settling on a definition we should understand that terrorism is a form of warfare carried out under conditions of asymmetric military capability.[6] That is, terrorists act against populations by utilizing rudimentary violence that includes kidnapping, hijacking, shootings, arson, and planted or human bombs. Much of the terrorism we see involves an organizational infrastructure that coordinates attacks through disguised agents, making detection difficult. Terrorists are generally supported by an underground organization and they do not wear insignia—all of which enables them to achieve tactical advantage by penetrating civilian areas and blending with the population.

Since terrorism is invariably connected to political objectives, it usually involves more than one person. From a conceptual view, the size of the organization is not crucial and it may vary from a cell of a few people to a full-blown hierarchically run apparatus. Certainly, terrorist organizations will differ in their political demands. Some terrorist demands are subject to negotiation while others are not. Prime Minister Tony Blair made this point in contrasting the political demands of the Irish Republican Army (IRA) versus those of al Qaeda. While these differences should be taken into account, it does not make one organization less "terrorist" than another. Differences exist, but so too do common denominators, and these are crucial for assessing terrorist warfare.

As is typical in social science, distinctions are not always tidy. There are times when conventional forces resort to terror, much as there are times when terrorists wage conventional warfare. Here I draw a line between one group legitimately being designated as "terrorist" because of its very frequent use of terror as its modus operandi, and another group not being considered as "terrorist" because of its rare or infrequent use of terrorist tactics. By and large terrorist warfare is distinguishable from guerrilla or conventional warfare. Guerrilla warfare is carried out by irregular fighters, aimed at other combatants, and relies on unconventional tactics. Guerrillas do share some attributes with terrorists, like hit-and-run attacks. Guerrillas and terrorists alike use surprise and long-term attrition to defeat more conventional foes. However, unlike those of terrorists, guerrilla targets are quite discrete and aimed at the military.

Whereas guerrillas seek to cause major disruption in the ranks of enemy armed forces and wear them down with costly losses, terrorists avoid open combat. This may well be because terrorists know they would lose in any military confrontation, so their logical recourse is to attack soft targets or assault the social order. Guerrillas operate as armed units that seek to hold and occupy territory, while terrorists try to prevent people from using their own established territory. Granted, there are times when lines between guerrilla and terrorist blur, especially when an organization conducts warfare through multiple means or when an organization is transitioning from one form to another. Terrorism can also evolve into guerrilla warfare or even develop conventional capabilities, much as guerrilla and conventional warfare can turn to terrorism. Hezbollah embodies this kind of transition. During the 1980s, its activities were heavily terrorist, involving abductions and assaults on civilians. In the last few years it has drifted toward building a guerrilla force, engaging the Israeli army in 2006 and developing the political trappings of a quasi state. Hezbollah's possible transition tells us that hybrids do exist and each case should be analyzed on the basis of its distinct attributes.

Still clearer is the conceptual distinction between terrorism and conventional warfare. As mentioned, terrorism's core features are its premeditated violence against noncombatant targets and its intent to influence a larger audience. By contrast, conventional military action has direct combat objectives that are aimed *primarily* at military targets. Mostly, conventional warfare is battlefield combat, designed to deprive the enemy of its fighters, logistical support, and will to carry on. To be sure, conventional warfare often results in civilian casualties, but this does not amount to terrorism. So long as this warfare is carried out without reckless disregard for the lives or sustenance of noncombatants, it remains as conventional military action, despite the fact that noncombatants are killed ancillarily or inadvertently as part of a larger effort. This principle pertains to lethal interceptions of terrorists ("targeted killings"), preemptive attacks, and other ways in which "ticking bombs" are stopped. When conventional military forces do revert to killing or injuring noncombatants as a primary objective, their actions should be assessed empirically to determine whether they qualify as acts of terror.[7]

Group Terrorism and State Terrorism: Same Genus, Different Species

The picture of terrorists operating surreptitiously to conduct indiscriminate violence evokes an image of outlaws and brigands. For some, this reinforces the notion that terrorism should be viewed as uniquely outside the state. Some scholars argue that since terrorism is aimed against governments and has an unusual structure of incentives, it should be seen as essentially a nonstate movement.[8] According to this view, states may commit atrocities, but by nature they should not be seen as terrorist entities. My own view is that such contentions are problematic because history is replete with states having conducted indiscriminate violence against civilians for political purposes. It therefore becomes difficult if not impossible to ignore the exercise of terrorism by states. Indeed, the modern genesis of the concept is couched in the government of revolutionary France and its notorious "reign of terror," to say nothing of state terrorism though previous ages.

Still and all, we should not conflate nonstate (or group) terrorism with state terrorism. There are substantial differences between these phenomena that embrace accountability, visibility, organization, resources, choice of targets, and immediate objectives.[9] Beginning with the most obvious distinction, group terrorists leave no address and they assiduously avoid being traced. By definition, all states (including those that engage in terrorism) are identifiable and reachable through addresses at their national capitals, their foreign embassies, and their membership in international organizations. While possessing an address does not assure accountability, it does mean that state actors are answerable to charges in ways that groups can ignore. Having a national or diplomatic address ordinarily promotes restraint. Second, and related to the previous point, group terrorists operate underground, they have little visibility, and very heavily rely on disguised agents to execute attacks. State actors are quite different. While they also possess the capacity to operate underground, states must demonstrate a modicum of visibility. They do this through uniformed troops, trained police forces, state-run media, political parties, bureaucracies, and the like. Third, group terrorism is generally built on less formal organizational structures. This organizational format may run the gamut from the more hierarchical apparatus that had been the hallmark of Hezbollah when it was exclusively a terrorist organization to the amorphous networks of al Qaeda.[10] Despite the variation, even groups with a substantial hierarchy bear no relation to the complex and extensive institutions possessed by nation-states. Fourth, because group terrorists have relatively low resources, their instruments of coercion are often primitive, makeshift, and low-tech.[11] Handguns, hand grenades, detonated explosives, and suicide vests are the usual weapons of choice. In sharp distinction, even poor states have high resources consisting of missiles, artillery, tanks, armored vehicles, boats, and aircraft. Fifth, these differences are also revealed in the contrasting ways group terrorists and state terrorists conduct violence. Group terrorism uses random, scattershot violence designed to strike generic targets like crowds, banks, transit systems, and large buildings. Quite apart from this, state terrorism is more likely to rely on collective punishment where retribution is taken against specific villages, neighborhoods, or communities. States are also more likely to mix their violence by using an assortment of force—military, police, and secret agents. Finally and most importantly, the immediate or medium-range objectives of group and state terrorism are quite different. Group terrorism seeks to upset a functioning society or overturn an existing state by "decontrolling territory" and producing social chaos.[12] This is why its violence is carried out surreptitiously and designed to arbitrarily shock mass publics. Compare this to state terrorism, which seeks to strengthen the existing state and reinforce its territorial control through more pinpointed violence. These contrasting features ramify into sharp distinctions in behavior and are summarized in Table 1.1.

So significant are these differences that group and state terrorism should be considered as separate species stemming from the same genus rather than as a single, undifferentiated category. Aside from the substantive differences, there are practical reasons for limiting a study to group actors. While state terrorism is much murkier and blends into a host of other kinds of violence, group terrorism is relatively easy to identify. The sheer scope of terrorism is enormous and its conception difficult enough without adding to it.[13] For these reasons, I have focused this study on the more common usage of terrorism as consisting of nonstate or group actors, organized for purposes of violence and political intimidation.

Locating the Urban in Urban Terrorism

While terrorism can be studied as form of general warfare, it can also be treated from a uniquely urban perspective.[14] This perspective is most applicable to cities that are located in what are commonly called liberal democracies. The reasoning behind this has to do with both the strengths and vulnerabilities of free and complex societies. The open qualities of liberal democratic states are often reflected in the fluid, unbounded social relations of their localities. These traits accommodate a chain of positive responses—first allowing cities to develop internal complexity, which in turn fosters mutual tolerance, which in turn nourishes the city's creative energy.[15] At the same time, a city's complex interdependence makes it vulnerable to abrupt and violent stoppage—which is a central tactic of urban terrorism. It is no accident that among the many different social systems of the world, liberal democracies absorb the majority of terrorist attacks.[16] To use some sharp examples, London has been more susceptible to terror than Beijing; Tel Aviv more vulnerable than Riyadh; and Mumbai (Bombay) more prone to attack than Singapore. This is not to say that there are no exceptions or that nondemocratic societies are free of terrorism, but rather that liberal democracies provide especially useful insights about terrorism.

Evidently cities do not *cause* terrorism, but their intrinsic characteristics make them a subject and target of terrorists. Here the emphasis is on urban distinctiveness, noting that this is not simply a matter of cities happening to be visible targets, but attacked because of their unique and inherent characteristics. Put somewhat differently, the connection between cities and terrorism is not just due to coincidental association, where targets are located in cities, but where cities qua cities become targets.[17]

Table 1.1

Distinguishing Group Terrorism from State Terrorism

Characteristic	Group terrorism	State terrorism
Accountability	Hidden headquarters, difficult to trace	Reachable "address" through national and international institutions
Visibility	Heavily clandestine or disguised	Often visible, uniformed troops and identifiable police
Organizational structure	Amorphous networks, often decentralized	Hierarchical leadership, bureaucracy, secret courts, armies and police
Resources	Makeshift, scattered, scarce, hampered supply	Relatively abundant weaponry, organized police, military forces, often easy to supply
Targets	Heavily random, indiscriminate	Generally discriminate and mixed with discreet assassination, abduction, and imprisonment of regime opponents
Immediate or middle-range objectives	Overturn existing states through territorial decontrol and social chaos	Reinforce the power of existing states through territorial control and a disciplined population

I define cities to mean high-density, mixed-use, continually developing, bounded environments. Through their diversity cities generate hosts of synergistic interactions.[18] These intrinsic features make a certain kind of terrorism effective and in many ways possible. Indeed, we shall see an extraordinary match between the urban characteristics of cities and the evolution of urban terrorism. Terrorists choose to target cities for particular reasons. We might consider terrorist warfare as functioning via different logics for targeting a particular site. Targeting logics are adumbrated here as (1) catalytic terrorism, (2) mega terrorism, and (3) smart terrorism.

By catalytic terrorism I mean the rapid and widespread transmission of attacks that shock the public.[19] The logic of catalytic terrorism requires that actions be viewed as spectacular, distressing, and widely communicated. A case in point can be drawn from a nonurban tragedy. In 2004 Islamists videotaped the beheading of a civilian captive, underscored by the caption "Al Zarquawi Slaughters an American Infidel."[20] Within twenty-four hours the video was downloaded half a million times and viewers witnessed the gruesome screams of torture by the knife. This was catalytic terrorism in the extreme. Other cases can be seen elsewhere. In 1994 and again in 2002, terrorists in France plotted to blow up the Eiffel Tower. Had this been successful, the attack would have startled the world and drawn attention to the terrorist cause. Catalytic terror often aims at key symbols, and the sight of France's cultural emblem lying in ruins would have been etched in memory. Symbol can be as important as substance, and this is one reason why catalytic terror targets iconic monuments. Whether it be a plot to blow up the Eiffel Tower in Paris or the actual destruction of ancient Buddhist statues in Afghanistan, catalytic terror seeks to announce itself while at the same time demoralizing the enemy.

As with other terrorist logics, fear also comes into play in catalytic terror. This is because fear so readily arouses those who are threatened and lubricates the flow of publicity. Terrorists play upon their own willingness to sacrifice themselves and their capacity to recruit endless numbers of volunteers so that apprehension is likely to continue until some kind of victory is achieved. Above all, catalytic terrorism is macabre theater and terrorists its showmen. In performing these acts, terrorists have converted warfare into a public spectacle. The more vivid spectacles occur when terrorists film testimonies of suicide bombers in preparation for attack; the most startling include visually recorded images of captured victims pleading for their lives or in the throes of being murdered. If cities are anything, they are crowded places that provide an audience where these spectacles can be witnessed and their messages transmitted.

There are many reasons why terrorists want to instill shock and fear. This kind of intimidation makes people aware of their own vulnerability (it could happen here). Public spectacles can also help in recruiting volunteers who are attracted by the opportunity of facing up to superior force. Last, we have the general motive of terrorists trying to gain recognition; the best way to accomplish this is to tie propaganda to deed. This idea of "propaganda by deed" goes back at least a century, when anarchists threw crude pipe bombs into crowds to attract attention.

Known as the *dynamitards*, these anarchistic terrorists comprised a homegrown European phenomenon that spread to the United States. Today, "propaganda by deed" has a much larger and reachable audience. The attack at the Munich Olympics by Palestinian terrorists debuted modern catalytic terror. It not only resulted in the killing of eleven Israeli athletes, but captured the attention of 600 million television viewers. World recognition was enhanced by what has now become the apothegmatic figure of a hooded terrorist peering down from a balcony at his newly acquired "audience."

As scholars point out, continuous broadcasts achieve the psychological effect of arousing the public and letting the popular imagination do the rest of the work.[21] This is particularly effective in environments where mass rallies can be held and where word-of-mouth communication can instantly convey witnessed events. Versions of catalytic terrorism can be seen in the images produced by terrorists. Organizations like Hamas hold mass rallies that feature black-hooded suicide attackers armed with canisters of explosives tied around their waists. Their willingness to die in order to kill is accompanied by religious chants roared in unison by their supporters. Al Qaeda operatives dress in traditional headgear with overlays of battle fatigues and guns at the ready. Some carry daggers in broad waistbands and publicize the beheadings of victims. In another part of the world, the Tamil Tigers employ different symbols, though with similar effects. Their flag contains a red background with a ferocious tiger leaping through the center. The tiger is armed with a round of ammunition crossed by two bayonets. These images designed for public consumption are also intended for mass intimidation.

The second targeting logic, mega terrorism, refers to the tactical advantage gained by heavy casualties, mass abductions, and large-scale damage, all of which are often caused by immense blasts. To most people these acts may seem like senseless mass destruction, but for terrorists mega attacks are indispensable for success. Few acts are as intimidating as the ability to instill an unceasing fear of death. As we shall see, over the years terrorism has become more lethal, with each attack creating heavier casualties. Terrorists work purposefully and diligently to magnify human tolls by targeting dense environments, maximizing the power of explosive devices, and loading those devices with metal shards designed to extend injury.

Mega terrorism also demonstrates the seriousness of attack. By increasing casualties, hostages, or damage, terrorists show that their actions are not a passing occurrence and cannot be ignored. Persistent acts of mega terror will produce unpredictable outcomes and arouse different responses. Mass murder may convince some that terrorism should be fought, but it will also convince others that terrorism should be negotiated. The responses become all the more complicated over the short and long term, though terrorists are convinced that, given enough time, established societies will capitulate. This was the intent of Chechen terrorists in 1999 when they blew up two apartment buildings in Moscow. The intent was explicitly stated again in 2002 when terrorists attacked Moscow's Dubrovka Theater, using the rational that it was "in the center of the city and there were lots of people there."[22] None of these sites possessed strategic or tactical worth, and it was apparent that terrorist objectives were to kill or maim as many Russian civilians as possible.

Turning to the third targeting logic, smart terror is used here to convey the notion that attackers can aim more precisely at high-value targets whose destruction has a much larger multiplier effect and causes large-scale instability. Smart terror often tries to destroy infrastructure or key financial institutions that lie at the synapses of the urban economy. Smart terror may also aim at a single bundle of nerves whose destruction has much wider ramifications. This type of terror exploits the complexity, interdependence, and fragility of urban society, which can be encumbered at any number of junctures. Even temporary paralysis is a reminder of terrorist presence, and this contributes to its longer-term effectiveness. More so, a single act of pinpointed destruction can leverage terrorism by disrupting society or wreaking havoc in the local economy. This can bring about large-scale helplessness, create widespread panic, or precipitate the flight of capital. The 2007 threat by four men to blow up fuel tanks at Kennedy Airport sought to wreck air transport and can be seen as an act, albeit futile, of smart terror. Had Palestinian terrorists succeeded in 2004 in slipping into the Israeli port of Ashdod and setting ablaze chemical tanks, the attack would have brought immeasurable calamity to Israel's shipping, energy, and core industries.

Banks, bridges, power-generating plants, fuel depots, airports, and reservoirs are often targeted for destruction. That seeming "peasants" can acquire the sophistication to reach the interstices of capitalism creates an enormous sense of power. Smart terror touches directly on destroying a key element in a vast chain of power, for if these targets can be so easily penetrated, victory is also possible. Indeed, one reason why suicide attackers are increasingly used across the globe is that they can penetrate and pinpoint targets. Suicide attackers make smart terror all the more possible.

Finally, these are heuristic distinctions used to underscore why cities figure so prominently in terrorist logic. While there are pure cases, a given target can be attacked for multiple reasons. The best example can be found in the 9/11 attack on the World Trade Center, which combined catalytic, mega, and smart terror. In point of fact, the more targeting logics provided by a site, the greater the wallop. From a terrorist viewpoint, certain sites are prone to repeated attacks because they hold the potential for greater yields.

Fear and Response

My central argument is taken from the essence of terrorism and applied to cities in particular ways.[23] That is, urban terror is based on the inculcation of mass fear and readiness to use martyrdom as a weapon. Fear is made all the more potent when it is induced by attackers whose inclination for destruction knows no bounds. Power lies in the credibility of this threat. The tactical ploy of terrorists is to convince others that their willingness to kill is exceeded only by their eagerness to die. When, just weeks after 9/11, an al Qaeda spokesman declared, "There are thousands of Islamic youths who are eager to die, just as the Americans are eager to live," he was bidding up the stakes in an effort to expand those fears and amplify terrorist power.[24]

The credibility of threat connects the uncertainties of Thomas Hobbes's medieval world ruled by "continual fear and danger of violent death" with the vulnerabilities of Daniel Bell's "post–industrial society."[25] Uncertainty robs individuals of security about what the next hour will bring, while vulnerability exposes every aspect of society to potential ruin. This is an enormously intimidating combination, made all the more dangerous by the escalating lethality and the potential use of chemical, biological, radiological, and nuclear weapons (CBRN). That any of these weapons of mass destruction could fall into the hands of terrorists is a distinct possibility. This is the point where terrorists reach the pinnacle of their power as a "weak force" against the fragility of "powerful societies."

Cities are ideal places where so much of this is manifest. Generally speaking, the largest and most important cities encounter the more frequent and most severe terror. Within these cities we can observe mega, smart, and catalytic terrorism working in tandem. The quantity of noncombatants killed, injured, or kidnapped by mega terror shocks people; the strategic or pinpointed destruction wrought by smart terror disrupts economies; and the dramatic transmission of gruesome acts by catalytic terrorism is a constant reminder to the larger public.

Cities facilitate catalytic, mega, and smart terrorism; or, to shift the emphasis, cities provide the elements that make modern terrorism so combustible. Their large populations, high-value assets, capacity to connect the world, strategic location, and symbolic importance have changed the course of terrorism, giving it a new form. Hence urban terrorism is about how terrorists turn the strengths of the city against itself. Tourist cities are particularly susceptible to terrorist exploitation because they are violence elastic. Once terror breaks out, travelers are very quick to change their plans and the tourist economy sinks. Besides, hitting a hotel with foreign guests transmits an international message. Terrorists have recognized both the vulnerability of tourist locales and the advantages of striking them in places like Bali, Luxor, Mombassa, and Djerba.

Aside from the target-rich aspect of cities, there are psychological and ideological reasons for striking urban environments. At least in liberal democracies cities are places that thrive on pluralism and heterogeneity. Cities force people with deeply different views to bump up against one another, in effect promoting mutual toler-ance and delegitimizing claims to an absolute or revealed truth.[26] This is precisely what disturbs absolutist, theocratic terrorists and provokes them. Demonstrating that open societies are a fiction is a victory for any absolutist movement.

Every action has its reaction, and urban terrorism has generated a train of re-sponses. Measures to prevent or thwart urban destruction are not just engendered at a national level but stem directly from city halls. In some instances the city's physical form has changed as high-value targets are covered by closed-circuit television, metal detectors, barriers, portable partitions, and police patrols. Cities have established special intelligence and anti-terrorist capacity that cuts across the globe. Once bombs had gone off in Madrid and London, members of New York's Counter Terrorism Bureau were either on their way to those stricken cities or already there. The same unit has established linkages with officials in Israel (Tel Aviv and Jerusalem), Russia (Moscow and Beslan), and Singapore. While the network overlaps with national authorities, it also has a distinct urban focus by concentrating on mass transit, entry ports, bridges, and high-value buildings.

While these measures may be comforting, they also compromise the qualities of free-flowing openness that make cities vital. Taken too far, they can weaken the city by robbing it of human assets, suffocating its social life, and dehumanizing its built environment. Every protective measure conveys a message that the public should beware and inadvertently promotes the very fear terrorists seek to inculcate. There is a danger that in combating terror, cities engage in a self-negation and become closed societies. Confronted by this dilemma, cities must find a balance between the requisites of security and those of a free society.

The issue of achieving balance is complicated, especially since we do not know the likelihood of a city being attacked, much less the location of a future attack. At one end of the spectrum the FBI, MI5, and other security agencies underscore that thousands of terrorists are lurking in cities waiting for an opportune moment.[27] At the other end, John Mueller and other critics suggest that terrorist threats are greatly exaggerated and that we are adopting excessive protections for an "enemy that scarcely exists."[28] As we shall see, ample data from around the world tell us that terrorism is deeply seated in a number of locales. But Mueller is talking about terrorist activity in the United States and he asks some pointed questions about why, after more than 300 million legal entries by foreigners, there has not been a single attack since 9/11? Investigative officials counter Mueller's claim by pointing to numerous attempts that have been thwarted. And Mueller offers the counter-claim that those who have been apprehended are either "mental cases or simply flaunting jihadist bravado."[29] While Mueller's point is well taken, investigators in New York and London claim nearly fifty terrorist attempts in the past half-dozen years. Is it likely that all of these were lone wolves? To date, the best answer for the United States is that we do not know and cannot ascertain the potential for future attacks. This makes for the seemingly contradictory conclusion that the threat of terrorism is at once considerably overstated and also very real.

There are, too, larger factors surrounding our domestic response. We live in a global culture, and both experience and hard data reveal that terrorism has an international dimension, is highly adaptable, and its success is imitated. This makes international terrorism very contagious and difficult to separate from its domestic roots. It is even more difficult to insulate a city from foreign infiltration. After all, the 9/11 attack was launched from Hamburg, Germany, and points farther east. Some kind of surveillance is both necessary and inevitable. How we might weigh surveillance against a suffocation of urban freedoms is addressed in a later chapter.

Focusing on the Terrorized

A study of this kind naturally focuses on the actuality of attack. This includes tactics, targets, and damage to people and places. Accordingly, I am concerned with how terrorists use cities, what kinds of places are attacked, how they are attacked, and the long-term effects of attacks. Unlike most treatments of terrorism whose concerns lie with grand strategies or with terrorists themselves, I often view terrorists through the lens of how their actions have affected the terrorized. This is quite necessary for a study of urban terrorism. Scholars and journalists have been mostly concerned with the makeup, motivations, and goals of terrorist groups. More recently, filmmakers have joined the ranks of other media by producing personal portrayals of terrorists.[30] Yet relatively few written or filmed accounts investigate the ruined lives of victims, their families, or what terrorism means for those who have to continue living and working in places that have been attacked. Invariably, conversations with victims of terrorism disclose the poignancy of memory. Take, for instance, the recollection of a father whose fifteen-year-old daughter lost her life in a Jerusalem attack:

> My daughter, along with other children of Israel, was on holiday. . . . She went to decorate the bedroom of her friend who was going to come back home from holiday. And then she went with her friend to downtown to have pizza. At 2 o'clock the pizza restaurant disappeared from the face of the Earth. And my wife, who was watching television, and got the first report, called me at work and told about the terrible things that had happened and she did not know where the children were. And this was a start of the process. We did not know that Malki was murdered until after 12 hours of visits to the hospitals.[31]

Or consider an altogether different situation faced by terrorist victims in a small city in Colombia. This instance involved killing coupled with kidnapping:

> I was kidnapped for 3 years, so were my mom and my brother. My mom is still kidnapped. And my father was killed two months ago. I was with my father, and was shot in my leg. I saw him dead. I do not know the reason. I mean, guerrillas killed because they think nothing about it. There are no reasons.[32]

Though these circumstances were very different and took place at opposite ends of the world, both demonstrate the destructive capacity of random violence and ensuing trauma. There is a point where individual trauma turns into collective trauma—where whole communities are conditioned by random violence. Given the nature of mass behavior, those cities that have been struck are likely to be faced with more intense or heightened shock. This may vary greatly, and terror-driven trauma will recede at differential rates, but it is likely to be manifest in how people behave, how cities are used, and how public policies are changed.

The principal points of this inquiry concern the targeting of people and places. In working through this approach, I focus on three key aspects of the urban environment, namely *territory*, *space*, and *logistics*. From the standpoint of *territory*, urban terrorism is directed against large swatches of land laden with strategic value. Because terrorists seek to decontrol as much territory as possible, they choose sites where mass disruption is likely to mushroom. Territorial decontrol also demonstrates that citizens are unprotected and their lives can be sabotaged. From the standpoint of selected *space*, urban terrorism targets smaller sites because hitting them will optimize damage. These spaces hold some importance—either as population centers and transportation junctures; or as hubs for business, finance, politics, religion, and media; or as places of strategic and symbolic value. Moreover, terrorists are apt to strike public spaces like squares, open markets, and recreational centers. These are the very spaces that are economically vital and lie at the heart of local democracy. Once under threat, the use of these spaces quickly withers, producing dead zones. The effects are portentous, sharply reducing human movement and ultimately shrinking the space available for normal interaction. Once terrorists succeed in shrinking urban space, they establish the power of threat. John Locke stated it best when he wrote, "what worries you masters you."

The *logistical* characteristics of urban terrorism are derived from its capacity for self-incubation, its ability to penetrate urban spaces, and its proximity to potential targets. Cities are especially well suited for furnishing terrorists with anonymity, safe houses, and supply depots in order to gain access to potential targets. This says a great deal about the linkage between cities and logistics. Taking a leaf from Mao Zedong, terrorists require a "sea in which to swim" or a population base close to potential targets. As a general rule, we expect that cities closer to sources of terrorism would experience a greater number of attacks as well as more lethal ones.

Discerning Global, Mega, and Major Cities

Not all cities are equal. They vary in size, function, importance, and symbolic value. In divergent ways, to different degrees, and for diverse reasons, cities may have particular experiences with terrorism. To get at these specificities some broad distinctions should be made between different types of cities; some ready illustrations can be seen by comparing *global*, *mega*, and *major* cities. Briefly put, global cities are best defined by their commanding position in world city networks; mega cities are best defined by their huge populations, large areas, and weightiness of size; and major cities are defined by a key function or unique attribute. While global, mega, and major cities differ from one another, they do share a distinctively common characteristic. All of them are "first cities," a designation conveying the notion that they are all preeminent urban entities within their respective nations. "First cities" of all types draw wide-reaching attention, and the consequences of attacking them often spill onto the world stage, though in quite different ways.

While *global cities* have substantial populations into the millions, they are better identified by their international profile.[33] Global cities such as London and New York lie at the core of the world economy, functioning as "switching stations" where capital is accumulated, bundled, converted, and traded. While the image of their being command-and-control centers can be overdrawn in a decentralized international marketplace, global cities nevertheless determine the flow of vast amounts of capital. As the locus for international business and stock exchanges, global cities function twenty-four hours a day conducting and negotiating international transactions. The internationalization of these cities ramifies into a huge inventory of office towers supported by infrastructure, large media outlets, and sizable immigrant communities.[34] Attacks or the threat of terrorism upon a global city ring very loudly. A single event could prompt international investigation, intercession from different national security agencies, and United Nations resolutions.

Mega cities are giant cities whose metropolitan populations encompass about 10 million or more inhabitants. Examples include Cairo, Jakarta, and Bombay. Demographics and development count for much in identifying mega cities. Often, the burgeoning population of a mega city outpaces the city's capacity to support its people. There are instances where mega cities are high-growth metropolises with limited development and endemic poverty. As such, they are impacted by congested inner neighborhoods (the slums of Calcutta) or overpopulated by migrants from the countryside (the shanties of Lagos), or ringed by squatter neighborhoods (the favelas of Rio de Janeiro). While their influence is limited, mega cities that are located in developing nations are often the sole source of national commerce (corporate headquarters) or hold commanding political power (presidential residences, legislative seats, army commands). At the same time, mega cities are the leading economic, cultural, or political centers within their respective nations. While mega cities are not necessarily "internationalized," their sheer size weighs heavily at national and supranational levels. Attacks upon these cities attract international notice, though only on occasion are they perceived as generating an international crisis.

Last, the populations of *major cities* vary greatly, ranging from 500,000 to many millions. Population size, however, is hardly an adequate identifier. Instead, major cities are better understood through their prominent roles as historic symbols, political capitals, great regional centers, or as places filled with religious legacies, contested by clashing national rivalries, or belonging to a great national power. Athens, Belfast, or Jerusalem are ready examples. Some major cities possess just a *single attribute* or play a single role—say, as a provincial capital. While there are some notable exceptions, attacks upon a single-attribute major city infrequently reach beyond national media or police forces. Other major cities hold a number of roles or *accumulated attributes*, and these magnify their importance. Attacks against a major city with accumulated attributes have a greater caché and attract wider public reaction.

Figure 1.1 displays examples of global, mega, and major cities within a Venn diagram. The figure is illustrative rather than exhaustive, and cities are placed within a sphere that best illustrates their characteristics. Some cities may fit within more than one category and the areas of overlap are designated.

Figure 1.1   **Global, Mega, and Major Cities**

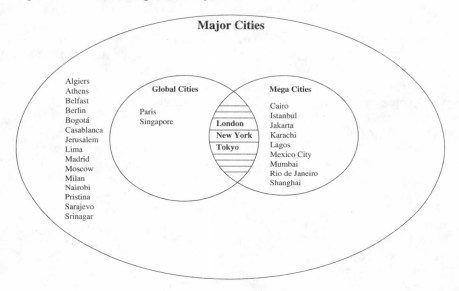

London, New York, and Tokyo are situated as global cities and fit at the intersection of all three spheres. New York's economic prowess makes it one of the few global cities, and its large, high-density population nested within sprawling suburbs also confers its status as a mega city. Finally, its cultural life gives it a persona as one of America's major recreational cities. Because their metropolitan populations are less than 10 million, global cities such as Paris and Singapore might not be thought of as mega cities, but their political status as national capitals and their cultural importance allow them to double as major cities.[35] Singapore is a unique global city, achieving its status because it is a gateway to Southeast Asia and because it combines the flexibility of a city with the authority of a state. It is a global and major city, but hardly a mega city because of its smaller population (4.5 million).

Mega cities also have qualities unto themselves. They possess some important prerequisites of a great city yet are seriously devoid of others. For example, Cairo, Lagos, and Mumbai (Bombay) do not have the economic caché of global cities, but as national and cultural capitals they have a great deal of visibility. Neither their power nor their potential for achievement should be underestimated.

Major cities are far more numerous and have variable qualities. Yet we should not mistake these cities as lacking in consequence. Major cities have a limited though very powerful national presence as political capitals (Algiers, Bogotá, Jerusalem, Lima, Madrid, Moscow, Mexico City, Sarajevo), or possess regional economic clout (Milan, Karachi, Mumbai, Rio de Janeiro, Shanghai, Tel Aviv), or are venerated religious centers (Jerusalem), or play a critical role at the seam of territorial disputes (Belfast, Jerusalem, Pristina, Sarajevo, Srinagar). Not only do cities with accumulated attributes attract greater world attention, but their chances of frequent and severe attacks are also greater. Thus, Jerusalem is at the very crux of numerous conflicts: it is a political capital claimed by two national groups, its boundaries are contested, and it is a highly disputed religious site. Palestinian terrorists of a more secular stripe as well as Muslim fundamentalists readily acknowledge Jerusalem as their greatest potential prize and have used its streets, buses, marketplaces, and plazas for extensive terrorist warfare.

Madrid also is important because of its accumulated attributes. Over the years, Basque separatists have seen it as a prime political target. An international cadre of Muslim fundamentalists also terrorized Madrid for irredentist reasons (hoping to regain the ancient glories of al Andalusia) or because it is a European crossroad. An attack upon Madrid conjures up a wellspring of attention—not just because it is Spain's capital and one of Europe's premier cultural centers, but because it holds accumulated attributes as the leading city in a nation with membership in the European Union and NATO, and because it experienced historic contact with Islam. Not surprisingly, an attack upon Madrid will be perceived in much broader terms.

Finally, it is important to recognize that in the post–9/11 zeitgeist, who attacks whom may be as important as what is attacked. Muslims attacking other Muslims will not arouse as much attention as Muslims attacking Westerners—at least not in Europe or North America. An attack by Basques in Madrid will not arouse as much world attention as an attack by al Qaeda. Likewise, IRA assassinations of minor functionaries will not arouse the same attention as an attack by Muslim fundamentalists against commuters. Terrorism has a context that is very much tied to its potential for metastasizing into larger warfare.

Global, Mega, and Major Cities as Targets

In one way or another, most global, mega, and major cities are sought-after targets or display a high degree of "target proneness" (see Appendix, Table A1). We can understand target proneness by illustrating how different cities might be chosen to realize different terrorist objectives. Generally speaking, global cities offer large payoffs in terms of lives (mega terror), resources (smart terror), and media attention (catalytic terror). Because of their characteristics, global cities will attract attackers engaged in foreign or exogenously based conflict. New York, London, and Paris belong to powerful nations that are often in the thick of overseas conflicts like wars, interventions, and controversial foreign policies. America's contemporary role as the world's superpower and Great Britain's and France's continuing roles as secondary powers put their cities at the crossroads of international traffic and immigration, making them suscep-tible to foreign intrigues. By comparison, a global city like Singapore has not been directly targeted, partly because it plays a very different international role and also because it is more authoritarian and subject to greater control than its global counterparts. Even under these conditions Singapore has been an unwilling host to "sleeper cells" and remains vulnerable to Islamist movements in Southeast Asia.

Mega and major cities are also valued targets but appeal to different priorities. These types of cities are more likely to refract different kinds of homegrown conflict. In such instances, cities have been used as battlefields. For example, ethno-religious clashes have occurred in mega cities like Cairo (government versus Muslim radicals) or Mumbai (Muslims versus Hindus), or in major cities like Belfast (Catholic versus Protestant) or Jerusalem (Arab versus Jew). Other mega and major cities have been battlegrounds for nationalist movements seeking political independence or territorial control. These include Istanbul (Turks versus Kurds) and Moscow (Russians versus Chechens) as well as Pristina (Serbs versus Albanians) and Sarajevo (Serbs, Croats, and Bosnians). A number of major cities have been venues for civil war or revolution. These include Algiers (army versus Muslim fundamentalists), Casablanca (government versus Muslim fundamentalists), Athens (government versus secular revolutionaries), and Lima (government versus secular revolutionaries). Finally, drug and criminal cartels have used terrorism as a weapon to control parts of Bogotá.

Urban terrorism is not monolithic. Rather, it is a complex and multifaceted phenomenon whose roots vary and whose branches reach in many different directions. Some of terrorism's many strands can be distinguished by whether it emphasizes local or international objectives, whether it has a popular base or one composed of a select few, and whether it is purely violent or is combined with a political movement. This being fully recognized, I also see urban terrorism as a method of warfare that is often driven by ideological extremism, and this gives it some common characteristics. Through much of this volume I focus on those commonalities, especially as they relate to the urban environment. One of terrorism's salient uniformities is the application of random violence and the manner in which cities have been used to inflict casualties and destruction. That violence continues to have a disproportionate impact both nationally and throughout the world.

Table 1.2 presents twenty-five global, mega, and major cities along with data on terrorist attacks. Also shown is the national share of incidents and casualties in each home country. The table covers a period of sixteen years between 1990 and 2005.

Note the highest number of incidents, found in certain major cities like Jerusalem or Athens—both of which have a string of accumulated attributes. Once we turn to casualties, major cities with accumulated attributes (Jerusalem, Moscow, and Madrid) are joined by global and mega cities (New York, Mumbai, and Istanbul). Especially interesting are the shares of national incidents and casualties held by these cities. In almost all cases the cities' share of incidents and casualties well

Table 1.2

Terror in Global, Mega, and Major Cities, 1990–2005

City	Incidents	Casualties	Share of incidents in total terror attacks in country (%)	Share of casualties in total terror attacks in country (%)
Algiers	37	83	51	39
Athens	133	12	70	40
Berlin	16	10	8	6
Bogotá	19	91	11	74
Cairo	23	182	36	22
Casablanca	5	134	55	96
Islamabad	11	143	12	14
Istanbul	85	1,021	52	91
Jakarta	14	378	41	37
Jerusalem	164	2,040	40	39
Karachi	22	178	24	18
Lima	83	147	75	59
London	41	806	85	99
Madrid	9	1,694	14	96
Milan	20	7	24	33
Moscow	15	885	31	98
Mumbai (Bombay)	1	1,517	3	82
Nairobi	1	5,291	14	98
New York	12	10,807	37	92
Paris	51	389	48	94
Riyadh	24	333	63	36
Rome	22	12	26	55
Srinegar	94	467	10	14
Tel Aviv	40	1,048	10	20
Tokyo	7	5,012	35	99

Source: A Comprehensive Databank of Global Terrorist Incidents and Organization. The National Memorial Institute for Prevention of Terrorism (MIPT), available at www.tkb.org.

Note: Type 2 data with the exception of Srinagar (Type 1 data). Global cities are shown in bold italics; mega cities are shown in bold; major cities are shown in regular type.

exceeds their proportion of the countries' population (see Appendix, Table A2). Thus, the percentage of incidents in twenty-four out of twenty-five cities exceeded these cities' proportionate share of the national population, while the percentage of casualties in all twenty-five cities exceeded their proportion of the national population. Looking at specific cities, the proportion of national incidents ranged between 50 and 85 percent in cities like Algiers, Athens, Casablanca, Istanbul, Lima, London, Paris, and Riyadh. Similarly, the proportion of national casualties ranges between 50 to above 90 percent in cities like Bogotá, Mumbai, Casablanca, Istanbul, London, Madrid, Moscow, Mumbai, New York, and Paris.

First versus Second Cities as Targets

Practically all global, mega, and major cities can be thought of as "first cities" within their respective nations or regions. It is useful to compare these preeminent first cities with their "second city" counterparts. As the term suggests, second cities are spatially and economically distinct localities that are next in line in national importance. Second cities are far less likely to be attacked than their preeminent cousins. Algeria's second city, Oran, incurred just 6 percent of national casualties while its first city, Algiers, absorbed 39 percent; Colombia's second city, Cali, had 2 percent of national casualties while its first city, Bogotá, encountered 74 percent; and Spain's second city, Barcelona, saw just 3 percent of national casualties while its first city, Madrid, absorbed 96 percent (see Appendix, Tables A2 and A3).

When we turn to "first cities" of global stature, the pattern of casualties is especially apparent. To cite specific instances, New York absorbed 92 percent of terrorism casualties while Los Angeles incurred less than 1 percent; Paris's 94 percent of national casualties sets it apart from Marseille's 0 percent; and Tokyo experienced 99 percent of national casualties while Yokohama stood at zero. The United Kingdom is unusual because of the conflict in Northern Ireland, but barring "domestic terrorism," it too conforms to the pattern of internationally designated terror. Thus, London encountered 99 percent of national casualties in contrast to Birmingham's 0 percent. Clearly, cities of global stature are in a category by themselves, and while their incidents are far fewer, the attacks are designed to have a much bigger bang.

Exactly why there is a large difference in targeting first cities rather than second cities can be explained by terrorist logic. First cities usually are the seat of media, thereby furnishing a rationale for catalytic terror; first cities usually have larger populations than second cities, thereby furnishing a rationale for mega terror; and first cities usually have a larger economic function than second cities, thereby furnishing a rationale for smart terror.[36] Aggregate all three logics and reasons for the disparity in targeting become clear.

The logic can be traced further. Where a nation has more than one city sharing preeminence, the differences in terrorist patterns dramatically narrow. In Italy, Rome experienced 55 percent of national casualties while Milan came closer than most second cities with 33 percent. In Israel, Jerusalem met with 39 percent of casualties while Tel Aviv also came closer with 20 percent. Similarly, Pakistan's two co-equal cities, Karachi and Islamabad, shared a similar portion of casualties, respectively—18 and 14 percent. Germany, which tends to distribute its urban pre-eminence among Berlin, Hamburg, and Munich, also experienced similarly close proportions of attack. This rather consistent pattern suggests that most terrorists rationally select their targets and are able, implicitly or explicitly, to select cities with certain criteria in mind. Terrorists not only choose cities that maximize their objectives, but where those choices provide mixed payoffs, terrorists will divide the violence.

This snapshot shows us that modern terrorism is not just a national or international problem but also an urban one. Cities are in the terrorist bull's-eye, with profound consequences for the nature of urban life. Further, the more important and visible a city, the greater will be its target proneness.

Comparing the Severity of Attack

Most of the world's great cities have been subject to terror attacks at one time or another. There have been periodic swings as terrorism became more or less ascendant. Since the mid-twentieth century and up through the present era, Lima, Bogotá, and to a lesser extent Buenos Aires, have sustained terrorist attacks. In Latin America, terrorism has secular roots with the greater part attributed to political causes (Lima and Buenos Aires) or criminal elements (Bogotá). The Indian subcontinent has also stood out since its partition in 1947 and continues to be a sore spot. Mumbai, New Delhi, Karachi, and Islamabad were seats from which terrorists operated with impunity. Much of the conflagration was ignited by sectarian strife between Muslims and Hindus and by a long-burning dispute over Kashmir. Istanbul has also experienced chronic episodes of terror, mostly stemming from secular/political movements and also related to territorial disputes related to Kurdish independence.

During the 1970s and through two subsequent decades, European cities were the focus of attacks. At the forefront were London, Paris, Rome, Athens, and Madrid. With the exception of Basque separatists in Spain, terrorists in Europe were less concerned with territorial ambitions and basically motivated by secular/political causes (often radical leftist). By the 1990s and up through the turn of the century, the locus of urban terror had shifted to North Africa and the Middle East with Algiers, Cairo, and Jerusalem at the forefront. Much of the terrorism took on a religious and Islamist cast, becoming progressively more severe as the century turned the corner into the current millennium. Over the years terrorism has become both more lethal and more often religiously inspired. During the last decade or so, casualties were more than twice as high as those inflicted during the previous three or more decades. The lethality for each attack was especially severe. Between 1995 and 2005, each attack brought an average of 30 casualties compared to the previous period between 1968 and 2004 where the average for each incident was fewer than 4 casualties. For the last decade, attacks by secular terrorists caused 6 casualties per attack, contrasted to the religious terrorist toll which averaged 166 casualties per attack. In total, religious terrorism, which is mostly Islamist, accounted for 86 percent of casualties (see Appendix, Tables A6 and A7).

We see here the increasing severity of terror. Severity can be defined as unrelenting violence coupled with the cumulative damage caused to human life. One way to measure severity is to assess the frequency of incidents as well as the fatalities and injuries caused by attacks. Even among highly vulnerable preeminent cities the severity of attack varies considerably. Bogotá has been struck more often and with greater casualties than Buenos Aires. Paris has sustained more terrorist as-

Table 1.3

Severity Index of Global, Mega, and Major Cities, 1968–2005

Cities	Raw index	Standardized index
New York	221	100
Jerusalem	220	100
Tel Aviv	207	94
Paris	206	93
Madrid	205	93
Istanbul	202	91
London	192	87
Rome	185	83
Lima	181	82
Islamabad	178	80
Karachi	177	80
Athens	176	79
Mumbai (Bombay)	176	79
Cairo	174	78
Moscow	171	77
Nairobi	170	77
Tokyo	169	76
New Delhi	164	74
Riyadh	162	73
Berlin	160	72
Haifa	160	72
Ankara	159	72
Washington, DC	157	71
Bogotá	156	70
Jakarta	153	69
Algiers	152	68
Frankfurt	149	67
Munich	137	61
Bali	134	60
Barcelona	133	60

Source: Terrorism Knowledge Base, available at www.tkb.org.
Note: Type 2 data. Global cities are shown in bold italics; mega cities are shown in bold; major cities are shown in regular type.

saults with greater costs to life than Frankfurt. London and Jerusalem are among the most heavily struck cities in world. Moreover, the severity of urban terror will change over time and from city to city.

Table 1.3 provides a view of how major cities across the globe compare on the issue of severity. Thirty cities are included. The period covers more than three decades of urban terror incurred by global, mega, and major cities. The table combines incidents, injuries, and fatalities by converting them into a single index of severity. Raw scores from the index are standardized so that the number 100 represents the highest score, with others in descending order.[37]

As can be seen in the case of New York City, a catastrophic mega event can shape the table's results. Notwithstanding an exceptional event like 9/11, the overall scores provide a reasonable account of how the world's leading cities compare to one another over the long term. Confirming our earlier observations, cities with the highest severity index tend to be global or mega cities and in many cases they are national capitals. Population size makes a difference. For each additional million inhabitants, the standardized score increases by 4.85 points on the severity index.[38] Using a similar group of cities, another study found density of population to be a significant predictor for the severity of attack. It established that for every additional increment of 1,000 people per square kilometer (.4 square mile) to the average density of the city, the standardized severity score increased by one point.[39]

Many cities suffering from severity of attack are located in nations involved in major territorial disputes. The Israeli-Palestinian conflict is reflected in indices for Jerusalem and Tel Aviv, and these cities respectively hold the second- and third-highest scores. The Indian-Pakistani conflict can also be seen in the severity of attacks in Mumbai and New Delhi The same condition is true for Turkey, where territorial conflict with the Kurds has put Istanbul high on the list and Ankara farther down. Russia's territorial conflict with Chechnya gives Moscow a significant index. Notably, Russia's second city, St. Petersburg, is absent from the list.

Note, too, that terrorism strikes cities in developed as well as less-developed nations. Terrorism appears to have abolished economic, social, or religious distinctions, making cities like Mumbai, New Delhi, Karachi, and Cairo as susceptible to attack as their more prosperous counterparts in Europe or North America. India and to an even greater extent Egypt and Pakistan have placed hopes for development on their leading cities. Cities with lower levels of development are more easily set back by a paucity of capital accumulation. Lacking a base of wealth, they are likely to find recovery more difficult.

The severity of terror has a disproportionate effect on cities perched at different levels of development. Also, the measures used to create a severity index tell us a great deal about the increasing lethality of urban terror. Severity provides a clue for understanding the trajectory of this type of warfare, enabling us to inquire whether terrorism has abated, gotten worse, or remained stagnant. Looking backward may help us understand today's challenges and tomorrow's threats.

Finally, the severity of terror is important because it bears directly on the capacity of cities to survive. Cities are threatened not so much by the rare mega attack but by the human toll and material cost of continuous attacks. The constant friction of terror is the real enemy of city resilience. Accounts of medieval history inform us that cities can disappear when they are placed under long-term siege. At least in our contemporary period, cities have proven themselves to be fairly resilient and recover quickly. Indeed, this is not the first time cities have adapted to external threats and their resilience is well established. The question is less of survival than the manner in which cities will continue to survive.

Conclusions

Terrorism is a complex phenomenon, defined as a type of asymmetric warfare that deliberately and indiscriminately employs violence against noncombatants and their sources of support in order to threaten or intimidate them for political purposes. The distinctions between group terrorism and state terrorism are sufficient to warrant studying them as different forms of warfare. Urban terror pertains to high-density, heterogeneous, mixed-use, continually developing bounded environments that generate hosts of synergistic interactions. Any study of urban terror should be concerned not only with the organization and tactics of terrorists but with the terrorized. Both the direct and the indirect victims of terror are very much part of the story, especially as it relates to personal costs and the large-scale suffocation of city life.

Urban terrorism can be understood as consisting of catalytic, mega, and smart terror. Catalytic terrorism attempts to broadcast the event by shocking a larger public. Mega terror is much larger in scope and attempts to inflict mass casualties and extensive property damage. During the last fifteen years or so, mega terror has taken on an increasingly religious cast. By contrast, smart terror is precisely aimed at vulnerable points of a city's strength, such as its economy or infrastructure. Urban terrorism contains all three elements of catalytic, mega, and smart terror. This made the September 2001 assault on the Twin Towers all the more potent.

Urban terror manifests itself and can be examined along three particular dimensions—territory, space, and logistics. Urban terrorists seek to decontrol large swatches of territory, inflict damage on smaller spaces, and obtain logistical access to potential targets. Finally, the most frequent targets of urban terror can be located within global, mega, and major cities. Generally, more populous and high-profile cities incur disproportionate attacks. These cities can be assessed by the frequency of incidents and the number of casualties due to terror, summarized in an index of severity.

The Evolution of Urban Terrorism

As 2001 began counterterrorism officials were receiving frequent but fragmentary reports about threats. Indeed, there appeared to be possible threats almost everywhere the United States had interests—including at home.

—9/11 Commission Report, "The System Was Blinking Red"

Mega Terror in New York, Madrid, and London

The event is all too familiar. September 11 happened on a crisp, autumn-like morning. Two hijacked passenger aircraft silhouetted against an azure blue sky came crashing into the twin 110-story towers of the World Trade Center. The North Tower was struck first as the American Airlines flight crashed into floors 93 through 99, igniting everything in its path. Seventeen minutes later a United Airlines plane hit the South Tower, cutting though floors 77 through 85, causing massive fireballs to surge through the building. Ten terrorists, five in each aircraft, succeeded in turning passenger planes into guided missiles, instantly killing 600 people on those floors alone. Others died as they became trapped in elevators and clogged the exits. Many more would fall as they struggled through fume-infested, smoke-drenched corridors and stairwells. The site came to be known as "ground zero," and its fatalities rose to nearly 3,000 people with more than twice that number of casualties.

In less than two hours, the twin giants of the World Trade Center (WTC) had collapsed, spewing concrete, glass, and massive amounts of ash onto the streets and into the air. As the buildings fell, crowds ran down the narrow streets for safety. Hours later, another building in the WTC complex capitulated, adding to the twisted and smoking wreckage already on the ground. On the other side of the island in Brooklyn, citizens watched in fright as part of New York's skyline disappeared. Days later the odor of human loss and flakes of debris still hung over lower Manhattan. The shock of 9/11 burrowed into peoples' minds and, years later, most Americans could recount how they came to remember that stunning day. What made 9/11 possible was mass. The scale and density of the city with its massive buildings, teeming streets, crowded hotels, and jammed mass transit presented enormous opportunities for terrorists. More than 50,000 people worked at the World Trade Center and another 80,000 visited it each day. Each floor of the towers covered more than

40,000 square feet, and the buildings contained over 200 elevators. The potential for immense gridlock and resulting casualties was alarmingly clear.[1]

According to available data, 9/11 was the first time more than 500 persons were killed in a single terrorist assault, though its consequences extended beyond that immediate loss.[2] The event showed that a great city could be brought to a halt by chaos and shock. Within a flicker of time the city shut down. Airports, tunnels, and bridges were blocked. The New York Stock Exchange closed, stopping all financial services. Nonessential government services were suspended while schools, theaters, and museums closed their doors. At the same time, a bomb threat forced the evacuation of the United Nations, obliging diplomats and personnel to seek safety.

Large cities are ideal battlegrounds for terrorists. While 9/11 was hardly the first episode in the terrorist saga, it was a dramatic instance of catalytic terrorism. It woke up much of the world by transmitting the reality of a giant attack and the possibility that it could happen elsewhere. Catalytic terrorism came to the fore by capturing public apprehension, catching media attention, raising intellectual debate, and absorbing the resources of governments. The attack on New York became the emblem of urban terrorism. Soon afterward, the language of 9/11 was expropriated with subsequent attacks on Madrid, called "Spain's 9/11," and London, called "Great Britain's 9/11." Officials in Jerusalem, whose cumulative experience with terrorism was lengthier than New York's, began to refer to its struck center as "Israel's ground zero."

To be sure, the attacks in Madrid on 3/11 (2004) and London on 7/7 (2005) were nothing near the scale of New York, but they did confirm a pattern that combined catalytic, mega, and smart terror. In all these cases, terrorists targeted high-value resources and congested spaces to sow panic. They also succeeded in transmitting the shock of these events to the rest of the world. Madrid's 3/11 occurred at Atocha Station, a huge complex located at the center of the city and near the Prado Museum—one of the country's great cultural landmarks. Atocha Station is the terminus for longer rail lines extending into the countryside as well as a local underground for shorter commutes.

Ten bombs had been placed on four trains, designed to detonate simultaneously as commuters entered the station during the height of the morning rush hour (7:37 A.M.). Each of the trains was filled with manual workers, office employees, older students, and younger schoolchildren. Had the trains not been delayed, the explosion would have occurred inside Atocha, possibly causing the entire structure to collapse on a much larger number of waiting passengers. Within minutes of each other, the packed trains burst from the explosions, causing 191 fatalities and 1,500 injuries. Transportation was disrupted for days and the catalytic effects were palpable. Soon afterward Spanish voters brought a more dovish government into office and announced the withdrawal of Spanish troops from Iraq (one of the ostensible reasons for the attack). The efforts by the new Spanish government seemed to be in vain, and just two weeks later explosives were discovered on train tracks.

The London attack of 7/7 was also aimed at mass transit. It too depended upon high-density crowds for effectiveness and bore many of the markings of Madrid. Approximately 3 million commuters ride London's Underground daily, while buses carry more than 500,000 passengers into central London each weekday. All the struck areas were transit exchanges within central London, close to office complexes, retail shops, or other areas of congestion. Four bombs were placed at different places—three along Underground lines at approximate points in Liverpool, Edgware, and Kings Cross stations, and a fourth in a double-decker bus at Tavistock Square. Like New York and Madrid, the explosions occurred at or near morning rush hour, when crowds were at or near their peak and set off within a close time frame (8:49 A.M. onward). Within 60 minutes 56 people were killed and 700 injured. Not all the dead could be counted or identified immediately, because they were caught in the smoke- and fume-filled Underground.

The train blasts were frightful, and eyewitnesses described large explosions that sent glass and debris in every direction. Darkened tunnels and electrical outages made recovery all the more difficult. Rescue workers had to use pickaxes in order to free trapped passengers. The Fire Brigade resorted to emergency triage by tending to those most likely to survive. The bus attack was equally shocking as the explosive force blew the roof from a double-decker bus.

Parts of London seized up. The entire metro system was closed, and buses and trains heading into London stopped short or turned back. Roads into central London were blocked off and vehicles commandeered for use as ambulances. One hotel was turned into an emergency care facility. Throughout the West End of London, shops and restaurants were shuttered. Even the mobile phone network was switched off for a time, as authorities feared that terrorists would use it to launch a follow-up attack. London's initial shock and subsequent response typifies the pattern of confusion, diversion, or semi-paralysis that can last up to a few days.

While 9/11, 3/11, and 7/7 received the widest coverage and are regarded as seminal events, they hardly touch the extent of urban terrorism. These dates are important because they constitute one of the rare times when events intersect with larger historical trends, producing a new realization. We can better appreciate the scope and severity of urban terror by turning to that recent past as well as looking across the continents to other cities.[3]

Attacks Around the World

Urban terrorism did not become a public specter with 9/11, 3/11, or 7/7. It has had a deep and persistent history, which most Americans had hardly noticed until it struck home. For Americans it is useful to remember that 9/11 was not the first attempt on the World Trade Center. The simple idea of collapsing two buildings in a highly populated, densely built "global city" occurred to a group of Islamic fundamentalists almost a decade earlier. In 1993, members of a cell based in Brooklyn and Jersey City parked a truck filled with explosives in a garage beneath the Twin Towers. The ensuing explosion opened a gap seven stories high, causing the death of six people and more than a thousand injuries. The man who planted the bomb, Ramzi Yousef, later claimed he had hoped to kill 250,000 people. Yousef's projections were exaggerated, but had it not been for an error in placing the explosives, the FBI estimated a death toll of 50,000.[4]

In that same year, the FBI managed to thwart a "summer of mayhem" planned by another group of Islamic radicals. Had the terrorist attacks been carried to success, that mayhem would have destroyed the United Nations building as well as the Lincoln and Holland tunnels, and Federal Plaza. International diplomats and American political leaders were also slated for assassination. Most, but not all, of the attacks in the United States were of international vintage. The situation across the Atlantic is quite different and those countries have longer experience with domestic or homegrown terrorism.

Great Britain's history of terrorism is far more extensive than the few dramatic events suffered on American soil. Taking London during several decades, more than 300 incidents have brought on the death of an estimated 119 people and injured over 1,500.[5] Most of these were launched by the Irish Republican Army (IRA) or its splinter groups. Attacks have been leveled against financial, social, political, and transportation targets. While London saw its fair share of attacks, some of the most severe terrorism occurred in Northern Ireland, in populated areas of Belfast, Londonderry (Derry), and Omagh. In recent years Arabs and Islamic groups have been responsible for an increasing number of episodes.

Madrid also has a long and painful history with terrorism, launched mostly by Basque Fatherland and Freedom (ETA). Other extremist groups also find Madrid to be a convenient target. These range from leftist revolutionaries to nationalist Arabs, Lebanese, Armenians, or Moroccans. ETA, however, has been the singular largest source of attacks, and during approximately four decades it has been responsible for more than 800 fatalities with more than twice as many wounded. Foreign-based terrorist organizations find refuge in Spain's liberal rules for asylum and its growing immigrant communities. Casualties from these groups have been light, however, and up until 3/11 the largest number of victims came from an assault by Hezbollah on a restaurant that catered to American servicemen. That attack resulted in eighteen dead and more than 80 wounded (mostly Spanish civilians).[6]

Up until 3/11, targets of choice in Madrid have included restaurants, embassies, tourist centers, and airline offices—almost all of which are in downtown locations. A handful of the attacks were executed through planted bombs or crude mortars and grenades fired from a distance. Spanish police now have special bomb squads and detonation teams that comb the city regularly.

Elsewhere in the world, cities have been subject to high levels of chronic violence. Istanbul is a packed city with a tumultuous atmosphere. Its mix of ancient tourist attractions, crowded bazaars, and modern office districts makes it particularly susceptible to large-scale attack. During almost four decades, 223 Istanbulians have been killed and nearly 1,288 wounded. Terrorism has been mounted by a number of groups across the political spectrum, including nationalists (the Kurdish Workers

Party or PKK), radical Islamic factions (Turkish Hezbollah and al Qaeda cells), and non-Kurdish leftists (Revolutionary People's Liberation Front). Major targets are often at busy commercial centers on the "European" side of the city where banks, foreign businesses, and consulates are located. PKK terrorists have also attacked the city's Old Bazaar (a main marketplace) as well as the renowned Blue Mosque and Hagia Sofia Mosque (main tourist attractions). On two separate occasions, Islamic radicals and al Qaeda operatives targeted Neve Shalom Synagogue, located in an older, crowded neighborhood. The Neve Shalom attack caused the deaths of forty-five people and many more injuries. During the past two years, terrorists have continued to strike Istanbul—with shooting attacks on the Asian side of the city and a detonated bus explosion on the European side.

Jerusalem's experience has been fairly continuous. Urban terrorism existed before the birth of modern Israel and has continued ever since. Casualties and incidents reached minor peaks toward the end of the 1960s, abated for a while at the dawn of the 1970s, peaked again in the mid-1970s, and rose intermittently through the 1980s. The 1990s were mixed. While the Oslo Accords brought about a respite, terrorism broke out again soon after the Camp David talks (1995). During this period, journalists were eager to see a light in the peace tunnel and called these attacks "terror's last gasp," but facts spoke otherwise and terror rose to unprecedented levels at the turn of the century.

Jerusalem also refracts the patterns commonly seen in other cities. Earlier attacks were mostly conducted by secular groups. Toward the end of the twentieth century, Islamist Hamas and Islamic Jihad joined the clash and terror became more lethal. Instead of individual knifings, high-powered explosives were employed, increasingly by youths who turned themselves into human bombs.

Also counted as a volatile area of the world is the Indian subcontinent, its conflict centered on Kashmir. During nearly four decades India's commercial capital, Mumbai (Bombay), and its political capital, New Delhi, sustained a combined total of 2,500 casualties. Some of the worst incidents have occurred in recent years. In 1993, more than a dozen coordinated blasts in Mumbai killed 300 people and wounded another 1,200. The attackers struck the Bombay Stock Exchange, banks, hotels, airline offices, and buses. In 2001, the bombing of the Parliament building in New Delhi killed fourteen people and wounded scores of others. This attack brought India and Pakistan to the brink of war. By July 2006, mega attacks returned to Mumbai when seven coordinated explosions ripped through trains on its busy commuter network. This most recent attack came to be known as "India's 7/11," leaving 188 dead and 800 injured. While Pakistan denied any role, Mumbai police attributed the attack to Islamists from Lashkar-e-Taiba and Jaish-e-Mohammed.[7]

These accounts barely scratch the surface. Terrorism goes well beyond a single group and some pockets of the world. It extends from the Americas into North and sub-Saharan Africa, through the Middle East to Asia and the Pacific Basin. Even in most recent times, terrorism has multiple exponents, and it would be a mistake to equate al Qaeda with its advent.

The Scope of Urban Terror

In 1999, a prestigious Washington, DC, think tank, the Woodrow Wilson International Center, held a conference on cities and security. Papers for the conference were sponsored by the U.S. Agency for International Development. Scholars from around the world were asked to select a major threat to urban security and write a paper on the subject. Some twenty papers were written, and over forty researchers attended the conference. The papers and discussion centered around crises of governance and citizen participation, water shortages and famine, migration and displacement, health and the environment, as well as crime and drug trafficking. The ensuing discussions covered a great deal on the subject of urban security, though hardly a person raised the issue of terrorism or chose to write about it.[8]

The Wilson Center's concerns were complemented by a domestic focus on urban crises undertaken by the Fannie Mae Foundation. In that same year, Fannie Mae published a study by Robert Fishman entitled *The American Metropolis at Century's End: Past and Future.* Using a survey of leading scholars, Fishman sought to assess historical as well as future factors that might influence cities. Fishman's respondents listed wealth disparities, suburban political majorities, the growing underclass, suburban deterioration, and the like. But again, there was no mention of terrorism or the threat it posed to cities.[9]

The general initiatives taken by both the Wilson Center and Fannie Mae were well founded and properly aimed. Cities play a growing role in world development and they are the pivotal points of change. A half-century ago, 29 percent of the planet's population lived in urban areas. By 1980 that percentage climbed to 39 percent. As we look at cities at the turn of the century, we find 49 percent of the earth's 6.4 billion people live in urban areas. Population densities have doubled, and they are likely to rise in geometric proportion in the coming decades. Forty years ago there were just eight cities in the world with metropolitan populations of more than 5 million. By the turn of the century that number had reached 42 percent. In the next 15 years, cities with metropolitan populations with over 5 million inhabitants are expected to grow in number to 61.[10]

While cities are swelling with population, they are also experiencing two polar tendencies—immense infusions of wealth coupled with large-scale poverty. One can visit large cities almost anywhere and see whole neighborhoods filled with luxury housing, while also discovering that 32 percent of the world's population lives in urban slums.[11] Two global cities illustrate the problem. In 1980, New York and London held several trillion dollars in stock market value. By the end of the last century, these two cities had roughly tripled that value to $12 trillion, enabling them to command the major portion of the world's corporate assets.[12] At the same time, New York's poverty shot up from 20 percent in 1980 to 24 percent by the end of the 1990s, while during a similar period London's poverty rose from 20 percent to 28 percent.[13] In these cities poverty is both spatially confined to particular neighborhoods and socially concentrated within particular minorities. The polarization has given rise to what some authors characterize as "dual or divided cities" where different social classes live worlds apart.[14] Granted, New York and London are extreme examples, but they do illustrate the growing disparity of wealth in cities around the world.

While we should be careful—indeed skeptical—about attributing the *causes* of terror to economic conditions, the *effects* are a different story. There is less doubt about what attracts terrorists. The incongruous mixture of growth, density, wealth, poverty, and immigration make these and other cities primary targets—both as venues of operation and targets of calculation. At one end of the urban spectrum, poorer, often immigrant, neighborhoods provide spaces where terrorists can embed themselves. At the other end of the spectrum, wealth and density provide desirable targets for attack. Not surprisingly, terrorism takes on an urban complexion. The attacks on New York, London, Madrid, Istanbul, Jerusalem, Mumbai, and other cities are a logical extension of these developments. With the benefit of hindsight, it might be easy to spot a trend toward urban terrorism, though years ago careful attention to the data also would have told the same story.

For all their substantial worth, the Wilson Center and Fannie Mae publications did not pick up on this trend. From a conceptual perspective, we can call this phenomenon the *scope of urban terrorism*. By the phrase *scope of urban terrorism*, I mean its geographical extensiveness and prevalence across nation-states. The scope of urban terrorism can be identified by the degree to which it has spread to many cities around the world.

Table 2.1 provides a picture of urban terrorism's spreading prevalence. The table portrays twenty-five nations and territories in terms of urban versus nonurban incidents between 1968 and 2005. Also shown are fatalities and casualties.

Of the twenty-five nations located in areas stretching from North America to South Asia, only three fell below a 50 percent rate of urban attack. During more than three decades, 76 percent of all terrorism occurred within cities. Given the range of urban-based population during the 1960s and 1970s (between 30 and 40 percent) and during subsequent decades (plus 40 percent) the pattern of urban concentration is striking. Of course there are countries listed whose urban populations are quite high—Great Britain at 89 percent, France at 75 percent, and the United States at 77 percent—whose rate of urban attack would be consistent with their urbanized inhabitants. But there are also many countries with very low urban populations—Algeria at 57 percent, Egypt at 45 percent, India at 27 percent, Morocco at 53 percent, and Pakistan at 35 percent—whose rate of urban attack far exceeds the proportion of people living in metropolitan areas.

Has urban terror actually increased across the globe as a proportion of all terrorism? A time line from 1968 onward would reveal that while cities have always been popular targets, up until 9/11 the trend was erratic. Before the big attack on New York, some years skewed overwhelming toward urban terrorism while other years

Table 2.1

Scope of Terror: Twenty-Five Nations and Territories, 1968–2005

Country/Territory	Incidents	Fatalities	Injuries	Casualties	Urban incidents (%)	Non-urban incidents (%)
Algeria	213	959	1,189	2,148	71	29
Canada	27	7	41	48	96	4
Chechnya	230	377	743	1,120	42	58
Colombia	1,608	1,410	2,098	3,508	54	46
Egypt	130	346	922	1,268	52	48
France	1,085	188	1,353	1,541	85	15
Germany	462	89	693	782	97	3
Greece	619	145	497	642	96	4
India	540	1,501	3,849	5,350	36	64
Israel	825	1,387	6,937	8,324	77	23
Indonesia	219	454	1,422	1,876	73	27
Italy	417	86	406	492	96	4
Japan	79	19	5,104	5,123	91	9
Kashmir	912	1,412	2,087	3,499	23	77
Kenya	11	320	5,166	5486	82	18
Morocco	25	52	103	155	52	48
Northern Ireland	683	68	195	263	78	22
Pakistan	657	1,482	5,330	6,812	77	23
Peru	363	174	390	564	88	12
Russia	417	1,396	3,450	4,846	74	26
Saudi Arabia	60	314	1,622	1,936	92	8
Spain	1,286	292	1,262	1,554	96	4
Turkey	1,152	512	1,960	2,472	80	19
UK	169	362	888	1,250	98	2
United States	552	3,235	8,775	1,2010	86	14
TOTAL	12,741	16,587	56,482	73,069	76	24

Source: Data from RAND database, available at www.tkb.org. Type 1 data.

saw a drop-off. After 9/11 and through the year 2005, cities accounted for at least 78 percent of incidents (see Appendix, Figure A1). All the same, this disproportion of urban terrorism constitutes just one aspect of its rise.

The Frequency of Urban Terror

In the summer of 2001, a former counterterrorism analyst named Larry Johnson wrote an op-ed piece for the *New York Times*.[15] Johnson titled his article "The Declining Terrorist Threat," and he introduced the article with an assurance that people were needlessly worrying about terrorism:

> Judging from news reports and the portrayal of villains in our popular entertainment, Americans are bedeviled by fantasies about terrorism. They seem to believe that terrorism is the greatest threat to the United States and that it is becoming more widespread and lethal. They are likely to think that the United States is the most popular target of terrorists and they almost certainly have the impression that extremist Islamic groups cause most terrorism.

Johnson went on to posit a counterargument, commenting that the numbers of terrorist incidents were declining, that fewer of these incidents were judged to be "significant," and that even fewer of the attacks "involved American citizens or business." He explained that most terrorism was foreign based and connected to business ventures. "The greatest risk is clear," Johnson advised, "if you are drilling for oil in Colombia—or in nations like Ecuador, Nigeria or Indonesia—you should take appropriate precautions; otherwise Americans have little to fear." The anti-terrorist expert brought his point home by concluding:

> Although high-profile incidents have fostered the perception that terrorism is becoming more lethal, the numbers say otherwise, and early signs suggest that the decade beginning in 2000 will continue the downward trend. A major reason for the decline is the current reluctance of countries like Iraq, Syria and Libya, which once eagerly backed terrorist groups, to provide safe havens, funding and training.

In the first instance, Johnson's reasoning was faulty because he assumed terrorism could be isolated. As a method of asymmetric warfare, terrorism can be adopted by any number of organizations in order to even out the odds. Terrorists learn from one another, and what works will spread to other underground organizations. Moreover, terrorism is mutable or, as Stern puts it, terrorism is a "protean enemy," able to change shape and flourish in many environments.[16] Terrorism occurs in many different places, in many different forms, and can be adapted to many different of conditions.

While Johnson miscalculated, from one vantage point he was correct. Within at least some particular time frames, the incidents of terror had declined. Figure 2.1 presents previously cited data in a different format. Taking the total number of

Figure 2.1 **Frequency of Terror: Incidents in Twenty-Two Nations, 1968–2005**

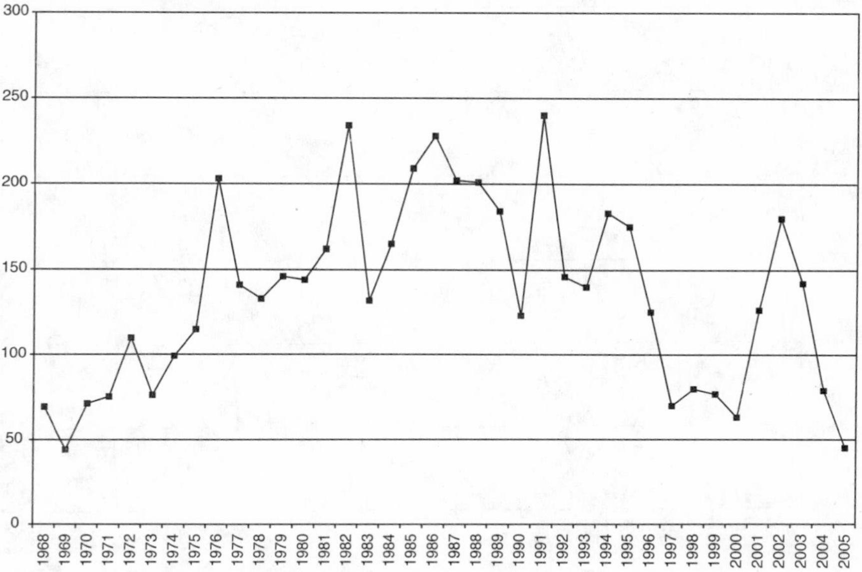

Source: Adapted from RAND database, available at www.tkb.org. Type 2 data.

incidents in twenty-two countries between 1968 and 2005, it presents the results as a line graph. Both urban and nonurban incidents are included.

Imagine Johnson from the year 2001 looking backward to the previous decade. Beginning in 1993 he would see a sharply plunging line culminating in a deep trough. Without attention to longer trends, the slight upward tilt of the line for 1998 could be interpreted as a glitch. Indeed, with some logic Johnson could have taken any number of limited time intervals in the record of terror and concluded it was on a downward slide.

Where Johnson went wrong was in not noticing the much longer time line, characterized by sharply upward peaks followed by plummeting downward lines. Taking a longer perspective, we see that in 1976 the number of incidents rose above 200 while just two years later it fell below 150. A decade later, incidents climbed to an all-time high of 228 only to fall by almost half in the mid-1990s. This pattern continued throughout the rest of the century, with terrorism hitting a steep decline in 2000.

The hard-won lesson is that the *frequency of terrorism* can be quite erratic. By frequency I mean the rate of occurrence. How often terrorism occurs or reoccurs is critical in assessing trends, and these rates should be examined over different intervals of time. Terrorism seems to occur in cycles or waves. Attacks tend to bunch up around particular targets and then recede for a time, only to reappear in the same or an altered form.

Figure 2.2   **Severity of Terror: Casualties in Twenty-Two Nations, 1968–2005**

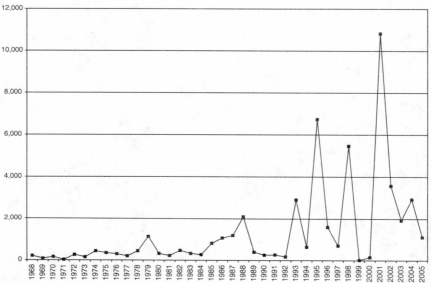

Source: Adapted from RAND database, available at www.tkb.org. Type 2 data.

As we shall see in later chapters, the reasons for this are numerous and connected to the purposes of urban terrorism. One of its core tactics is to inculcate fear, and as such, the shock of attacks is more effectively released in clustered and repetitive assaults, rather than attacks that are spread out. For this reason alone, one can see changes in the frequency of terrorism. At times it will be extremely active and at other times it will lie dormant, perhaps varying by places across the globe.

The Severity of Urban Terrorism

Johnson also might have systematically examined casualties, or what is here called the *severity of attack.* As noted in an earlier chapter, severity refers to incidents, fatalities, and injuries caused by attacks. In seeking to inculcate fear, terrorists will assess the "payoff" of any given attack in terms of its human casualties. The general notion behind measuring severity is that terrorists have grown more efficient and are able to achieve a bigger payoff with fewer attacks. Thus, even if incidents appear to be falling in number, total casualties may be rising. Accordingly, we turn our attention to that aspect of severity dealing with casualties. Figures 2.2 and 2.3 portray the severity of terror in twenty-two countries across the globe between 1968 and 2005. Figure 2.2 displays total casualties while Figure 2.3 shows casualties per attack. Included in the figure are both urban and nonurban casualties.

Figure 2.3 **Severity of Terror: Casualties per Attack in Twenty-Two Nations, 1968–2005**

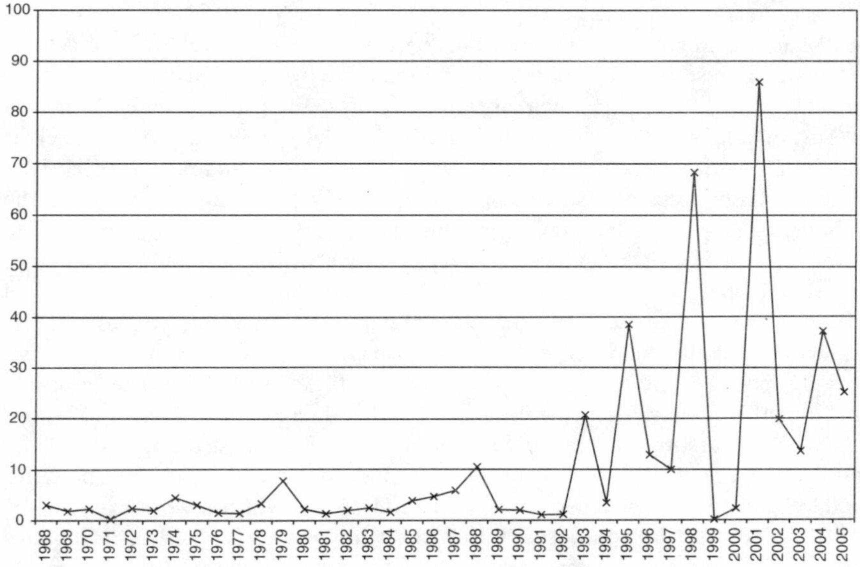

Source: Adapted from RAND database, available at www.tkb.org. Type 2 data.

Notice the modest ratcheting effect of casualties—extremely low through the 1970s followed by a slight rise, with each successive dip followed by a slightly higher jump until the radical jump due to the 9/11 attack, followed by irregular movements. Looking at absolute numbers, Figure 2.2 tells us that in the 1970s casualties peaked at 1,126; by the 1980s they had hit 2,102; by the 1990s over 6,000; and by the turn of the century over 10,000, only to drop down again below 2,000.

This ratchet effect is even clearer in Figure 2.3 when examining casualties per attack. Here, the jumps stand out for the entire time trajectory. As time goes by, the severity of attack increases, albeit in erratic patterns. For example, in the early 1970s terrorists exacted a high of almost 4 casualties per attack; by the late 1970s, the high rose to almost 10 casualties per attack; by the 1980s it had risen slightly above 10 casualties per attack; by the 1990s that rose to more than 60 casualties per attack; and by the turn of the century it peaked at more than 80 casualties per attack, only to fall by 2005 to less than 30 casualties per attack.[17]

That terrorists are exacting bigger payoffs is corroborated by other studies, many of which use a different methodology and rely on different databases. Using a time series analysis, Enders and Sandler show that over the years, victims are 17 percent more likely to be killed or injured in terror attacks.[18] More people are being more severely injured by terrorism, and this makes it all the more lethal. We can best conclude that while it is possible for frequency to decrease, the lethality of terror may very well increase.

What else might we learn from this? For one, terrorists are "rational actors" interested in results and willing to pay a high price to achieve a certain outcome. Second, suicide terror is a particularly effective way to bring this about. In Hoffman's words, suicide is the "ultimate smart bomb."[19] Attackers willing to blow themselves up can recognize strategic targets, pinpoint large crowds, and penetrate barriers. Further, the chances of a suicide attacker succeeding are much greater than the chances of those wielding guns or planting explosives.

So long as terrorists can draw from a population willing to supply recruits (not always possible), suicide attacks are likely to be resorted to because they are optimal killers (creating mega terror) and capture attention (creating catalytic terror). The trend lines bear this out. Over the last two decades, high-risk attacks (where terrorists might expect to be killed by others) and suicide attacks (where terrorists purposely kill themselves) have dramatically increased. While a number of terrorist groups claim to have first employed suicide decades ago, its current use has spread globally by al Qaeda, on the West Bank and Gaza by Palestinians, in Russia by Chechens, and in Iraq by numerous insurgents recruited from the Muslim world.[20]

Third, and for our purposes, this is most important: High severity requires mass and soft targets that can best be found in cities. Poorly defended, densely inhabited, high-value sites make the best targets. Once terror evolves from small to large scale, it requires the city—particularly the mega city. We now turn to a closer look at these targets.

Global, Mega, and Major Cities

Ask what kinds of cities are likely to experience terror in the future, and some of the answers will vary, but others will not. By and large, mega terror and smart terror are likely to target or exploit cities with *high density and thick infrastructure*, and *concentrated high-value commercial assets* while catalytic terror would target cities with a *global or international profile*.[21] Global, mega, and major cities contain most of all of these possible vulnerabilities, which are amplified below.

Density and Infrastructure

- clustered, congested environments, large crowds
- skyscrapers, office towers, or large public buildings
- tourist or visitor attractions (hotels, restaurants, nightclubs, retail malls, marketplaces, and historic sites)
- bridges, tunnels, metro systems, rail stations
- major airports, docking stations, seaports, and transit interchanges
- theaters, museums, sports arenas, pubs, discos, and cultural centers

Concentrated High-Value Commercial or Political Assets

- center of world and national commerce
- large financial centers with big stock exchanges
- major banks and lending institutions
- government buildings, diplomatic offices like embassies, consulates, and international organizations
- large-scale tourism and tourist attractions like historic sites, hotels, cafes, beaches

Global or International Profile

- a city belonging to a state involved in international conflict
- a global reputation, a capital city, a political seat
- major media (newspapers, radio, television)
- an intellectual community that fosters debate
- multiethnic neighborhoods, large foreign communities
- a reputation for granting asylum to immigrants

As mentioned. terrorists target *density and infrastructure* because a single attack maximizes casualties. The methods of assault vary and include detonated explosives, shootings, and suicide bombing. The most frequently attacked sites are packed city centers, encompassing restaurants, hotels, retail outlets, and mass transit lines. Before the big attack in New York there was Oklahoma City (1995), where American terrorists planted explosives in a parked van at a large federal office building. That attack killed 168 people and left over 500 wounded. Manchester (1996) also suffered a similar attack through an explosive-laden van parked outside a downtown shopping center, resulting in 200 casualties. Tokyo (1995) experienced a sarin gas attack in its metro system, killing eleven commuters and causing thousands of injuries.[22]

Densely populated cities in less developed nations have been chronic victims, among them Bogotá, Cairo, and Casablanca. Bogotá has a history of terror connected to its drug trade as well as political insurrection. Bombs were set off in downtown Bogotá and its marketplaces (2002 and 2003), killing scores of people and injuring many more. Cairo has an extensive history of direct assaults; in 1996 and 1997, gunmen opened fire on tourists outside their hotels, killing a total of eighteen and wounding sixteen others. Sometime later, attackers threw bombs and opened fire on tourists outside a museum, killing ten and wounding scores more. Casablanca experienced a series of coordinated attacks in a two-day period (2003) that killed twenty-nine people and injured hundreds. The attacks were aimed at a foreign consulate, a restaurant, a hotel, and a Jewish center.

Terrorists are especially keen on targeting *concentrated, high-value assets.* More so than ever globalization has turned cities into "nodes" for a vast international network of transactions. Economic complexity and international interdependence have converted cities into powerful command centers, directing billions of dollars in investment, managing millions of people, and controlling thousands of work sites around the globe.[23] This may be a sign of enormous power, but it is also a very visible sign of vulnerability. A well-placed explosion can produce catastrophic reverberations and paralyze a city.

September 11 is the most conspicuous example of terror's ability to create a contagion of economic rupture. The initial attacks in New York caused stock exchanges in the United States and other countries to fall. Gradually, stock exchanges have become inured to these shocks and are able to quickly recover. The same tactic of economic assault has been employed in London and also in Istanbul and Jerusalem, though with narrower economic repercussions. During the early 1970s, planted bombs exploded in central London hotels and banks. By the 1990s, economic targets in central London were struck again. One bomb blew a ten-foot breach in the stock exchange, located in the financial district, the "City." A large bomb was also found and defused at Canary Wharf, the site of London's new business district. From the standpoint of financial and banking assets, the most notable attack was the bombing of the Baltic Exchange in the heart of London. That event brought into question the safety of conducting business in the City, raised insurance costs throughout the City, and precipitated massive efforts to protect its buildings and thoroughfares.[24]

In 2003, serial assaults were launched in Istanbul on the British consulate and HSBC bank. Using trucks filled with explosives, the terrorists detonated their cargo within two minutes of each other, blowing out vital economic functions. Jerusalem has been subject to its most intense attacks, generated by al Aqsa violence in 2000. Most of the attacks were aimed at the center of the city and carried out by suicide terrorists. For at least a time, the cumulative effects of terrorism have devastated downtown, small business, and the city's tourist industry.[25]

Moreover, tourist areas with historic sites (Istanbul, Jerusalem, and Luxor) or with attractive beaches and resorts (Bali, Djerba, Nairobi, and Sharm al-Sheikh) have been struck time and again. Several factors contribute to the vulnerability of tourist cities, including the presence of Westerners living an affluent or "decadent" life-style, the resonance created by inflicting casualties on an international clientele, the highly elastic nature of tourism that induces consumers to cancel vacations because of danger, and the immediate impact of those cancellations on foreign exchange revenues. An attack on a "tourist city" also puts in question government contentions about stability and security. Thus, devastating attacks in Bali brought Indonesia under suspicion as a hotbed of Islamic radicalism while Sharm al-Sheikh made Egypt's claims of being the "Red Sea Riviera" ring hollow.

Last, terrorists are apt to both operate in and target cities with a *global and international profile*. Part of this profile stems from a city's belonging to a nation with high levels of international involvement or conflict. During the 1990s, Paris was attacked because of France's involvement with its former colonies in North

Africa, particularly Algeria. Moscow and Mumbai have been a targeted because of international disputes over territory and religion. The most obvious cases of 9/11, 3/11, and 7/7 in part were due to American, Spanish, and British involvement in the Middle East.

Immigrants, guest workers, and international communities can also be a significant source of risk. While social pluralism provides rich synergies, under certain conditions it can be a nesting ground for terrorist organizations. Terrorists find safe houses, material support, and recruits within ethnic communities or with co-religionists in local mosques. Global, mega, and major cities not only supply these conditions in abundance, but furnish the anonymity for terrorists who wish to "get lost."

There are instances as well where heterogeneous cities provide a battleground for intergroup conflict—sometimes fought out by using terrorism. A sense of relative deprivation sharpens as different groups come into closer proximity. Word gets around more quickly and socialization proceeds more rapidly in densely packed environments. Beirut provides a ready example of how different groups living under conditions of hopelessness and in proximity to one another can engage in mutual attack. Similar ecologies of terror have pervaded Belfast, Londonderry, Sarajevo, and Hyderabad. Rather than being directed vertically, warfare occurs laterally and between groups operating at the same level—Hindus fighting Muslims in Mumbai, Albanians fighting Serbs in Kosovo, or rival criminal gangs fighting each other and the citizenry in Bogotá. Ethnic, religious, or underworld gangs simply battle it out.

Even more than this, the media plays an enormous role in the exercise of terrorism. In Iraq, a priority of the insurgents is to film an attack and download the footage for distribution. The insurgents have now honed that process to a science so that within thirty minutes the attack is broadcast to other parts of the world.[26] Few places enable terrorists to reach an audience more than a city with a prominent media and intellectual establishment. As one terrorist in Algeria expressed his logic: "Is it preferable for our cause to kill ten enemies in an *oued* (dry river bed) of Telergma when no one will talk of it . . . or [is it better to kill] a single man in Algiers, which will be noted the next day in the American press?"[27]

A blast in a mountain town or in the countryside may arouse local concern, but is generally of little or no consequence for the rest of the world. But an attack on Wall Street, a massacre in Piccadilly Circus, the bombing of the Eiffel Tower, or poison gas in a Tokyo metro arouses international alarm. Any such event will be instantly telegraphed to a larger world and provoke a much larger audience. If terrorists thrive on anything it is media attention and widespread recognition. Graphic images of terror can be used to both intimidate the public and enlist its sympathy. Publicity acquired through less violent means also serves the terrorists' cause—not just because it introduces them to the world, but also because it induces a sense of vulnerability into the population at large. There are two sides to this tactic. On one side, vulnerability entails the dread of attack and mass fear. On the other side, it softens up the opposition, predisposing it to try to "understand" the terrorist cause. Liberal societies accustomed to tolerance are apt to wonder why individuals would resort to such brutal, impersonal acts. Intellectuals and academics ask questions, raise issues, and sometimes blame their own societies for provoking terrorism.[28] When society is under pressure, politicians who were once on the fringe can gain credibility. After 7/7, London mayor Ken Livingstone blamed British and American foreign policy for the attacks, suggesting that those nations reverse themselves for their alleged misdeeds.[29] Broadcasting the other side's position makes the public sensitive to the grievances that motivate terrorists. Media attention and constant publicity also impart terrorist causes with quasi legitimacy. The more one hears about a set of grievances, the greater the chance those grievances will gain a place on the public agenda and become part of a wider discourse.

These incentives may explain why terrorism would be so prone to attack global, mega, or major cities. Global cities like London, New York, and Paris hold a cumulative abundance of features that make them desirable and vulnerable targets. They convey a powerful "international message" that attracts potential attackers.[30] Cities capable of an "international message" magnify the conflict; they broaden its meaning and engulf more participants. A strike at any one of these ramifies through the world.

Further, as globalization proceeds, the number of "global cities" is likely to increase—both from major cities located in growing economies and from mega cities in burgeoning nations. Cities that were once in the mega city camp, like Beijing, Shanghai, or Mumbai, will connect with the rest of the world and also become global cities. Other candidates for global status in South America include Mexico City, São Paulo, and Buenos Aires; in Africa, Johannesburg and possibly Cairo stand out; and in Southeast Asia and the Pacific, Jakarta and Sydney are reasonable choices.

Many of these cities, particularly those located in South America and Africa, have been impacted at their peripheries by large numbers of squatter settlements. Consisting of tin-roofed shanties with no plumbing, these settlements subsist through informal economies where people labor at whatever menial jobs they can find or earn money with whatever goods they can sell. With more and more people leaving the countryside and migrating to cities, a swelling urbanization of poverty now threatens urban stability. The estimates vary, but mainstream projections say that 40 to 65 percent of big-city populations live in substandard conditions.[31] While there is no credible evidence to suggest that poverty leads to terrorism, it does create desperate conditions and mounting chaos—both of which may be precursors for recruiting.[32] For mega cities, the danger lies in a pervasive atmosphere of lawlessness where any method of survival gains social acceptance. At bottom, terrorism feeds on potential recruits becoming accustomed to breaking social norms. Once a person has transgressed moral codes, it becomes easier to do so within a framework of asymmetric warfare.

Conclusions

September 11 is noteworthy because it constituted the quintessential moment for catalytic, mega, and smart terror. For the first time in the modern history of terror, fatalities exceeded 500 in a single attack and the shock was transmitted around the world. New York's 9/11 was followed by similar mega terrorism in Madrid's 3/11, London's 7/7, and India's 7/11. From the standpoint of modern terror, 9/11 was unique, but it was also part of a larger train of urban terror rooted in the 1960s. These incidents can be traced by examining the scope, frequency, and severity of urban terror—respectively defined as the spread of urban incidents, the chronological occurrence of those incidents over the long term, and the toll in casualties. An examination of the scope of terror shows that an overwhelming proportion of incidents took place in cities, and during the post–9/11 period these numbers rose even higher. The frequency of terror has also risen, erratically, in an upward ratcheting of incidents. The severity of terror tells us that terrorists have exacted more *total casualties*, having reached a high in 2001 (due to the 9/11 attack). They have also become more efficient in creating more *casualties per attack*. While the post–9/11 period has not reached the highs created by the attack in New York, urban terror has continued to escalate compared to all other time intervals. Finally, we can observe a certain coincidence between the exercise of urban terror and the presence of global, mega, and major cities. Terrorists are likely to target or exploit cities with *high-density and thick infrastructure*, *concentrated high-value commercial assets*, and a *global or international profile*. The accumulation of these characteristics and their attributes are most available in cities like New York, London, Paris, Mumbai, Istanbul, and Moscow.

The Fear Factor

If thought corrupts language, language also corrupts thought.

—George Orwell

Politicians, Media, and the "T" Word

All too frequently, hot-button issues are used to advance political agendas. Terrorism is an ideal candidate for this because it is based on fear and easily manipulated to mislead people. The manipulation crosses the ideological spectrum, and politicians as well as journalists have been the foremost prestidigitators. The word magically extends far and wide, but two examples are worth noting. The American White House manipulates the "t" word to prop up its "war on terror," and the British *Guardian* uses it to satisfy its own addiction for blaming the victim. While we may not be able to avoid the rhetorical manipulation, we can try to speak straightforwardly about terror. The remedy is not to becloud but to clarify, and we can start with language.

More than a few mainstream media outlets, including the British Broadcasting Corporation (BBC), Reuters, the *Washington Post*, the *New York Times*, and National Public Radio, insist on using words other than "terror" to describe political violence against noncombatants. The insistence is especially pronounced when assaults take place in countries other than their own.[1] The stated reasons for not using the "t" word are driven by a common rationale. Reuters was one of the first to announce that "terrorism" would be abolished from its lexicon because the news agency wanted to be accurate and free from emotive terms.[2] The BBC cautions its correspondents that the "word terrorist can be a barrier to understanding."[3] A spokesman for the *Washington Post* devoted an article to the issue, claiming that "terrorism" is a label "that does not convey hard information" and suggesting that its use meant the newspaper was "taking sides" instead of reporting what was actually "seen and said."[4] Besides, wrote the spokesman, some alleged terrorists may also be part of a "nationalist movement that conducts social work."[5] The *New York Times* also avoided the "t" word in reporting an interview with Secretary of State Condoleeza Rice. Where Rice had repeatedly and clearly used "terrorist organizations" to describe Hamas and similar groups, the *New York Times* substituted the phrase "Palestinian factions."[6]

Other media representatives explain that describing some organizations as terrorist "ignore[s] their complex role in the Middle East drama" and is a "bias" that "runs counter to good journalism."[7] A reporter from National Public Radio also felt the terrorist nomenclature was not appropriate for Hezbollah because it has "a very important status" and "is a very important political party."[8] France found itself caught in the discourse when former foreign minister Dominique de Villepin repeated much the same reasoning. In opposing the European Union's classification of Hamas as a terrorist organization, Villepin argued that because Hamas was a "mass movement" it should be exempt from the terrorist designation.[9]

Presumably news outlets and others are seeking to convey a type of violence or a method of warfare. Accurate and objective descriptions of this violence have nothing to do with whether its progenitors possess a "popular base," much less whether they are engaged in "social welfare." History tells us about an assortment of political organizations with large popular bases as well as their prominence in taking up the cause of social welfare. This runs all the way from political conservatives promoting "faith-based" charities, to social democrats endorsing social security, to the Soviet Communist Party sponsoring the Young Pioneers, up through Germany's Nazi Party using summer camps to recruit the Hitler Youth. Hamas and Hezbollah may be major players who actively recruit a following, but this is entirely unconnected to their method of warfare, how they attack, or whom they choose to target. Similarly, attempts by the left to describe group terrorism as "resistance" or by the right as an effort to create a "caliphate" do not address its unique use of violence. Rather, these are attempts to characterize political motives or objectives.

More serious is the debate over the application of the "t" word, and this is far from a quibble over semantics. Words chosen to describe a critical event have a profound impact on how that event is internalized, perceived, and ultimately treated. The most commonly used substitute for the terrorist noun is "militant"; less frequently used are descriptive terms akin to "fighter" or "armed faction."[10] Much, though not all, of the world's mainstream media favor these nouns because they are supposed to better portray the facts.[11] But do they really? The media's chosen substitute, "militant," is either vague or misleading. By most standard definitions, the term denotes a broad range of actions that encompass fighting, aggressive behavior, forceful action, stridency, or intolerance. While "militant" might also be applied to someone who took up arms, the array of possible actions could include almost anything. Traditionally, "militant" has been used to describe striking unions, civil rights picketers, pacifists who blocked doorways, and hard-line political movements. Coal miners who marched on the offices of government or corporate executives were known as "militants"; truckers who blocked highways were called "militants"; doctrinaire political movements like London's "Militant Tendency" called themselves "militants"; and radical members of the Women's Liberation Movement referred to themselves as "militant feminists."[12] While all of these movements possess a common aggressiveness, their conduct is a far cry from the Red Brigades, the Irish Republican Army, Hamas, Palestinian Islamic Jihad, Lashkar-e-Taiba, or al Qaeda.

Terms like "fighter" or "armed faction" are even more ambiguous and generally pertain to engaging in a battle or contest. This could apply to armies, guerrillas, or civilians. Using these words among others as synonyms for terrorists is reasonable. But without mentioning a larger context of terrorism, terror, or terrorists, the media's preferred euphemisms are not only meaningless, but they confound a host of behaviors that have nothing to do with real acts of terror. If anything, choosing euphemisms to describe individuals who carry out the mass, deliberate killing of civilians is a distortion of the very act a journalist might be trying to describe. Euphemisms obfuscate rather than clarify, they conceal more than reveal, and they camouflage raw facts. Purposeful ambiguity has always been used by propagandists to fool audiences, and wittingly or not, news services propagate the very propaganda they seek to avoid.

News outlets may feel intimidated, fall prey to wishful thinking, or have political reasons for treating the subject as they do. But the words chosen do not always match the acts taken. A failure to describe terror properly means not being able to report on it properly. Too often the media miss the significance of a particular act or linkages between seemingly different acts. The conclusions on how to report the mass killing of noncombatants are not just a matter of positivist, empirical social science but also common sense. Take, for example, the following acts and how they might be described.

- In July 2005 at Sharm al-Sheikh, vehicles laden with explosives were driven into a resort district and nearby hotels. The synchronized blasts killed nearly 100 tourists and workers and left many more injured. A group calling itself the Tawhid Wal Jihad claimed responsibility, saying "Jews and Christians are our targets at any time by any means and that Muslims are not permitted to mingle with them."[13]
- In September 2004 in Jakarta, a car bombing killed 10 people and injured more than 180. The incident occurred just meters from the Australian embassy and was intended to kill or maim nationals of that country. A terrorist organization known as Jemaah Islamiya, thought to be affiliated with al Qaeda, took responsibility for the attack, explaining, "We decided to settle accounts with Australia, one of the worst enemies of God and Islam."[14]
- In the spring of 2002, during the height of "al Aqsa violence," Palestinians launched a series of suicide attacks in buses, markets, and pedestrian malls located in central Jerusalem. Other mass killings occurred in the resort of Natanya, a restaurant in Haifa, an entertainment hall in Rishon Le Zion, and elsewhere. The attacks were carried out by young men and women disguised to meld with the crowds, and they resulted in thousands of casualties. A spokesman for Hamas claimed responsibility, saying "Your children and your women, everyone is a target now." Referring to the wave of al Aqsa

violence, Yasir Arafat urged his followers, "We will make the lives of the Infidels hell. . . . Find what strength you have to terrorize your enemy and the enemy of God."[15]

- In August 1998 American embassies in Nairobi and Dar es Salaam were blown up, causing hundreds of civilian deaths and many more casualties to local inhabitants. Months later, Osama bin Laden took credit for the attacks and explained, "Every state and every civilization and culture has resorted to terrorism under certain circumstances for the purpose of abolishing tyranny and corruption. . . . The terrorism we practice is of the commendable kind for it is directed at the tyrants and the aggressors and the enemies of Allah. . . ."[16]

- In October 2002 in Moscow, more than 800 people were taken hostage in a theater by a Chechen suicide squad. Forty-one Chechens conducted the attack, which included women accomplices ("black widows"). The women hid suicide vests under their cloaks and guarded the hostages while the men took charge of exit points and gave instructions. More than 100 hostages were killed as Russian troops stormed the theater. Now-deceased Chechen leader Shamil Basayev claimed responsibility, and in an interview stated his "main goal will be destroying the enemy and exacting maximum damage." Basayev also remarked, "I admit, I'm a bad guy, a bandit, a terrorist . . . but what would you call them [the Russians]?"[17]

The lesson to be derived should be obvious. Out of any possible choice, the word "terrorism" is "hard information" that most accurately conveys *a type of warfare whose major intent is to target noncombatants for purposes of political intimidation.*[18] Whether attacks are carried out against Egyptians in resorts, Israelis in buses, Australians, Indonesians, Kenyans, and Tanzanians in foreign embassies, or Russians in theaters, journalists interested in reporting what is "seen and said" have ample evidence at their disposal. In describing the actions of their own followers, Yasir Arafat, Osama bin Laden, and Shamil Basayev have readily used the descriptive "terror" or its derivative.

No doubt, all these incidents differ. They were conducted by groups with different histories, different grievances, different compositions, and different goals. But they also bear similarities. All are part of a pattern involving indiscriminate multiple killings, maimings, or hostage taking; all are geared to optimize casualties; all are carried out by invisible or near invisible attackers with camouflaged or concealed weapons; and all involve an enemy whose modus operandi is to ignore rules of warfare. Furthermore, terrorists of all stripes are able to learn from each other ways to optimize catalytic, mega, or smart terror, and they draw inspiration from each other's successes.

There is also another characteristic these disparate groups share and that total the media have yet to fully portray. Terrorism works by intimidation, and intimidation requires the inculcation of fear. It is not only the fear of terror but the terror of fear that enhances the power of a small minority. Fear has multiple dimensions and can be a powerful bargaining chip. Terrorists readily apprehend this and understand that public trepidation can be traded for substantial concessions.

The Rhetoric of Fear

The fear factor may contribute to an understanding of why it is that some mainstream media shy away from the "t" word. Fear manifests itself in different ways, depending upon the proximity of attack. When seen from a distance or reported to a faraway constituency, people have a tendency to rationalize terrorism and discount the fear factor. By this rationale, terrorists act because there are no other ways to deal with deep-seated grievances. Their resort to mass intimidation is seen as due to the absence of a means for conducting civil discourse or attributed to socioeconomic privation. There is also another reaction to terrorism stemming from a direct or painful experience with it. Once having encountered terror firsthand, perspectives can radically change. Terror moves from political abstraction to personal bloodshed.

One principle seems to endure. Proximity to acts of random violence makes fear difficult to deny and more realistic rhetoric difficult to escape. Examples of rhetorical transformation can be gleaned respectively from the *New York Times* and the British Broadcasting Company (BBC). Once New York and London were attacked, the rhetoric began to change. The *New York Times* referred to the "horror" of terror during the 9/11 attack, and the BBC made denunciatory profiles of "terrorists" in the wake of 7/7.[19] While both mainstream outlets openly reported events close to home as inherently terrorist, both just as freely used words like "militant" to report on comparable events in Russia and elsewhere.

The most striking confirmation of the proximity to actual attack and use of the "t" word can be found in public opinion surveys conducted in Jordan. In November 2005, al Qaeda struck three hotels in Amman, turning the immediate area into rubble, devastating a wedding party, killing 60 people, and injuring over 100 (overwhelmingly Jordanians and Arabs from other nations). The attack shook Jordanians, who, while a peaceful people, had before the attack shown some sympathy for al Qaeda. Prior to the attack, only 11 percent of Jordanians chose to describe al Qaeda as a "terrorist organization." After the attack, Jordanian public opinion had decisively reversed, with 50 percent choosing to label al Qaeda as a terrorist organization.[20] Jordanians also took to the streets with large-scale demonstrations in angry protest against al Qaeda.

Jordanian public opinion also changed toward terror in other lands and so too did their rhetoric. Prior to the attack in Amman, only 34 percent of Jordanians regarded the attack on the World Trade Center as "terrorist"; after the attack the proportion grew to 61 percent. Interestingly, there were also shifts in attitudes about terrorism in Israel. Prior to the Amman attack, 24 percent regarded attacks against Israeli civilians as "terrorist"; after the Amman attack, that proportion doubled to 48 percent. Not surprisingly, the proportion of Jordanians labeling the attack on their own city as "terrorist" rose to near unanimity at 94 percent.[21] As we shall see, a direct experience with terror brings fear to the fore and along with it a willingness to use the "t" word. Direct experience will also influence perceptions, and this too is mediated by residential distance from the event.

The Tactics of Fear

While strategy emphasizes long-term, broad-based objectives, tactics play to shorter and immediately achievable steps. Because of their immediate impact and tangibility, there are times when tactics displace strategy. This is especially true for urban terrorism, where tactics have a marked and profound impact on urban life. Notice that all the incidents described above took place in congested, highly complex environments. Hotels, embassies, commercial/cafe districts, and theaters are crowded venues that contribute to the making of an intricate urban fabric. Cities thrive on conditions where large populations function amid clustered diversity and interdependence—all of which are sustained by an elaborate infra-structure of interconnectivity. Together these aspects of the urban environment constitute what organizational theorists call "tightly coupled" societies—that is, highly complex mass entities containing many points of interaction that are highly sensitive to disturbance of any kind (accidents, catastrophes, warfare).[22] While in the United States newer "Sun Belt" cities are less likely to be tightly coupled, more traditional cities in the Northeast, the Midwest, and some in the South fit the tightly coupled pattern.

To be sure, cities are powerful and dynamic, but despite their economic prow-ess, tightly coupled, densely populated societies are difficult to defend. Spotting vulnerabilities is the key to effective tactics, and cities are the soft underbelly of an aggressive capitalism. Few situations provoke hostility more than an object that is perceived as both menacing and weak. A single well-placed terrorist strike can unhinge a city's interconnectivity while at the same time turn its towers of financial might into cascades of destruction.

As good tacticians, terrorists understand their environments and figure out ways in which the overwhelming conventional power of their foes can be turned against them. The basic idea is to prompt the enemy's self-destruction by resorting to a militarist jujitsu. The trick is to apply inordinate pressure to a small though crucial area and watch everything turn upside down. For instance, office towers can be turned into massive blocks that crush their own inhabitants, transit systems can be used to plug up a city, theaters can become holding cages for ransom, and foreign tourists can transmit shock. These effects can also be compounded by forcing local officials and police to overreact with indiscriminate arrests, massive shutdowns, trivial regulations, and ineffective measures that do more harm than good. Citizens might see these restrictions as a necessary nuisance, but as time goes by they may also grow restless and irritated. Even at a tactical level, terrorists hope to wait things out until a society splits, citizens begin to dissent, and politicians search for relief.

Whether this tactic works or not is a different question, and part of the answer depends on the ability of terrorists to sustain attacks as well as the resilience of a local population. By and large, cities have shown themselves to be quite capable of withstanding these pressures.[23] Nevertheless, we should not underestimate the efficacy of the terrorist arsenal.

Terrorist weapons may be primitive, but their tactics are quite sophisticated. To mistake terrorism as the weapon of the weak is to miscalculate its potential for causing urban society to implode. Terrorism is power made possible by fear. The issue is not whether terrorists are "weak" or "strong," but the effectiveness of the resources they are able to use against their enemies.[24] Indeed, terrorists can be quite effective and are better thought of as having low resources employed in optimal ways. Well-placed attacks upon major cities have changed whole nations and in many ways transformed the world. They also demonstrate that the more robust a society grows, the more complex and fragile it becomes. Witness the large-scale panic and overreactions brought about by 9/11, 3/11, and 7/7 where whole areas were closed down, substantial numbers of people were investigated or arrested, and mass transit was temporarily frozen.

Recall that soon after 9/11, "white powder" was delivered in envelopes to congressional and public offices. Some of this turned out to be anthrax and it captivated America. Postal services slowed, employees rushed to the hospital, and parts of government offices were put off-limits. Some workers did not report to duty stations and others refused to open packages of unknown origin. The reaction was instantaneous when two years after 7/7 a plot was uncovered to blow up airplanes leaving from London's Heathrow Airport. Other airports around the world were put on hold, aircraft were detoured, and passengers made to stand on lines for hours on end in order to search baggage. Extreme measures to safeguard security reached Frankfurt, Paris, New York, and as far away as Auckland. Liquids, pastes, gels, and anything that could conceal a detonator were confiscated. The security panic went as far as requiring mothers to sip their own breast milk before being able to board.

Large-scale, massive populations are also precious targets—not just because they yield more casualties (mega terror) but because, in the context of those casualties, they are able to transmit endemic fear (catalytic terror) and because masses of people can trigger economic disruption (smart terror). Tightly coupled cities make fear especially contagious—in the rapidity though which they transmit personal messages, the breadth of their media, and the attention they give to human emotions. Attacks create waves of anxiety because those who have escaped also walk away believing they could be next. These reactions are most visible in the aftermath of an attack. Mass transit loses riders, people hesitate before entering large buildings, patrons are less prone to linger in marketplaces, and even parks seem emptier.

Added up, these tactics are designed to wreck the urban environment, constrict city space, and create an atmosphere of ambient suspicion. While attackers harbor more distant strategic considerations, their tactical ploys of smart or catalytic terror are designed to break down the city. These tactics constitute a form of persistent, low-level warfare, or what has come to be called "the friction of terror." In the long term this friction feeds insecurity, precipitates disinvestment, and seeks the atrophy of civil society.

Fear and Weapons of Mass Destruction (CBRN)

We know that terrorist weaponry has gradually become more lethal—going from shootings and kidnappings, to explosive-laden vehicles, to the use of nerve gas and crashing aircraft into buildings. This trajectory would suggest that chemical, biological, radiological, or nuclear agents (CBRN) could be used in the future. Terrorists around the world have experimented with CBRN weapons of one kind or another. Sarin gas, anthrax, ricin, and hydrogen cyanide appear to be the weapons of choice. The most aggressive terrorists have expressed an interest in "dirty bombs" or even nuclear suitcase bombs. In a 1998 interview, Osama bin Laden asserted that it was a religious duty for Muslims to acquire weapons of mass destruction.[25] The use of CBRN is particularly suited to cities, and depending on the type of attack, would have variable effects.

A radiological attack in the form of a dirty bomb (nuclear waste wrapped around conventional explosives) could continue the upward ratchet of weaponry. While the fallout would be geographically limited, its consequences would go well beyond attacks with conventional weapons. A pea-sized morsel of cesium from a medical gauge could be encapsulated within ten pounds of TNT and its detonation would contaminate 300 city blocks. Buildings within the targeted area would become "poisoned" and radioactive material could not be washed or blown away, but require weeks for removal. Detonating a dirty bomb within certain spaces, such as New York's Wall Street, could paralyze the nation's financial center, causing a domino collapse in capital markets. Detonating a dirty bomb in parts of Washington, DC, would contaminate congressional buildings, the Supreme Court, and precipitate a parallel chain of political chaos.

The 1995 chemical attack in the Tokyo metro caused considerable havoc. Images from the scene were broadcast throughout the world, and for many Japanese the response was one of consternation and foreboding. Clinical reports showed that more than 600 people who came into contact with sarin gas were afflicted by hampered vision, numbness, loss of muscle control, convulsions, and severe pain.[26] The fears evoked by this kind of attack have a basis elsewhere in the world. A number of threats involving deadly chemicals like cyanide or ricin have been uncovered in Jerusalem, New York, Paris, and London.

Chemical terrorism has its limitations. While the potential for damage and loss of life is very serious, attacks of this kind are not likely to bring about large-scale or long-term destruction. By current thinking, a chemical attack would be geographically limited as well as contained by the availability of antidotes, gas masks, and the ability to seal off contaminated areas or water supplies.

In the longer term, worse scenarios with weapons of mass destruction are possible. Terrorists might seek to destroy one city as an object lesson, thereby demonstrating a heightened threat capacity. Nuclear or biological attack could realize the ultimate fear of total destruction. The smuggling of a "suitcase nuclear bomb" into a city and its detonation is not beyond the realm of possibility.

Still more likely is the potential for spreading deadly biological agents throughout a city. One of the earlier uses of biological agents occurred in the fourteenth century. At the time, the Mongols took corpses contaminated with the Black Plague and catapulted them over the city walls into Kaffa (Crimea). During the nineteenth century, blankets ridden with smallpox were distributed to American Indians, causing widespread death. Nowadays, smallpox bacteria are difficult to obtain, but their mass use could cause millions of casualties. In the post–9/11 era anthrax has been used to terrorize smaller numbers of people. If anthrax spores were successfully deployed on a large scale, they could produce millions of casualties. Any rebirth of germ warfare would create intolerable panic and collapse, especially in the absence of full-scale medical preparation (vaccination of health responders, knowledge of the biological agents or toxins used, suitable methods of treatment, and so on).

Graham Allison points up the massive destruction such an attack would entail.[27] This is not an abstract proposition. In a survey of eighty-five intelligence and other experts, most believed that if weapons of mass destruction were targeted on American cities, terrorists would more likely be the attackers than any single government. A majority of these respondents estimated the chances of nuclear attack within the next ten years to be between 10 and 50 percent. Many of the same experts estimated the risk of a radiological or biological attack in the next ten years to be at least 40 percent, while they judged the risk of a chemical attack to be lower.[28] No doubt experts will disagree and the prognosticators are making judgments on the basis of scattered evidence.[29] In the meantime, city planners are preparing for the worst. A survey by the National League of Cities showed that biological or chemical attacks were regarded as the most serious terrorist threat. An attack by a "dirty bomb" was seen as the next most serious, followed by a suicide bombing; a hijacked airplane strike was last. Most cities claimed these threats were addressed in anti-terrorism plans.[30]

The concerns are rooted in uncertainty about terrorist capacity and intentions. All the more so because well-trodden rules and understanding no longer apply. Traditional deterrence was rooted in a belief that the other side would not risk the destruction of its own territory and thereby refrain from launching weapons of mass destruction. But international jihadists have no bounded territory, and deterrence may be irrelevant. Moreover, the leading objective of urban terror is to decontrol rather than consolidate territory, so here, too, deterrence might not work. Any terrorist acquisition of CBRN weapons would radically alter the asymmetry of power between legitimate authority and rogue terrorism. Here is where the most significant dangers lie.

Public Fear

One thing is clear—the purpose of having a capacity for mass destruction is to inject fear into the public psyche. Fear is the germ that creates pervasive mistrust and has a corrosive effect on urban life. Nothing better illustrates this than an essay by journalist Gene Weingarten. In the midst of al Aqsa violence, Weingarten took the "terrorist tour" on a Jerusalem bus. He wanted to understand the psychology not of terrorists but of those who had been terrorized, and he posed some penetrating questions:

> Would you ride a bus in Jerusalem? Right now? Here's your five and one half shekels, go take a bus to market, buy some figs. Pick a bad day, after the Israelis have assassinated some terrorist leaders and everyone is waiting for the second sandal to drop. There are lots of buses in Jerusalem—the odds are still in your favor. Do you take that dare?[31]

Weingarten's message goes well beyond an apprehensive bus ride. Once people begin to interpret normal activities as "a dare," they have converted personal trepidation into a nub of civic distrust. That breakdown can metastasize and make cities hazardous places in which to live, luxuriate, or conduct business, ultimately robbing urban environments of their raison d'être. These hazards are manifest in the stares bus passengers give each other as they size up people with bulky overcoats. It was evident in Paris during the 1990s when security officials in that city placed lids on all public trash cans because terrorists had used them as explosive canisters. It left ominous signs in London when a national newspaper captioned its front page with the headline "City of Fear." Another newspaper featured a cartoon with a redrawn map of the Underground and its stations designated as "Panic and Fear Leading to Doom: Dread and Worry Leading to Cold Sweat."[32] Those fears were transformed into tragedy when a young man, an immigrant from Brazil, was mistaken for a terrorist and shot by police in London's Underground. Within a month after 7/7, police believed on 250 separate occasions that they might be dealing with a suicide bomber. On seven of those occasions they nearly opened fire.[33] Alarm can be seen in random searches conducted by police in New York's subways or by security guards at Los Angeles sporting events.

It is by now commonly believed that 9/11 changed America and because of that event, the United States changed world politics. Aside from the palpable shifts in foreign or defense policy, 9/11 also reconfigured public attitudes. The threat of terrorism became part of the fabric of American life, woven into it by newscasts, alerts, security checks, metal detectors, first responders, and opinion polls. The attacks on the World Trade Center caused tens of thousands to flee in panic, and an estimated 100,000 witnessed the crashing planes from a distance. Within days, the entire nation had seen footage of the towers and the Pentagon lying in wreckage.

Few events in American history have had so profound an impact on the public. A year after 9/11, more than two-thirds of those interviewed said the event had a great deal of emotional impact on them, though these effects were more deeply felt in cities than elsewhere.[34] So powerful were those images that years later a survey done in Providence, Rhode Island, revealed that 60 percent of residents were willing to reallocate funds for better anti-terrorist protection, 28 percent of residents had taken emergency steps in case of a terrorist attack, and 45 percent of residents indicated they had become more careful when terrorism alerts were announced.[35]

Perception of imminent danger feeds fear, and the closer one's experience with attack, the greater the psychological impact. While these impacts are collective and are significant for public policy, they also have a strong personal dimension that affects city life. In the United States, a number of surveys conducted after 9/11 showed that concern about terrorism varied directly with whether the respondents lived in cities, whether respondents lived closer to Washington, DC, or New York, and whether respondents had relatives or friends living close to the sites of attack.[36] Even after a national outpouring of sympathy for those victimized by the al Qaeda attack, public opinion remained divided over how to interpret its dangers. People living on either coast felt more vulnerable than those living in the interior of the country, and with the passage of time the gap widened.[37]

These differences are durable. Five years after 9/11, New Yorkers continue to feel less safe about terror than Americans living elsewhere.[38] Local government officials reflect much the same pattern. Those working in large cities report a higher likelihood of being attacked by terrorists than their counterparts in smaller-sized cities. These officials also report feeling more threatened by terrorism.[39]

Proximity feeds knowledge and knowledge shapes attitudes. Fully 59 percent of New Yorkers and 27 percent of Washingtonians reported knowing someone who was killed or hurt in the attacks. Compare this familiarity to the national figure of just 11 percent. Intimacy with 9/11 was also concordant with whether people were willing to move from the city, whether they thought about terror daily, and whether they experienced sleepless nights.[40] Personal experience, then, is critical and can encompass numerous kinds of familiarity, including physical or geographic proximity, human or social proximity, and recognition of a point in time or chronological proximity.

Table 3.1 presents this proximity in terms of geographical, social, and chronological distance. The table is a composite of various surveys conducted with respect to New York's 9/11 and London's 7/7.[41] It is designed to demonstrate how fear of terrorism as measured by stress or depression reflects various proximities in both the United States and the United Kingdom.

Beginning with geographic proximity we see that a higher percentage of individuals feeling stress or depression lived closer to the crash sites in New York or Washington, DC. Those residing in metro areas also felt slightly more anguished than those living in the rest of the nation. While the differences in residence are noticeable, they are still relatively modest. If we place the focus on Manhattan, these differences enlarge. Here we find a sharp break between individuals living farther from the crash site in upper Manhattan as opposed to those residing in the

Table 3.1

Public Attitudes in the Wake of Attack: Proximity to Sites of Attack

	Percentage affected
Geographical proximity	
Fear (stress, depression, worry):	
Area's proximity to crash sites	
In New York City metro area	16.6
In District of Columbia metro area	14.9
In other major metro area	12.3
In remainder of United States	11.1
Residential proximity	
Upper Manhattan	16.1
Lower Manhattan	36.8
Social proximity	
Fear (stress, depression, worry):	
Directly witnessed the events	
Yes	21.2
No	14.8
Friends or relatives killed	
Yes	29.1
No	15.7
Acquaintances injured or killed	
Yes	23.3
No	11.0
Chronological proximity	
Worried by greater chances of attack:	
Pre–9/11	
Yes	36
No	30
Post–9/11	
Yes	51
No	12
Pre–7/7	
Yes	35
No	63
Post–7/7	
Yes	55
No	44

Sources: "Changes since September 11," *New York Times*, June 11, 2002; CNN/USA Today/Gallup Poll, *USA Today*, 12 July 2005, available at www.usatoday.com/news/washington/2005–07–11-bush-poll.htm; A. Etzioni, "American Society in the Age of Terror," The Communitarian Network Papers and Reports (2002), available at www.gwu.edu/~ccps/news_american_society.html; S. Galea et al., "Psychological Sequelae of the September 11 Terrorist Attacks in New York City," *New England Journal of Medicine* 346, 13 (2002): 982–987.

vicinity of the World Trade Center in lower Manhattan. On this count, lower Manhattan registered more than twice the proportion of residents experiencing stress or depression than upper Manhattan.

Once we turn to social proximity the pattern continues. Clearly, those individuals who either directly witnessed the attack or whose friends or relatives suffered death or injury were much more pained by the event. Apparently, directly witnessing the attack took its toll, though that emotional toll rose further once a more intimate connection was drawn.

Last, as we can see from the data on chronological proximity, the tangibility of experience has a great deal to do with anxiety. It is one thing to hear about terrorist threats or read about their frequency, but quite another to feel their presence. As we saw in the last chapter, terrorism was quite prevalent before 9/11 or 7/7, but only after the strikes in New York and London did a majority of citizens begin to worry about further attacks. Here we see that before 9/11 only 36 percent of respondents worried about a terrorist attack, while after 9/11 that proportion jumped to 51 percent. Much the same tendency is evident in the United Kingdom. Before 7/7, only 35 percent of respondents worried about an attack, whereas after 7/7 that proportion climbed to 55 percent.

Since 9/11 and 7/7, those fears have subsided somewhat, but remain high. Shortly after the September 11 attacks, 75 percent of New Yorkers felt another attack within the immediate future was "very likely or somewhat likely." Five years later, the proportion of respondents expressing those fears dropped to 57 percent.[42] A hiatus in the frequency of attack will reduce but not eliminate this apprehension. The obverse is also true—continuity of attack reinforces trauma and any new strike would rapidly increase the fear quotient.

This is why residents of cities that have incurred sustained attacks experience far greater anguish than residents of cities that have experienced irregular attacks. There is a considerable difference between the chronic experience of Belfast during the 1980s or Srinagar and Jerusalem during the last decade as opposed to the more intermittent occurrences of New York, London, or Madrid. Indeed, sustained violence that entails geographic, social, and chronological proximity can bring about mass trauma of the citizenry. Put somewhat differently, geographic, social, and chronological proximity become telescoped within smaller, frequently, and severely attacked cities, thereby leading to much greater public anxiety.

Jerusalem is a case in point. The Jerusalemite's awareness of terror is extraordinary, and Israel's history of warfare with neighboring countries causes its citizenry to absorb every bit of news. In many ways the city's reaction to terrorism is a function of population and geographic size. Jerusalem's 700,000 inhabitants live in compact and distinct neighborhoods whose municipal boundaries encompass an area of 50.4 square miles (126 square kilometers). In area alone, Jerusalem is one-tenth the size of London, one-seventh the size of New York City, and one-twelfth the size of Istanbul. Given the differentials between these cities, casualties in Jerusalem would be magnified ten times compared to London or New York and twelve times compared to Istanbul. An attack upon this limited spatial configuration reverberates throughout the city.

A number of studies were conducted in the autumn of 2000 when al Aqsa terrorism struck the city. These studies concerned the frequency of experience with terror and its effects on public attitudes. One survey found that nearly 22 percent of Israeli Jews had family or friends who had died in a terrorist attack or a war. That same survey indicated that 15 percent of Israeli Jews had been injured or had an acquaintance injured during the course of al Aqsa terror.[43]

With nearly an entire civilian population experiencing pervasive fear during the worst years of the violence (2000 to 2004), Jerusalem has been beset by trauma.[44] More than 90 percent of Israeli adults indicate they have grown more fearful of terrorism, and similar proportions of children in elementary and high schools express the same apprehension.[45] Phrasing the questions somewhat differently, another scientific study found that almost two-thirds of respondents felt their lives were in danger and more than half the respondents (58.6 percent) reported feeling "depressed" or "gloomy." Still another 28 percent of those interviewed felt "very depressed."[46]

Jerusalem's intensified experience stirs the imagination to wonder how other cities might respond under similar circumstances. The issue remaining is how citizens translate those apprehensions into behavior—how do their feelings manifest themselves in everyday life and political attitudes?

Translating Fear

Regardless of the nation, most citizens are willing to take extraordinary steps to assure their safety. In the United States the availability of open land translated into an urge to flee from concentrated settlements in the event of a national emergency. The prospect of a mass exodus became known as "defensive dispersal" and was designed to deprive the enemy of urban targets. Defensive dispersal gained popularity as American and Soviet leaders traded threats with one other over nuclear warfare. A path for dispersing population was cleared in the 1950s by a colossal interstate highway system designed to spread families and commerce into America's hinterland.[47] Talk of defensive dispersal resurfaced soon after 9/11 as a way to deprive terrorists of easy targets. Naturally, mayors, local politicians, journalists, and academics resist this thinking and offer reasons why the collective benefits of remaining in cities outweigh any impulse to escape. While some would suggest that we fight fear by bravely "bunching up" in cities, human behavior does not work that way.[48] Moral suasion can go just so far and unfortunately evaporates when it comes to individual survival. Should downtowns be subject to attack, rational choice will most likely result in a flight of people to the nearest dispersed suburb.

The reasons for this kind of reaction can be discerned in data gathered on terror's victims. People who in one way or another have been exposed to terror are likely to undergo fairly long-term personality changes. The accepted medical terminology for this is post–traumatic stress disorder or PTSD. Its major symptoms include a feeling of helplessness and lost control coupled with behaviors of avoidance, hyper-vigilance, and startled reactions. Having once been exposed to trauma, the simplest reminder can trigger extreme distress. Fear is a signal for future avoidance and can be taken to an extreme.[49] PTSD sufferers will stay away from any news, sights, sounds, or aromas connected to an attack. The behavioral consequences of terror-induced PTSD are to resist areas with a history of attack. Thus, it is quite possible for PTSD subjects to avoid crowded places, rail stations, or tall buildings.[50]

There are, too, cognitive symptoms associated with PTSD such as panic, pes-simism, irritability, and excessive concern with safety. Living in this state of ap-prehension can reduce one's openness to the outside world and induce various kinds of hostility toward the unfamiliar. Exaggerated beliefs, xenophobia, and reduced ability to cope with these feeling are common. All this is bound to affect one's beliefs about how to deal with terrorism as well as shape political attitudes.

We should remind ourselves that most Americans have not experienced an incident of terror—either directly or through a close acquaintance. The results of any scientific survey are likely to be quite skewed, with some feeling intensely while the majority of respondents remain minimally affected. At the same time, intense minorities can have a disproportionate impact on public opinion and vivid portrayals of an event like 9/11 can leave a lasting impression even on those who had no experience with it.

Table 3.2 shows some attitudinal and behavioral responses in the wake of 9/11.[51] The table divides these into two basic responses. The first deals with spatial re-sponses, or how citizens treat particular kinds of urban facilities. The second deals with political responses, or willingness to curtail civil liberties.

The table instructs us to be careful about judging the proportion of individu-als who perceive trauma. While substantial minorities retain a good deal of ap-prehension about urban spaces, the majority of respondents still feel comfortable within these spaces. Nevertheless, the minority results are significant. Upward of a quarter of responders felt uneasy about entering traditional urban spaces. After 9/11, a significant proportion of New Yorkers felt uncomfortable about going into crowded areas while smaller proportions were uncomfortable in subways and sky-scrapers. Some of these fears translated into a desire to live elsewhere, while others were reflected in a connection between 9/11 and increased insomnia.[52] Five years later, the proportion of New Yorkers who felt nervous about an attack had hardly changed.[53] The size and scope of 9/11 left an enduring impression, and suddenly a tremendous assault on the city not only became plausible, but most likely in the minds of residents.

Stress produces a desperate search for a reprieve and for solutions—some of which can be incommensurate with the size, content, or scope of the problem. The toll often falls on civil liberties. It may also be that fear translates into anger and anger releases itself by placing the onus on suspect behavior. The immediate period after 9/11 saw an 8 percent jump in the proportion of Americans willing to

Table 3.2

Public Attitudes in the Wake of Attack: Responses to Attack

	Percentage affected or holding opinions
Spatial response	
Uneasy about crowded areas (New York respondents)	
Yes	41
No	57
Uneasy about traveling by subway (New York respondents)	
Yes	36
No	51
Uneasy about going into skyscrapers (New York respondents)	
Yes	26
No	60
Political Response	
Relinquish some liberties for more security (national respondents)	
Pre–9/11	
Yes	58
No	23
Post–9/11	
Yes	66
No	24
Require metal detector searches for office buildings (national respondents)	
Yes	81
No	18
Require Arabs to undergo special checks at airports (national respondents)	
Yes	53
No	46
Require Arabs to carry special identification (national respondents)	
Yes	46
No	53
Government searches for borrowed library books (national respondents)	
Yes	37
No	60

Sources: "Changes since September 11," *New York Times,* June 11, 2002; CNN/USA Today/Gallup Poll, *USA Today,* 12 July 2005, available at www.usatoday.com/news/washington/2005-07-11-bush-poll.htm; A. Etzioni, "American Society in the Age of Terror," The Communitarian Network Papers and Reports, available at www.gwu.edu/~ccps/news_american_society.html; S. Galea et al., "Psychological Sequelae of the September 11 Terrorist Attacks in New York City," *The New England Journal of Medicine,* 346, 13 (2002): 982–987; W. Schlenger et al., "Psychological Reactions to Terrorist Attacks," *Journal of American Medical Association,* 288, 5 (2002): 586; "On Security, Public Draws Blurred Lines," *USA Today,* August 3, 2005, available at www.usatoday.com/news/nation/2005-08-03-security-lines-public-opinion_x.htm?csp=N009; "Two Years Later, the Fear Lingers," The Pew Research Center, September 17, 2003, available at http://people-press.org/reports/display.php3?ReportID=192.

curtail civil liberties. The range of responses on public restrictions is considerable. Eighty-one percent of those surveyed were in favor of using reasonable precautions like metal detectors, and this is not surprising. More surprising is the proportion of Americans willing to predesignate people solely on the basis of national or ethnic characteristics. More than half of Americans were willing to single out Arabs and American nationals of Arab descent for special searches regardless of place or circumstance. Significant minorities were willing to infringe on civil liberties by requiring these same groups to carry special identification or by monitoring borrowed library books.

Some of these attitudes find their parallels in British society. Polls show that a majority of Londoners feel more terrorism is inevitable and a significant portion of the population are bracing for multiple attacks. Londoners are willing to accept more aggressive restrictions on freedom and are inclined to give more discretion to the police. In response to a question about whether the police were "right" or "wrong" in shooting a Brazilian man thought to be a terrorist, more than 50 percent of respondents believed the police action was correct. Only 20 percent faulted the police. A similar majority voiced support for police and showed a marked disposition toward viewing the police favorably since 7/7.[54]

Elsewhere in Europe, public opinion also appears to be supporting greater restrictions on civil liberties, and much of this stems from fear. A poll of twelve European countries shows that 66 percent of respondents see terrorism as an "important" or "extremely important" threat.[55] A majority of respondents support various kinds of government intrusion on private citizens that include monitoring Internet communications and banking transactions. Concomitantly, larger numbers of Europeans are suspicious of Muslims residing in their countries. Overall, 56 percent of Europeans believe the values of Islam are not compatible with those of their own nation's democracy. The highest percentages of those holding these views occurred in Germany, Slovakia, Spain, and Italy.[56]

Aside from the democratic implications of these attitudes, they also engender pragmatic inferences for city life. Freedom of movement, tolerance, and the compatibility of diverse populations are what cities offer. The lifeblood of cities lies in their differences, not their similarities. Without the freedom to pursue those differences, urban life withers. We see here a profound contradiction: by embracing public restrictions for the sake of quelling public fear, we undermine the very kind of public we seek to preserve.

Manipulating Fear

Perceptions are not passive objects derived from external events, nor are they always formed by accident. Perceptions can be manipulated or arise from elites. They can be shaped by individuals who profit from a particular version of an incident. One does not have to see conspiracy in any of this. On the contrary, manipulation can be seen as the outcome of multiple, discreet agendas derived from different officials and aimed at different publics. The process by which this takes place is akin to a version of Norton Long's "ecology of games," where different parties interpret their needs and promote their own versions of an event.[57] Adapting Long's terminology, we might see perceptions as advanced by politicians, bureaucrats, and local leaders—each using their version of terror in order to advance their own "game." Terrorism is the perfect symbol to manipulate because it is subject to glaringly simple slogans. Politicians may make the most of people's anxiety, sometimes exploiting the citizens' impulse to surrender reasoned judgment to zealous reaction. Manipulation crosses party lines. Politicians on the right may exaggerate threats in order to morph local threats into international causes. Conversely, politicians on the left may discount real international threats in order to placate a local constituency. In the wake of terror, those on the right may want to launch foreign wars, while their counterparts on the left are prone to blame those very same wars for causing terror. Even those in the center will use terrorism to advance their own political careers by offering seemingly pragmatic, middle-of-the-road solutions.

Urban terrorism mixes national with local politics. Tip O'Neil's axiom that "all (national) politics is local" also means that all local politics is national. Territorial issues can mix in inextricable ways. Politicians at all levels jump into the fray with their own versions of terrorism. America's George Bush and Russia's Vladimir Putin—both of whom could be counted as either on the political right or as nationalists—rode to their reelections on the fear of terrorism. Bush and Putin each conducted his own "war on terror" by defining it in particular ways. Both men gained a reputation as "hard liners" by using military force and by their unrelenting pursuit of "insurgents."[58] U.S. Republicans in particular continued to play the "terror card" through the elections of 2006 and are likely to do so in 2008. Spain's former prime minister José María Aznar, also on the right, was quick to blame the Basque ETA for the Madrid attack of 3/11. Aznar was known for a tough policy against ETA, and a terrorist incident in the midst of an election campaign would have bolstered his support. As it turned out, Aznar was caught manipulating 3/11 for his own political gain and when his charges against ETA proved wrong he went down to defeat.

Nor does the left lack demagogues. Shortly before 7/7, London's mayor Ken Livingstone found justification for the prevalence of suicide attacks in Jerusalem, but soon after the attack on London expressed dismay about similar acts. Livingstone unabashedly charged London's 7/7 bombers with cowardly acts, yet failed to see the same cowardice in terrorists who struck elsewhere. The mayor attributed the attacks to "80 years of Western intervention into predominantly Arab lands because of the Western need for oil."[59] Livingstone's reasoning has been echoed by George Galloway, a member of the House of Commons elected from a heavily Muslim East London constituency. Galloway also sought to deflect local fears onto a larger arena. He faulted British and American aggression in the Middle East as well as the "globalised capitalist economic systems." According to Galloway, these were the real things to fear, not terrorism, which would "dry

up" as soon as the West mended its ways.[60] While Galloway is a marginal politi-
cian, elected from a narrow base, Livingstone is a visible member of the Labor
Party and has a substantial following within London.

Closer to the center of the political spectrum, New York's former mayor Rudolph
Giuliani's public standing massively improved as a result of 9/11. Prior to that event,
Giuliani had run into trouble on issues of police brutality and a downturn in the
city's economy. At the time, the mayor's approval ratings had plummeted as low as
26 percent. Once catastrophe struck, the mayor took charge and his performance
shined. He not only managed the emergency with aplomb, but put the city back on
its feet in the last months of his mayoralty.[61] Giuliani was transformed. His approval
ratings skyrocketed to 50 percent, and after he left office they continued to rise to
72 percent.[62] A man who had been pilloried in the press for letting the police go
wild was now cited as one of America's most inspirational leaders. Giuliani has
gone on to become a popular presidential aspirant for 2008.

Portrayals of fear change as the issue of terrorism wends its way into the maw
of bureaucracy. Ministries, departments, the courts, investigative offices, and police
forces promote particular versions of what has transpired or is about to transpire.
Bureaucracies adopt standard procedures for dealing with terrorism. Large-scale,
rule-oriented organizations are bound to take excessive precautions and overstate
the danger. The result: a pervasive and grating admonition about the imminence
of an attack that is at the same time glaringly unspecified and confusing. Missing
are details related to when, how, or where. Public reaction to these signals can only
swing between the extremes of bland disregard and distorted apprehension.

In the United States, the Department of Homeland Security issued various color-
coded alerts without seeming to know what to do about them or telling the public
what to expect. Almost daily announcements were broadcast and the warnings hung
in the air. Over time, the department became an object of ridicule, and while color
codes remained, the frequency of announcements sharply abated. Other countries
have created special courts or police to deal with terrorists. Bureaucracies in the
United Kingdom, France, and Spain are particularly active. Investigations, raids,
and prosecutions serve as constant signals that terrorism is very much part of daily
life, though again the public is left feeling helpless.

Down the line, local and national authorities follow different trajectories for
responding to threats. In San Francisco, local and state officials sounded public
alerts because of threatened attacks on that city's bridges. Teams of security officials moved into key locales, only to be rebuffed by the federal government and
told that their actions were unnecessary. Similarly, local officials in New York put
the city on alert because of reports of an imminent attack on the city's subways.
Police fanned into subway stations as transit workers searched riders. The search was
extensive—from those wearing shoulder bags to those pushing baby carriages—only
to be discounted by Washington, DC, as a false alarm. These disparate signals leave
citizens alarmed, cynical, or indifferent.

In the immediate aftermath of 7/7, armed guards with automatic rifles patrolled

London's Underground. Police helicopters hovered overhead and riders on mass transit dropped by as much as 15 percent.[63] Within a short time London recovered its normal patterns, though for months police rounded up suspects and warned the public to be watchful. In Rome, citizens have rehearsed planned responses to an attack. In Paris, Operation Vigilance has placed a canopy of surveillance across the city that includes cameras, patrols, entry searches, barriers, and the closure of public toilets and trash bins. In Athens, security measures for the Olympic Games included a dirigible flying over the city and scanning key locations with high-powered cameras. All of these exercises key up the public and tell citizens to take extreme caution, yet at the same time political leaders urge the citizenry to behave normally. New York's mayor opined that the best way to help the city was to go out and shop. Exactly how one is supposed to be cautious and be ever watchful, while also going about ordinary business, is never quite explained.

Conclusions

Perceptions of threat and fear vary and are manifested in behavior. At least some of the mainstream media portray terrorism in vague, if not misleading terms. At times, terrorism's threat value and its concomitant fear may not be mentioned or fully understood. At other times it may be confused with features of ordinary politics that are beside the point. Terrorist politics differs from ordinary politics much as terrorist warfare differs from conventional warfare. Mistaking terrorism for a weapon of the weak misses its relationship to those being attacked as well as its effectiveness as a type of warfare. A better way to understand terrorism is to see it as low-resource warfare that can be very consequential. Some of the more devastating consequences of terrorism lie in the potential of terrorists to acquire chemical, biological, radiological, or even nuclear weapons (CBRN). At the very least these weapons can boost the threat value of terrorism and can reverse the relationship between rogue groups and legitimate authority. At worst, they can lead to calamity for modern civilization.

Constant intimidation and fear can wear down civil society. Survey evidence shows that individuals experiencing stress may withdraw from social life, become overcautious, or resort to repression. While all this may be done in the name of public safety, the effects actually undermine the basis of a viable urban society. Inadvertently or not, politicians, bureaucrats, and local government may feed the public's fears—often in different or contradictory ways. Just as the usage of fear varies, so do the responses to it. Nonetheless, while cities have briefly succumbed to fear, they have recovered and remain remarkably resilient. There is a difference, however, between cities experiencing chronic as opposed to intermittent terror.

Intimidation is one matter and actuality of attack another. The chapters in the next part point to groups responsible for the spread of urban terrorism. These chapters also examine the geospatial features of terrorism, namely efforts to decontrol territory, launch repetitive attacks, and implement logistics.

_____ Part 2

The Geospatial Features of Urban Terrorism

Terror's Spaces:
Identity, Haunts, and Nodes

It's a bottomless pit. The more we advance the less progress we make.
With each discovery we find endless permutations and with each step
we see myriad associations.

—French anti-terrorist policeman

Identity Is Not Always Destiny

Terrorism takes many forms, varying through time as well as across continents. It is a protean force whose metamorphic ability baffles those who study it and daunts those who fight it. While terrorism has always been inspired by multiple sources (anarchistic, secular, religious), each age has produced its waves of terror. To simplify, "four waves" can be identified that run concomitantly with different periods. The "first wave" occurred during the nineteenth and early twentieth centuries when terrorism became a weapon of anarchistic revolutionaries, most of whom were of European origin. By the middle of the twentieth century, a "second wave" of terrorism had migrated to Africa or Asia and been put to use by anti-colonial nationalist movements. Once abandoned by Africans and Asians, terrorism found its way back to Europe and took root in the Middle East. The 1970s and 1980s saw a "third wave" of terrorism take root in Europe and veer strongly toward the extreme left (Marxist-Leninism) or extreme right (neofascism); in Northern Ireland and the Middle East terrorism arrived in the guise of a nationalist agenda. By the turn of the century, terrorism had entered another phase. Strains of Islam joined with terrorism, and terrorism took on a religious cast in what Rapoport calls the "fourth wave" of terrorism.[1]

Far from disappearing, the historic roots of terrorism continued to influence practices through much of the current period. The Anarchist Faction (Greece) and Revolutionary Offensive Cells (Italy) maintained the ardor of nineteenth-century anarchic revolutionaries. The Irish Republican Army (Northern Ireland) and the Shamil Basayev Gang (Chechnya) follow along the path of mid-twentieth-century nationalist anti-colonialism. The Revolutionary Armed Force or FARC (Colombia), the Red Army Faction (Germany), and the Red Brigades (Italy) have pursued a Marxist vision. Down through history, various religious strains were joined with terror and in many ways terrorism was used to advance politico-religious causes.[2] Today, most religious terrorism draws its strength from a fundamentalist version of Islam. As they have come to be called, Islamists are hardly of a single stripe. They continue to be a major force and many operate legally in Lebanon, Syria, and Iran. Islamist organizations can range from the domestic jihadist Hamas (West Bank and Gaza) to the Iranian-linked Hezbollah (Lebanon) and the global jihadist al Qaeda. Religious terrorist groups of the non-Islamist variety are more isolated from mainstream co-religionists. These organizations often fuse religion with an apocalyptic or racist doctrine and are often outlawed in their home countries. They include Aum Shinrikyo (Japan, Buddhist) as well as Arm of the Lord and Christian Patriots (U.S., Christian), and Kach (Israel, Jewish).[3]

The organizational longevity and form of terrorist organization also differ. Some groups consist of small cliques that soon vanish only to arise again a short time later under a different name. This is especially the case with leftist and fascist factions, like the Baader Meinhof (Germany), Direct Action (France), or Russian National Unity (Russia). Other terrorist groups, like Colombia's FARC or Peru's Shining Path, are mass political organizations with a long-time presence in the country. Hamas and Hezbollah have a mass political base, social service outlets, and operate under a defined hierarchy, while al Qaeda works mostly through violence and has a very amorphous structure. Al Qaeda in particular has become more of a holding company that emphasizes "leaderless resistance" than a specific organization.

Some would argue that because terrorism is a strategy or set of tactics, it cannot be treated as an "enemy"—how, after all, can one fight against a method of warfare?[4] While the premise is correct, the conclusion does not necessarily follow. For all their differences, terrorists also share notable similarities that stem from the type of warfare they choose to conduct.[5] Terrorism requires an abundance of disciplined brutality and an eagerness to deliberately violate accepted norms of warfare. Moreover, terrorists can be treated as belonging to a class apart because they are usually motivated by ideological extremism that demands a great deal of them. These traits allow us to recognize terrorists by what might be called their underlying characteristics encompassing a rigid belief system, a sharply curtailed view of the world in terms of good and bad, a propensity to sacrifice human life, and a messianic belief that emphasizes purification through violence. Terrorist organizations are more likely to embrace authoritarian leaders, more likely to obey dogma, and more likely to pursue uncompromising or "true-believer" paths to achieve their goals.[6] No doubt, these characteristics will pertain more or less by type of organization and by the tactics they emphasize. Some fair assumptions are that terrorists who destroy human life rather than property are more apt to hold the most rigid positions; similarly, terrorists who conduct suicide attacks rather than abductions are more inclined to hold extreme views.

Nor does it necessarily follow that once having achieved power, terrorists change their viewpoints or evolve into nonviolent politicians. Some former terrorists most certainly have evolved, such as the leaders of the Algerian or South African revolutions, and it currently appears that members of the Irish Republican Army or the Basque ETA have moved toward nonviolent politics. But some terrorists never did evolve and instead interpreted earlier successes as a way to enhance power. Witness the accession to power of Nazi Brown Shirts in Germany's Third Reich, the behavior of the Taliban after taking control of Afghanistan, the jihadist fervor of Hezbollah after taking seats in the Lebanese government, and Yasir Arafat's continued flirtation with terror after achieving legitimacy. There is, then, no hard and fast rule about how terrorists will behave after acquiring power.

Targeting by City Type

We can get a better grip on terrorist behavior by comparing terrorists' identity with both their choice of cities and their exercise of violence. To better explain this relationship, Table 4.1 lists a variety of terrorist organizations that have operated over the last forty years. Notice that particular identities are used to describe each organization. These identities are listed in a specific form as nationalist, leftist, Islamist, and so forth, but later discussed as three broad categories (anarchist, secular, and religious). Also, the identities listed in the table are used as markers representing an ideology, a belief, or a rationale. No causal connection is perforce made here related to the rise of a belief and the rise of terrorism (i.e., that nationalism or religiosity necessarily leads to terrorism). Whenever possible, organizations and their identities are listed by approximate chronology, with earlier groups (1960s to 1980s) listed first and more current groups (1990s to 2005) shown thereafter. The table shows these organizations relative to the cities they have attacked, some cities having attracted attention from more and a greater variety of terrorists than others. Displayed in the table are 27 cities and more than 100 terrorist organizations.

Starting with the first column, urban locations can be classified as (1) cities subject to attack by relatively few and similar groups, (2) cities subject to attack by a large number of similar groups, and (3) cities subject to attack by a large number of dissimilar groups. The first of these groupings consists of cities located across the world (Algiers, Casablanca, Grozny, Lima, Nairobi, Riyadh, Srinagar, and Tokyo). Most of these places fall into the designations described earlier as single-attribute *major cities* (see Chapters 1 and 2). Cities in this grouping experienced attacks from relatively few organizations, and their attackers usually bear a religious identity of one kind or another. The second grouping of cities also can be located in a geographical belt stretching from South America to Europe and through to the Middle East (Belfast, Bogotá, Islamabad, Jerusalem, Moscow, and Tel Aviv). These cities also fall into the category of *major cities,* though they tend to have multiple attributes and hold considerable importance. These places have been subject to extensive factional attacks, stemming largely from a combination of nationalist and religious organizations. The third grouping holds the largest number of cities that also reach across the world (Berlin, Cairo, Istanbul, Karachi, London, Madrid, Milan, New York, Paris, and Rome). Most of these places are either *global*

Table 4.1

Terrorist Organizations and Identities

City	Organization	Identity
Algiers	Islamic Salvation Front, Armed Islamic Group	Islamist
Athens	ASALA, Black September, Revolutionary Organization 17 November, Anti-Establishment Nucleus, Anarchist Faction	nationalist/ separatist, leftist, anarchist
Berlin	PFLP, Black September, Red Army Faction, Anti-American Arab Liberation	nationalist/ separatist, leftist, other
Belfast	IRA, Ulster Defense Association/Ulster Freedom Fighters, Loyalist Volunteer Force	nationalist/ separatist
Bogotá	Revolutionary Armed Force of Colombia (FARC), National Liberation Army of Colombia, Popular Liberation Army, April 19, United Self-Defense Forces of Colombia	leftist, right-wing
Cairo	PFLP, al-Gama'a al-Islamiyya (GAI), Islamic Liberation Organization, Thawrat Misr	nationalist/ separatist, Islamist
Casablanca	Al Qaeda, Salafia Jihadia	Islamist
Grozny	Shamil Basayev Gang, Riyad us Saliheyn Martyrs	nationalist/ separatist, Islamist
Istanbul	PFLP, ASALA, Turkish People's Liberation Army, Abu Nidal Group, PKK, 28 May Armenian Organization, DHKP-C, Islamic Great Eastern Raiders Front, al Qaeda, Turkish Islamic Jihad	nationalist/ separatist, leftist, Islamist
Islamabad	Amal, al-Gama'a al-Islamiyya (GAI), Moslem Commandos, Hindu Sena	nationalist/ separatist, Islamist, Hindu
Karachi	PLO, Abu Nidal Group, Amal, Lashkar I Jhangvi (LJ), Mohajir Quami Movement, Jaish-e-Mohammed (JEM)	nationalist/ separatist, Islamist
Jakarta	Free Aceh Movement, al Qaeda, Jemaah Islamiya	nationalist/ separatist, Islamist
Jerusalem	Al Fattah, PLO, PFLP, Democratic Front for Liberation of Palestine, Black September, Abu Nidal Group, Kach, Palestinian Islamic Jihad, Hamas, Tanzim	nationalist/ separatist, Jewish, Islamist
Lima	Shining Path, Tupac Amaru	leftist

City	Organization	Identity
London	IRA, al Fattah, Black September, Abu Nidal Group, Amal, DHKP-C, Hezbollah, Abu Hafs al Masri Brigade (Mohammad Sidique Khan et al.)	nationalist/separatist, leftist, Islamist
Madrid	al Fattah, ETA (Basque Fatherland and Freedom), PLFP, Black September, ASALA, Abu Nidal, Hezbollah, al Qaeda (Abu Hafs al Masri Brigade)	nationalist/separatist, Islamist
Milan	ETA, Black September, ASALA, Red Brigade, Angry Brigade, Hezbollah	nationalist/separatist, leftist, anarchist, Islamist
Moscow	Dagestan Liberation Army, Islambouli Brigades, Movsar Barayev Gang, Russian National Unity	Islamist, nationalist/separatist
Mumbai (Bombay)	PFLP, Abu Nidal Group, Azad Hind Sena, Lashkar-e-Taiba (LeT), Jaish-e-Mohammed, Students' Islamic Movement of India	nationalist/separatist, Hindu, Islamist
Nairobi	al Qaeda	Islamist
New York	PLO, Black September, JDL, Liberation Army Fifth Battalion (Ramzi Yousef/Sheikh Rahman), al Qaeda	nationalist/separatist, Jewish, Islamist
Paris	IRA, ETA, Black September, ASALA, PKK, DHKP-C, Action Directe, Hezbollah, Armed Islamic Group (GIA)	nationalist/separatist, leftist, Islamist
Rome	ETA, Red Brigade, Black September, ASALA, Japanese Red Army, Hezbollah	nationalist/separatist, leftist, Islamist
Riyadh	al Qaeda	Islamist
Srinagar	Hizbul Mujahideen, Lashkar e Jhangvi	nationalist/separatist
Tel Aviv	Black September, Palestinian Islamic Jihad, Hamas, al Aqsa Martyrs Brigade	nationalist/separatist, Islamist
Tokyo	Maruseido, Aum Shinrikyo	leftist, religious (cult)

(continued)

Table 4.1 *(continued)*

Source: Terrorism Knowledge Base, available at www.tkb.org. Type 1 database.
Names and abbreviations of terror organizations:

ASALA	Armenian Secret Army for the Liberation of Armenia
DHKP-C	Devrimci Halk Kurtulus Partisi-Cephesi—Revolutionary People's Liberation Party-Front
ETA	Euzkadi Ta Askatasuna—Basque Fatherland and Freedom
JDL	Jewish Defense League
PFLP	Popular Front for Liberation of Palestine
PLO	Palestinian Liberation Organization
PKK	Partiya Karkeran Kurdistan—Kurdish Workers' Party

Names and years of operation of terror organizations:
Abu Hafs al Masri (2003–current); Abu Nidal Group (1974–1994); Action Directe (1982–1999); al Fattah (1950s–current); al-Gama'a al-Islamiyya (1977–1998); al Qaeda (1980s–current); al Qanoon (2002); Amal (1975–1998); Anti-American Arab Liberation (1986); April 19 Movement (1970s–1998); Armed Islamic Group (1992–2001); ASALA (1970s–1990s); Aum Shinrikyo (1987–1995); Azad Hind Sena (1982); Basque Fatherland and Freedom (ETA) (1959–current); Black September (1971–1988); Dagestan Liberation Army (1999); Democratic Front for Liberation of Palestine (1969–current); DHKP-C (1978–current); Free Aceh Movement (mid-1970s–current); Hamas (1987–current); Hezbollah (1981–current); Hizbul Mujahideen (1989–current); IRA (1919–2002); Islambouli Brigades (2002–2004); Islamic Liberation Organization (1974); Islamic Great Eastern Raiders Front (1970s–2004); Islamic Salvation Front (1989–1992); Jaish-e-Mohammed (2000–2004); Japanese Red Army (1970–1988); Jemaah Islamiya (1993–current); Jewish Defense League (1968–1992); June 16th organization (1987–1989); Kahane Chai (1990–1995); Kach (1971–current); Lashkar-e-Taiba (2000–current); Lashkar I Jhangvi (1996–2004); Liberation Army Fifth Battalion (1993); Loyalist Volunteer Force (1996–2003); Maruseido (1974); May 28 Armenian Organization (1977); Mohajir Quami Movement (2001–2001); Moslem Commandos (1982); Movsar Barayev Gang (2002); National Liberation Army of Colombia (1964–2004); Palestinian Islamic Jihad (1970s–current); PFLP (1967–current); PKK (1974–current); Popular Liberation Army (1967–2002); PLO (1964–1991); Real IRA (1998–2004); Red Army Faction (1978–1992); Red Brigade (1969–2003); Revolutionary Armed Force of Colombia (1964–current); Revolutionary Organization 17 November (1975–2002); Riyad us Saliheyn Martyrs (2004); Salafia Jihadia (1990–2003); Shamil Basayev Gang (1995–current); Shining Path (1960s–2002); Students' Islamic Movement of India (2000–2004); Tanzim (1993–2004); Thawrat Misr (1984–1987); Tupac Amaru (1983–2001); Turkish Islamic Jihad (1991–1996); Turkish People's Liberation Army (1971–1980); Ulster Defense Association/Ulster Freedom Fighters (1971–2004).

or *mega cities* and have generally incurred attacks by a larger number of diverse groups that include left (Marxist-Leninist), right (fascist, nationalist), and religious (mostly Islamist). Not surprisingly, *global* and *mega cities* have incurred attacks by the largest number and variety of groups, the foremost of which have a world jihadist or an "international" outlook. As mentioned earlier, *global* and *mega cities* are rich targets with the capacity to rapidly transmit catalytic terror with ramifications across the world. Obviously, too, the more heterogeneous cities are likely to attract and house a multiplicity of terrorist organizations.

Most instructive are issues of who attacks what, with what frequency, and whether different patterns of attacks can be associated with particular organizations. Two different databases are enlisted to answer these questions: long-term data between 1968 and 2005 that include *only international events*, and short-term data between 1998 and 2005 that include *both domestic and international events*. Again we use a representation of twenty-seven cities to verify a number of observations. Short-term data are displayed in the text while long-term data can be found in the appendices.[7]

Beginning with the first observation, most incidents were small and of unknown origin. This trend can be seen in Table 4.2. The table shows twenty-seven cities along with incidents, casualties, the generic identity of the organization (anarchist, secular, religious, or unknown), and casualties per attack.[8] Incidents and casualties are separated by a slash.

We can see that during just eight years these cities encountered 1,652 incidents, and a large proportion of attacks (74 percent) were carried out by "others" or "unknowns"; here too, the unknowns/others accounted for relatively few casualties (13 percent). In other words, during these years most attacks were minor and often intended as a violent statement rather than a deliberate attempt to inflict bodily harm. The long-term data verifies this notion. Taking the much extended period between 1968 and 2005, our 27 cities encountered more than 2,400 incidents; slightly more than half of these were carried out by "others" or "unknowns," though attacks falling in this category account for just 10 percent of the total casualties (see Appendix, Tables A4 and A5).

The second observation is that actual casualties tell us much more about terrorism's enduring legacy than incidents. We know from previous discussions that across the world terrorism exacted a higher human toll with each successive decade. The bulk of these occurred during the most recent eight years, when casualties surpassed 26,000 (Table 4.2). To be sure, the tallies clustered in a number of cities, with the highest casualties found in Istanbul, Jerusalem, Madrid, Moscow, Nairobi, New York, and Tel Aviv. Many of these cities continue to confront violent Islamic fundamentalism. It is also the case that co-religionists are often the victims, so that these acts represent Islamist on Islamic violence.

The third observation is that religiously inspired terrorists were responsible for most of the casualties. While accounting for less than 7 percent of the incidents during the short term, religious terrorism produced 79 percent of the casualties. This proposition basically holds for a previous long-term period with religious terrorism continuing to be responsible for a minority of incidents but the lion's share of the casualties (see Appendix, Tables A4 and A5).

The fourth observation stems from the preceding one and turns on those cities most frequently attacked by particular identity groups. By scanning Tables 4.1 and 4.2 we can compare anarchistic and secular terrorism with their religiously inspired counterparts. Here we find that cities with the most casualties per incident include Algiers, Casablanca, Islamabad, London, Madrid, Moscow, Mumbai, Nairobi, New

Table 4.2

Terrorist Identity and Attacks in Twenty-Seven Cities, 1998–2005

City	Incidents/ Casualties	Anarchist	Secular	Religious	Other/Unknown	Casualties per attack
Algiers	19/294			2/30	17/264	15.5
Athens	154/7	26/0	43/6		85/1	0.1
Belfast	242/69		52/20		190/49	0.2
Berlin	0					0.0
Bogotá	67/635		26/362		41/273	9.4
Cairo	3/32			1/22	2/10	10.7
Casablanca	6/135			5/131	1/4	22.5
Grozny	79/659			2/370	77/289	8.3
Islamabad	16/324		1/109		15/215	20.3
Istanbul	353/1,126		33/201	14/449	306/476	3.2
Jakarta	43/516		3/35	7/377	33/104	12.0
Jerusalem	151/1,634		17/403	23/909	111/322	10.8
Karachi	113/828		11/176	5/44	97/608	7.3
Lima	12/52		7/48		5/4	4.3
London	20/285		6/9	4/276	10/0	14.2
Madrid	68/1,001		38/210	5/791	25/0	14.7
Milan	26/2	2/0	11/2		13/0	0.1
Moscow	64/1,678		4/5	8/1,478	52/195	26.2
Mumbai	9/358		1/80	1/202	7/76	39.8
Nairobi	1/5,291			1/5291		5,291.0
New York	8/9,755			2/9,749	6/6	1,219.0
Paris	14/11		4/0		10/11	0.8
Riyadh	28/393			18/245	10/148	14.0
Rome	29/6		6/4		23/2	0.2
Srinagar	92/466		10/20	6/99	76/347	5.1
Tel Aviv	25/802		11/400	6/364	8/38	32.1
Tokyo	10/1		3/0		7/1	0.1
TOTAL	1,652/26,360	28/0	287/2,090	110/20,827	1,227/3,443	15.956
Percentages:						
Incidents		1.7%	17.4%	6.7%	74.2%	
Casualties		0%	7.9%	79%	13.1%	
Casualties per attack		0	7.2	190	2.8	

Source: Terrorism Knowledge Base, available at www.tkb.org. Type 3 database.

York, Riyadh, and Tel Aviv. In many of these cities Islamists were responsible for the highest ratios of casualties per attack.

That said, religious terrorism is not limited to Islamists. While the numbers are quite small for other religions or cults, spiritually inspired terrorism does share a propensity to produce large numbers of casualties. For example, Hindu terrorists operating on the Indian subcontinent have an extensive history of violence (Hyderabad). In the United States, fringe Christians have caused casualties in their drive against abortion clinics. In Israel, outlawed Jewish terrorists have attacked Palestinians, with one instance of a devout settler causing dozens of casualties. Also, Tokyo is listed as having very few incidents and negligible casualties because Table 4.2 did not cover the 1995 sarin gas attack on its metro system. That particular attack was launched by the Buddhist-inspired Aum Shinrikyo and caused more than 5,000 casualties. By contrast, most of Tokyo's secular attackers caused relatively few if any casualties. The only exception to this observation was the leftist Maruseido, whose attacks brought a spike in Tokyo's casualties during the 1970s (see Appendix, Tables A8 and A9).

The fifth observation is that there is a difference in the terror executed by secular as opposed to religious groups. We can better appreciate this by taking another perspective on the human toll and turning to the casualties per incident located in the bottom row of Table 4.2. For the years shown, secularists accounted for just 7.2 casualties per incident, while religiously motivated terrorists exacted an astounding 190 casualties for each attack. A similar pattern also holds for a previous long-term period (see Appendix, Table A5).

It does appear that terror carried out by secularists pays greater heed to the destruction of property or individual assassinations rather than indiscriminate targeting large groups. There are major exceptions to this generalization. During the 1980s, Italian neofascists killed 84 people and wounded 200 in a Bologna bombing and leftists committed similar atrocities on the streets of Paris. Through this same period, nationalists like the Basque ETA, Irish Republican Army, and Ulster Loyalists were responsible for more than three thousand deaths.[9] Nevertheless, secular groups have been known to warn noncombatants to evacuate premises that are about to be bombed. Other secular terrorists were more likely to resort to abductions or specific murders rather than mass killing or maiming. This is particularly true of Marxist revolutionaries, who turned to terror after the failed attempt to overthrow the French government in 1968. Some would think it fitting that radicals chose to destroy property or a member of the bourgeois elite rather than killing large numbers of ordinary people.

This kind of terror was different than the suicide-driven mass killing that arrived in later years, mostly because it was concerned with committing the act and getting away with it. Writing about this period, C.J.M. Drake could caution that "the main risk to a terrorist is of being seen on CCTV and either captured at the time or having his movements recorded and being identified."[10] The rise of religiously inspired suicide attackers summarily dispensed with Drake's concern and terrorism became a far more efficient killing machine. While not all suicide attackers have been recruited though religious terrorism, many have been and religion has played a role in sanctifying their acts.[11] By the mid-1990s, suicide had become an indispensable tool of mega and smart terror.

Exactly why mass killing and injuries are so closely linked to religious terrorism is subject to a number of educated guesses.[12] Religion can do what secular belief systems cannot, namely, eliminate the emptiness connected to death by rationalizing it as a sacred act. Religion can promise martyrdom for suicide attackers and bless their accumulation of casualties. Divine sanctions that assure promises of a future filled with rapture for suicide bombers and hell for their victims can be a powerful source of legitimization. Elaborate rituals and indoctrination back up this belief. In the Palestinian territories, impressionable youths have been told that as martyrs they will enter paradise, live in beautiful gardens, and enjoy the company of seventy-two virgins. After a youth blows him- or herself up, sweets have been distributed and posthumous weddings have celebrated the occasion.

Religion can also claim to represent certainty, assuring terrorists that killing is justified. Holding to a single absolute truth is extremely appealing to people in doubt or those who do not have the social capacity to question received doctrine. This is the case for Christian fundamentalists who attack abortion clinics because they believe that abortions are against the will of God. It is also true for Buddhist cults like Aum Shinrikyo, whose name translates into "Supreme Truth."

Moreover, the most extreme fundamentalism can flourish in a number of seemingly different environments. These run the gamut from second-generation immigrants relegated to public housing in their host societies, to alienated Muslim immigrants living on the margins in Western cities, to indigenous populations living in squalid villages. These conditions provide fertile ground for recruiting hapless youth to a religious utopia.

Roger Masters offers an account of suicide terror based on demography and available resources that may shed additional light on this issue.[13] He explains that rampant poverty, high birthrates, shorter life expectancy, and low investments per child make self-sacrifice palatable. This is especially true when families must compete for scarce resources and martyrdom provides an opportunity for redemption. While these are nonreligious factors, they can also work in tandem with religion. Spiritual and material rewards provided by local clergy, operatives from al Qaeda, or theocratic supporters in Iran can go very far within desperate environments. Parts of Lebanon, Pakistan, and the Palestinian territories roughly fit these criteria and have also spawned high rates of suicide terror.

No single set of propositions provides complete answers. Masters's hypothesis might explain Gaza City, but would not apply to Riyadh. Nor does it explain why terrorism would take root in and be directed toward Western cities. Nagging questions remain about the background of suicide terrorists who do not fit Masters's demographic/scarcity hypothesis. This is particularly true for wealthier, well-educated

Saudis and Egyptians, or for Western converts who frequent radical mosques, hook up with al Qaeda, or become "mujahadeen."

The explanations behind terrorist recruitment are far from complete, but as we review the information, the most basic distinctions do hold between cities attacked as well as distinctions between secular and religious terror.[14] During the latter half of the twentieth century, political attacks on European cities like Athens, Paris, and Rome took the form of smaller-scale urban terror. At that time most political terror focused on property, the abduction (or sometimes killing) of select elites, and the attacker's own need to escape. By contrast, the latter-day mostly Islamist attackers of Cairo, Casablanca, Karachi, Moscow, Mumbai, Nairobi, and New York were less discrete, conducting mega terror centered on human casualties and self-sacrifice. In addition, a handful of cities with a longer history of terror experienced both the secularist smaller-scale terror and religious mega terror; these include Jerusalem, Tel Aviv, London, and Madrid.

Old Small-scale versus New Mega Attacks

There is, too, something else to be derived by comparing secular to religious terrorism. At least in Western Europe, old-fashioned secular terrorism appears to be fading.[15] It has been years now since leftist and nationalist factions like the Red Brigades (Italy) or the Revolutionary Organization of 17 November (Greece) have been eliminated. Had secular terrorism continued to be vital, we might expect these factions to have been replaced, but no such regeneration has occurred. Another harbinger of deeper trends can be found in the recent renunciation of violence by secular terrorists. The abandonment of violence by Northern Ireland's IRA and possibly by the Basque ETA certainly works in this direction. Some of the leftist decline could be felt in individual cities like Berlin, Milan, and Paris, where in recent years terror attacks and casualties have dramatically declined.

The most significant trends can be detected by examining proportionate shares of secular and religious terrorism during two periods—1968 to 1994, and 1995 to 2005. It is also useful to do this for the overall picture of 25 nations (or regions) and more specifically for our 27 representative cities. Beginning with the national level, in the period between 1968 and 1994 secular terror accounted for 45 percent of total incidents and 36 percent of total casualties (see Appendix, Table A6). Since 1995 and up through 2005, these proportions shrank to 23 percent of incidents and just 5 percent of casualties.

We now narrow the picture down to our twenty-seven cities. The pattern is very much the same with both incidents and casualties declining over the two time periods. In the pre-1995 era, secular terrorists committed 45 percent of the incidents and 50 percent of the casualties. By the post-1995 period, we find that incidents shrink to just 16 percent and casualties also wither to just 3 percent (see Appendix, Table A8).

If secular terrorism is exhausting itself, this cannot be said for religious terror-

Figure 4.1   **Distribution of Attacks by Terrorist Identity in Twenty-Seven Cities, 1968–1994 and 1995–2005**

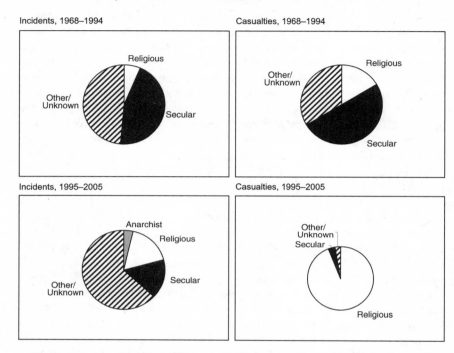

Source: Terrorism Knowledge Base, available at www.tkb.org. Type 2 database.

ism. Here the trend lines are upward, telling us that the vacuum has been filled by jihadists. Typifying this brand of terrorism, casualties far exceed incidents, though both have climbed. The national picture brings religious terrorism into stark relief. During the pre-1995 era, religiously motivated terrorism accounted for just 5 percent of incidents and 12 percent of casualties. Since 1995, religious terrorism had risen to 16 percent of incidents and skyrocketed to 86 percent of casualties (see Appendix, Table A6).

Again, our twenty-seven cities reflect and perhaps magnify these broader trends. This more focused city picture reveals that in the pre-1995 period, religious terrorists accounted for just 6 percent of incidents and 16 percent of casualties. After 1995, religious incidents rose to 17 percent and nearly monopolized the total number of casualties at 94 percent (see Appendix, Table A8).

The distribution of differently inspired terrorism is shown in Figure 4.1. Data are drawn from the earlier listing of twenty-seven cities (see Appendix, Table A8). The figure displays the two time periods discussed above relative to incidents and casualties for each identity (anarchist, secular, religious, other/unknown).

Note that the bulk of incidents still remain in the category of "other" or "unknown." As mentioned above, the incidence of religious terror increased, but by the more recent period it accounted for only slightly more episodes than secular terror. The real expansion for religious terror has been in its proportion of casualties. Here the "pie chart" graphically depicts for 1995–2005 the overwhelming share of casualties by religious terrorism.

Concomitant with increased lethality are bigger attacks on larger spaces, or what have been called mega attacks. Attacks of this kind are critical events. Like 9/11, 5/11, and 7/7, most mega attacks precipitated a deep sense of awareness, often galvanizing the nation in which the attack took place. There is little doubt about the profound impact of mega terror on public policy—especially in the West. Residents of Madrid were stunned by the 5/11 attack, the ruling party was turned out of office, and that country reversed its commitments to the Iraq war. Londoners wondered how the sons of immigrants could have turned on them, and the United Kingdom enacted highly restrictive laws to counter terrorism.

But mega attacks have long occurred in cities outside the West. There too, the response has been mixed. In one sense, mega attacks drew the affected population closer to the American experience and evoked sympathy from abroad—hence the reference to India's or Russia's or Turkey's 9/11. In another sense, some nations struck by mega terror refrained from taking aggressive military action outside their borders, and these countries were inclined to be more critical of the U.S. response. Whatever the reation and wherever the cities struck, mega attacks brought to the fore a host of emotions and punctuated people's experience. For this reason alone they are worth a collective review.

Table 4.3 illustrates the presence or absence of mega terror in twenty-three nations and regions. Some areas experienced more than one such event while a few had none at all. The list contains 21 watershed events, defined by having caused at least 199 casualties. Almost all attacks caused extensive property or infrastructure damage.

Of the twenty-three nations and regions, all but eight experienced mega attacks. Targeted spaces included central business districts (CBDs), downtowns, city centers, and resort areas. Within these spaces, the favored structures for attack were government headquarters, hotels, retail or entertainment facilities, and public transit systems. Most of the attacks were launched by religious terrorists, and a majority occurred after the year 2000. Just six of the attacks were predominately domestic—that is, undertaken by terrorists whose origins and sources of support came from within the country. This was the case in Chechnya (Grozny), Egypt (Sharm al-Sheikh), Indonesia (Bali), Japan (Tokyo), Saudi Arabia (Dhahran), and the United States (Oklahoma City). The majority of attackers were of foreign derivation. The prime venues for these were Germany (Berlin), India (Mumbai), Israel (Jerusalem), Kenya (Nairobi), Pakistan (Karachi and Islamabad), Russia (Moscow and Beslan), Spain (Madrid), and the United States (New York). Usually foreign nationals required a base from which to house, coordinate, and supply attackers.

Table 4.3

Mega Attacks in Twenty-Three Nations and Regions

Nation	City	Space	Date	Casualties
Algeria				
Chechnya	Grozny	City center: headquarters building of federal government	December 27, 2002	352
Colombia				
Egypt	Sharm al-Sheikh	City center: Old market, Ghazala Gardens Hotel, Ocean Bay Hotel	July 23, 2005	206
France				
Germany	Berlin	City center: La Belle discotheque in Schoenberg district	April 5, 1986	199
Greece				
India	Mumbai (Bombay)	CBD: Bombay Stock Exchange, the headquarters of India's airline, three luxury hotels	March 12, 1993	1,517
	Mumbai (Bombay)	City center: gateway of India monument, Hindu temple of Mumbadevi	August 25, 2003	202
Indonesia	Bali	City center: entertainment district of Kuta Beach	October 12, 2002	502
Israel	Jerusalem	CBD: Yehuda shopping mall	September 4, 1997	207
Italy				
Japan	Tokyo	City center: Tokyo subway system	March 20,1995	5,012
Kashmir				

Kenya	Nairobi	City center: U.S. embassy	August 7,1998	5,291
Morocco				
Pakistan	Karachi	City center: shopping area	July 14,1987	322
	Islamabad	Weapons dump	April 10, 1988	1,200
Peru				
Russia	Moscow	Outer neighborhoods: five-story building	September 9,1999	295
	Moscow	Near city center: Palace of Culture Theater "Dubrovka"	October 24, 2002	812
	Beslan	Neighborhood, school compound	September 1, 2004	1,065
Saudi Arabia	Dhahran	Khobar Towers housing complex	June 25, 1996	521
Spain	Madrid	City center: train stations at different locations	March 11, 2004	791
Turkey	Istanbul	City center: Neve Shalom and Beth Israel synagogues	November 15, 2003	325
	Istanbul	CBD: British consulate and HSBC office	November 20, 2003	428
United Kingdom	London	City center: London Underground system, Tavistock Square	July 7, 2005	752
United States	Oklahoma City	Downtown: Murrah Federal Building	April 19, 1995	668
	New York	CBD: World Trade Center	September 11, 2001	9,749

The most salient examples of this included India (Mumbai), Pakistan (Karachi), Spain (Madrid), and the United Kingdom (London).

Most interesting is the international character of almost all mega attacks. Even attacks classified as domestic have some foreign linkage, either because of training done abroad or explosive material smuggled from abroad. Many attacks have involved coordination between locally based terrorists and international sources. This was true for the bombing in Berlin, where Germans worked with Libyans to execute an attack in a discotheque frequently patronized by American military personnel. It is also true for attacks in India where local Muslims were enlisted by Pakistanis. Transnational linkages were especially important in the Madrid metro bombing. In that instance locally based immigrants collaborated with terrorists from Morocco, Algeria, Tunisia, and possibly India and Syria.

The international character of attacks often meant that terrorists were imported to attack citizens on their home soil. For example, Chechens attacked Russians in theaters, schools, and apartment buildings; Palestinians struck Israelis in cafés and commercial/entertainment strips; al Qaeda assaulted Turkish Jews in synagogues or struck Turks and Westerners in a business district. Some attacks inverted this scenario, so that foreigners were attacked once they set foot on local soil. This occurred in Bali, where mostly Australian tourists were struck by a locally based cell of Jemaah Islamiya. A similar attack occurred in a Sinai resort area, where European tourists were killed or injured by car bombs and explosive-laden suitcases planted by terrorists based in Egypt. Finally, there were instances of state terrorism in this mix. Earlier attacks in Karachi (1987) and Islamabad (1988) were alleged to have been carried out by Soviet intelligence, anxious to thwart Pakistan's support for the mujahadeen in the Afghan war.

Reviewing the components of the mega attack we can conclude that most terrorism was fueled by a fiercely defined identity (Islamist interspersed with nationalist), coupled to distinct international connections, and framed by tactical objectives to envelope large numbers of people and property within the ensuing carnage. It is hardly coincidental that some of the largest attacks had an international presence. This may very well be an extension of the notion that internationally organized attacks require a bigger bang than locally initiated assaults. Turkey provides a ready example of the largest attacks being conducted by al Qaeda and much smaller ones executed by separatist Kurds. It may also be that international terrorism possesses the capacity to take on mega attacks. Groups appear to be learning from one another across boundaries about how to conduct mega terror. They even have managed to reduce their costs. The 9/11 attacks are said to have been carried out for approximately $500,000; 3/11 was supposed to have been carried out for a fraction of that sum; and 7/7 was thought to have been executed for just $14,000.[16]

This most recent brand of mass violence has been identified as Islamist-dominated "fourth wave terrorism."[17] The religious distinctiveness of this movement is derived from the spread of Islamist ideology in North Africa, the Middle East, and parts of Asia. Rather than examining terrorism solely from the vantage of *who* does the attacking, we also take the perspective of *where* those attacks originate and *what are* the sites of attack. Judged by this criterion, fourth wave terrorism is not simply a matter of religious inspiration, but also based on cities as both targets and sources of attack. We now turn to what may lie within cities that makes them so convenient for world jihadists.

City Haunts

It is not easy to precisely identify, much less predict, the kinds of neighborhoods or city haunts that terrorists will choose. Some choices will be dictated by pure accident. Rather than having been carefully calculated, the berthing of terrorist cells has something to do with happenstance. The main factors include where co-religionists have settled, their places of congregation, the existence of supportive institutions like mosques or sports clubs, access to religious bookshops, and the presence of a "terrorist entrepreneur" who acts as an organizer and mentor. A city that evolves along these lines may have a university that has attracted foreign students and subsequently provides an atmosphere where sectarians can organize for social or religious purposes. These conditions simply grow up in a place and over time evolve into full-blown communities. Coincidence, however, goes only so far, and there are also structural characteristics connected to cities that determine why some places are especially desirable.

Experience shows that fourth wave terrorists are likely to flourish in a city that is open, contains a marked degree of ethnic diversity, manifests a good deal of sociopolitical tolerance, and has a permissive attitude toward immigration. More often than not, the city chosen has a mixed urban fabric, an abundance of old neighborhoods, and the availability of cheap rental housing. The best candidates are not prohibitively expensive central cities, but less expensive localities that are close to them. These tend to be old, smaller industrial cities or working-class suburbs that lie in the shadow of their larger neighbors.

For urban terrorists, the idea is to find a location either within or close to a major city, where one can find support, that is affordable and most of all contains places where people can get lost. The ability to get lost while freely operating is an art form that is best practiced in faceless urban environments. In South Asia, bustling Karachi has supplied an abundance of city haunts because amid so much public display, so much is also kept secret. "Who could not hide," one observer comments, "in a place where everything is hidden?" In the United States, Brooklyn and Jersey City are superbly located within striking distance of Manhattan. They also contain dense, pluralistic neighborhoods that provide anonymity within a context of liberal values.

Terrorist haunts can also be found in most West European cities from Madrid to Rotterdam to Brussels and well beyond. For various reasons, some cities stand out more than others and these would include Paris, Milan, Leeds, London, and Hamburg. Each of these cities is inhabited by distinct communities and each has its particular traits. A thumbnail sketch of each city illustrates how terrorist cells adapt to their particular environments. The great majority of neighborhood residents are peaceful and law abiding. This makes it easier for terrorists to shield themselves or mask their activities. This is often accomplished by building a niche within a neighborhood, establishing a network of relations, and reconstituting a common identity (often through radical Islam).

Roubaix and the Parisian Maghreb

More than most European nations, France is a nation of immigrants and many from North Africa's Maghreb have settled there. Over past decades, immigrants made their homes in northern industrial cities like Roubaix where factories have closed and unemployment reaches 22 percent. The city is known for having spawned the Roubaix gang, reputed to have carried out waves of bombings in Paris during the 1990s and years later attempted to blow up the U.S. embassy.

On the outskirts of Paris, a host of working-class suburbs have also been transformed. Once known as the Red Belt because local residents voted the Communist ticket, these suburbs now have a distinct ethnic and religious flavor. Immigrants from the Maghreb live in the aged and torn housing stock of Seine-St. Denis or the huge blocks of public housing in nearby La Courneuve. For decades, gangs of unemployed youth sometimes turned to minor theft and delinquency. In Seine-St. Denis, the Tablighi Mosque introduces young men to fundamentalism, often with mixed results. A number of gang members have taken up fundamentalist Islam, changed their habits, and lead religious lives. Others have used their experience with street violence and converted it to religious terrorism. While there is no evidence to suggest the Tablighi has been involved in any kind of illegal activities, the sect has produced conspicuous jihadists who have gone off to fight in foreign wars. The Tablighi also serves as an ideological way station to venture into the more aggressive strain of Salafist Islam. Salafists are known to have harvested proceeds from armed robberies to finance the activities of France's notorious terrorist organization, the Armed Islamic Group (GIA).[18] No clear leader has emerged among these jidhadists, though a religious head named Abu Doha has organized volunteers for service abroad. Afghanistan, Pakistan, Chechnya, and most recently Iraq are favored. A number of raids carried out by French anti-terrorist units have turned up large quantities of material used to manufacture explosives as well as caches of explosives and chemicals.[19]

Terrorism in France falls under the purview of La Direction de la Surveillance du Territoire, or DST. In December 2002, the DST raided two safe houses in La Courneuve and uncovered gas canisters, fuses, chemicals, and a protective suit. The suspects have since been brought to trial and convicted of a criminal association with terrorism. Meanwhile, Judge Jean-Louis Bruiguiere, who presides over special courts that try terrorists, forthrightly states, "The level of threat is incontestably high. Radicalization has never been this strong."[20]

Milan's Fortress Zone

Italy's northern industrial cities serve much the same purposes as those in France, and immigrants have migrated to cities like Turin or nearby Milan. As the country's most important commercial hub, Milan is well suited as a haunt for terrorists.[21] Its winding, back-alley streets bustle with traffic, restaurants, countless businesses, and thousands of passers-by. Milan is thick with politics and packed neighborhoods. During the 1990s it became a hotbed of terrorist cells that recruited jidhadists for civil wars in Algeria, Bosnia, and Chechnya. Milan's terrorist cells are sustained by religious institutions—mostly mosques along Viale Jenner and Via Quaranta. During the last decade, cells were organized by a terrorist entrepreneur named Anwar Shaban, who led sermons at local mosques. Another terrorist entrepreneur, Ahmed Rabei (alias Mohammed the Egyptian), has been convicted of terrorism charges in Italy and has since been extradited to Spain on charges of having masterminded the attack in Madrid.

Rabei cast a long shadow over terrorist circles in Milan and elsewhere. Once having arrived in Milan he became intensely pious. Wearing a full-grown beard and traditional garb, he frequented various haunts preaching violence. Rabei was put under police surveillance and overheard celebrating the beheading of an American hostage as an example of how to kill Westerners. Armando Spatero, a Milan prosecutor with years of experience fighting leftist terror and Mafia crime, looks at Rabei with incredulity, "How is it possible," he exclaims, "that here in a democracy that welcomes immigrants, there could be someone who harbors so much hatred that he could consider taking his own life to kill others?"[22]

Milan's jihadists put secrecy above all else and created their own niche environment. Porta Venezia shows how a densely populated, self-sustaining, mixed-use community provides an air of normality that can also protect a terrorist underground. With increased immigration, Porta Venezia became a "fortress zone" ringed by an extensive network of lookouts and trained agents. Consider the following description of this particular place:

> [A] member of the cell spent hours in a little Arabic restaurant posing as a customer, the Tunisian barber keeping an eye on a junction, the Algerian seller watching over a possible escape route; they were the sentries with eyes and ears everywhere. They noted the faces of all "suspect" persons: Italian law enforcement agents, but above all spies from Arabic intelligence agencies.[23]

A combination of local operatives, transplanted immigrants, and foreign contacts makes for a very viable and effective network. Locals and long-term immigrants can act at the margins of different communities. As merchants or artisans they assimilate into the mainstream while also maintaining friendships with more recent arrivals. Urban neighborhoods furnish a fertile ground for insulating ethnic or religious communities, while at the same time allowing them necessary contact and intelligence from the outside world.

Leeds and the Pakistani Diaspora

Great Britain's northern industrial cities share much the same role as those in France or Italy. Leeds exemplifies this for Pakistani immigrants. The 7/7 bombers hailed from industrial Leeds, where unemployment among the city's seventy different nationality groups can reach 40 percent. Beeston is Leed's most diverse neighborhood, with a high transitory population. It is largely residential, laced with rows of back-to-back terraced housing, and serviced by local shops and three mosques.[24] By British standards, the neighborhood could be described as run-down.

It was in Beeston where Mohammed Siddique Khan, Shehzad Tanweer, Hasib Hussain, and Jermaine Lindsay made plans for earlier attacks. Khan's name was linked to an earlier and foiled attempt to detonate a truck bomb in London. Israeli sources also reported that Khan had visited Israel prior to the deadly suicide bombing of a discotheque in Tel Aviv. Two British citizens of Pakistani origin were involved in that attack, leading to speculation that Khan had been in touch with another group of terrorists.

Kahn and Tanweer also came into contact with terrorists who were apprehended in the midst of planning an attack in London. In what has become known as "Operation Crevice" a half dozen other men were discovered to have stashed away 600 kilograms (1,320 pounds) of ammonium nitrate fertilizer to be used in a massive explosion. Like the Leeds cell, the Operation Crevice terrorists chose London targets and had discussed the relative benefits of destroying a shopping center, a nightclub, water and gas utilities, a soccer stadium, and even the Houses of Parliament. At least some members from the Leeds and Crevice cells had met in London on four separate occasions and once in Pakistan. These cells saw their mission as the furtherance of jihad, some members received training in Pakistan, and contacts became more elaborate from locality to locality and across national boundaries.

Local geography is the building block of domestic terrorism, and the pattern in Leeds typifies the larger process of recruitment, planning, and implementation. A long-term resident of Leeds, Khan was employed as a "learning mentor" at a local school and set up a gymnasium at a local mosque. He used his position to advocate radical Islam and befriend troubled youngsters. After being expelled from the mosque for his radical views, Khan opened another gymnasium and continued his work. He worked with distraught youngsters to reorder their lives, fill their spirits with purpose, and win their loyalties. A local Islamic bookshop also served potential recruits. The shop sold disks, tapes, books, and conducted sessions on Islamic radicalism. Mosque, gym, and bookshop stood as supportive institutions for these men.

Gradually, Khan became a terrorist entrepreneur by taking initiative and operational control. During his previous trips to Pakistan, he was thought to have traveled to adjoining border areas of Afghanistan, where he established links with al Qaeda. By November 2004, Khan made another trip to Pakistan, this time accompanied by one of his younger followers, Shehzad Tanweer. It was during this last trip that both men are thought to have prepared for the 7/7 bombings. Other men who traveled between Karachi, London, and Leeds were also suspected of collaborating with Khan.

Back in the United Kingdom, the four men needed a place to conduct operations and they chose an area near the University of Leeds because its high turnover student population provided good cover and cheap rent. After letting an apartment from an Egyptian chemistry student at 18 Alexander Grove, Khan and his followers set to work. At 18 Alexander Grove they converted a ground-floor flat of a two-story building into an explosives factory. Khan and his accomplices labored day and night to prepare their ultimate act. It appears that the four men worked with the windows open in order to avoid fumes from the chemicals, though the windows were covered by net curtains in order to avoid detection. From all indications, the men could come and go, purchase the needed chemicals, and work freely without arousing suspicion. Under the collective name Abu Hafs al Masri Brigade, a few disaffected youth traveled to London and set off their cargo, taking their own lives in the process. For a some people, their legacy lives on.

London's Finsbury Mosque

Well before 9/11, London was reputed to hold the most extensive and robust group of religious radicals in Europe. Islamic fundamentalists were clear about their views and brazen in their speech. They posted calls for jihad on public billboards, spoke openly about evils committed by Jews and Crusaders, and told new recruits that killing nonbelievers would be a passport to paradise. This caricatured behavior evolved from the Hyde Park traditions of free expression, where anyone could say almost anything. So pervasive was religious radicalism in London that it was thought to have become the "crossroads of terrorism" and some nicknamed it "Londonistan."

It may be that because London was a place where the extremes of free speech could be tolerated, even worse things had not occurred. It is precisely because the sound of world jihad was so loud and clear in London that the city became so conspicuously identified as a terrorist haunt. As one of the world's great media capitals, London would remain a catalyst for jihad while Hamburg would be the city where the actual plot for the world's biggest mega attack would be hatched.

At the heart of the call for jihad was the Finsbury Mosque. The mosque is located at the intersection of three London boroughs—Islington, Haringey, and Hackney.[25] Once a working-class neighborhood, Islington has gone through large-scale gentrification and become one of London's most fashionable areas. Notwithstanding its upscale status and low unemployment (5.8 percent), the borough is relatively diverse, with nearly 20 percent of its population from Africa, the Caribbean, or Asia. Haringey is less upscale, though it shares similarly low unemployment rates and holds comparable proportions of nonwhites. Hackney is less well off than its sister boroughs, with higher rates of unemployment (6.9 percent), a more diverse population, and a non-European population of more than 40 percent.

The Finsbury Mosque is just a twenty-minute bus ride from central London. The mosque draws from surrounding boroughs and services a multiethnic community of Pakistanis, Bengalis, Algerians, and Egyptians. For six years a radical imam named Abu Hamza preached out of Finsbury. Egyptian-born Hamza has one eye, and because of a lost hand he wears a metal prosthesis in the shape of a hook. Hamza's unusual physical appearance was more than matched by menacing words. His sermons were not only meant for congregants, but addressed to crowds in decayed neighborhoods like Whitechapel in nearby East London. The radical preacher called for "bleeding" the enemies of Islam and doing away with Jews, gays, tourists, the royal family, and women in bikinis.

Whether Hamza's words led to any actual attacks is unclear.[26] Convicted 9/11 terror accomplice Zacarias Moussaoui and shoe-bomber Richard Reid had been in contact with Hamza and the mosque. Upon raiding Hamza's apartment, police found a manual for waging terror called the *Encyclopedia of Afghan Jihad*, plus thousands of tapes advocating war against the West. Interestingly, the *Encyclopedia* focused on symbolic targets like Big Ben, the Eiffel Tower, and the Statue of Liberty. Also uncovered were forged passports, bio-nuclear-chemical protective suits, minor weapons, and a CS canister. Hamza has since been convicted of soliciting murder and causing racial hatred.[27]

Hamburg's/Harburg's Al Qaeda

If London is the place from which the fury of urban terror originated, Hamburg and Harburg are where its biggest event was planned. Hamburg is one of Germany's wealthiest cities. It has long been Germany's media capital, and since the country's reunification it has recaptured its roles as a leading port and gateway to Eastern Europe. Hamburg's elegant buildings, parks, rebuilt harbor, and smart streets appear to justify its long-held claim of being home to most of Germany's millionaires.[28] The adjacent city of Harburg, lying to the south, tells a much different tale. Harburg is a drab, gray industrial suburb with few landmarks or attractions. Many of its factories and houses were destroyed by Allied bombing during World War II. Upon close inspection one can spot weather-beaten plaques on the walls of buildings, inscribed with dates of destruction and reconstruction.

While much has been written about the Hamburg Cell, the nearby offshoot of Harburg is where much of 9/11 was planned. The plot's leader, Mohammed Atta, lived in Harburg, and was joined there by three major accomplices—Ramzi Binalshibh, Marwan al-Shehhi, and Ziad Jarrah. This core was later joined by four other accomplices.[29] For at least a time, three of these men shared the same apartment at Marienstrasse 54. Like most of the buildings around it, Marienstrasse 54 is vintage 1950s, constructed when there was little money in Germany and people were grateful for a place to live. It is a plain, square four-story house with a yellow façade, squeezed into rows of identical houses.

Some of the men used the local university's facilities to meet with comrades and host events. Marienstrasse 54 is a short walk from the Technical University of Hamburg-Harburg (TUHH), where Atta studied urban planning. Apartments in the vicinity rent quickly and inexpensively to foreigners and students. Anyone renting can be sure they will attract little notice. As one shopkeeper describes the environment chosen by the 9/11 attackers:

> I don't recall those guys. . . . All I can tell you is that there were many of them. . . . I do know that it is possible to live in a Harburg neighborhood for years without befriending, or even recognizing, a single soul. If you pay your rent on time and don't cause any trouble, you can become invisible.[30]

The city's high tolerance for privacy was supplemented by an indulgent attitude toward criminality. Conscious of the country's Nazi past and sensitive toward allegations of racism, police shied away from investigating complaints against foreigners—even when those complaints involved petty crime or drugs. Police were especially reluctant to target suspect mosques. This allowed Islamic radicals to enjoy near immunity from investigation.

Members of the Hamburg Cell were drawn from North Africa and the Middle East. From the early 1990s onward, more than a half-dozen young men from the Arab world settled in Hamburg-Harburg as foreign students. While different individuals would join the cell, they would soon disappear. This meant that membership was held to a core of seven steadfast individuals, retrospectively described as "a bunch of guys." The seemingly innocuous "bunch of guys" was made up of lost young men who upon finding themselves in an unfamiliar setting would reconstitute their own collective identity.

The activities of the "bunch of guys" revolved around al Quds Mosque, situated near a train station, a red light district, and police offices. As in other city haunts, their religious orientation was guided by a radical imam—this one known only by the surname al Fazazi.[31] The al Quds Mosque was not only a center of prayer, but of bonding and indoctrination. Congregants regularly visited an Islamic bookstore just two blocks away. A special entrance was reserved for a select few who could enter a backroom and purchase jihadist books and tapes.

Along with other comrades, Atta made ample use of the university. Fees for foreign students were low and rules allowed them to pursue academic degrees at a leisurely pace. Atta himself had arrived in 1992, taking nearly eight years to complete a master's degree. For both Atta and his accomplices, the extended time was spent in other pursuits. At TUHH he founded an Islamic students' association that soon turned toward militancy. Led by Atta, the students obtained permission from university officials to reserve a room for common prayer. The student Islamic association soon formulated strict rules for attendance and engaged in animated political discussions. According to evidence discovered later, the discussions revolved around calls for world jihad, attacks on the United States, and punishment for members who did not pray regularly.[32]

The cell seemed to be able to flourish in some of the most run-down, transitional neighborhoods. Everywhere Atta looked he was surrounded by ugliness; the mosque in a seedy neighborhood, the sterility of TUHH, and the nondescript building where he lived were all strange and depressing.[33] Despite this, the city haunt allowed for anonymity, freedom, friendship, a code of behavior, purpose, and portals to the outside world. From this haunt "the bunch of guys" traveled to parts of the Middle East and Asia. September 11 may have been sanctioned by Osama bin Laden or Khalid Sheikh Mohammed, sitting in the harsh landscape of Afghanistan, but much of it was formulated in a niche environment—a city haunt—where the cell could comfortably function.

City Haunts as Reconstituted Places

Writing about what makes a world jihadist, Marc Sageman observes that alienated young men turn to apocalyptic notions of a holy war "precisely because [they] lack any anchor to any society."[34] He sees these men as part of a minuscule diaspora, ripped away from their former society and living in a strange land. These alienated individuals find each other, form a new group, and live apart from the host society. As Sageman puts it, they "become embedded in a socially dis-embedded network."[35] Yet while Sageman offers astute insights, he discounts the role of place in assessing these networks. Far from being "socially disembedded," jihadists are connected in critical ways to their surroundings. Connections come in many different forms like marginal contacts, friendships with assimilated co-religionists, relationships with sympathetic or converted nationals, and the ability to lead "double lives." Those connections may be erratic and they are often unusual, but they are the terrorist's lifeline to the outside world.

Indeed, the tangential nature of connections allows jihadists to work or learn within mainstream society, take recreational or cultural advantage of conventional facilities, and propagandize or recruit new followers. Moreover, the lines between local and international jihadists are not always clear. Locals serve as an informational and supply channel for their international comrades. Long-standing locals may mix with recent foreigners and those who were once indigenous may "go foreign" and vice versa. Even some "sleeper cells" were never really "sleepers" in the sense that adherents lay in quiescence and waited for the day when they could attack. Rather, much of what passes for a "sleeper cell" really consists of semi-assimilated locals who began helping Islamists and were later converted to radicalism. To be sure, the blending of different actors is very selective and it may be complicated by Europeans of long-standing generations. British intelligence estimates that 1,200 jihadists have received training abroad and that a portion of them are European converts.[36] Other intelligence reports have identified 1,600 individuals who are "actively engaged in plotting, or facilitating terrorist acts," either in the United

Kingdom or overseas.[37] Rough estimates also indicate that 100,000 sympathizers could offer support or cover of some kind.

Certainly, social blending occurred for local jihadists in the Parisian suburbs and Leeds. In both places, "bunches of guys" led two lives—working, studying, engaging in sports and social relations within the larger society, while also planning attacks at home and spending time abroad. The head of the Leeds group worked at local schools and studied at the university while he also indoctrinated youth and traveled to Pakistan. Likewise, in Milan, London, and Hamburg, those who might be described as international jihadists had ample connections to the social order. In Milan, local intermediaries assisted terrorists cells; London's Finsbury Mosque was constantly fed by locals, while its radical imam preached in East End neighborhoods; Hamburg's cell drew much of its support from the local university, while one of its members frequented the city's nightspots and married a German woman.

The more complex and alarming feature of Islamist terrorism is that its most exuberant followers are not foreign but homegrown products. It is the homegrown nature of terrorism that is particularly elusive and that surprises authorities. The Leeds cell consisted of British citizens who were born and raised in that country. Similarly, the "bunch of guys" from St. Denis or La Courneuve were born and raised in France and were very much a part of their communities. The concerns about homegrown terrorism not only pertain to Europe but to North America. In the United States, six Yemeni Americans traveled to Afghanistan in order to undergo training in al Qaeda camps. Known in their hometown outside Buffalo as the "Lackawanna Six," the men were convicted in 2003 of providing "material support" for terrorism. In Toronto, charges were made against seventeen individuals for conspiring to commit terrorist acts. Dubbed the "Toronto Seventeen," they were accused of plotting to blow up buildings and landmarks. Canadian agents managed to infiltrate efforts to purchase explosives and substituted a harmless look-alike before apprehending the suspects.

The connections that allow urban terrorism to flourish were made possible by the element of "place," or more precisely, a specific locale where the group enjoyed freedom, exercised control, and could form social bonds. Without "place" jihadists could not socialize, recruit, organize, coordinate, supply, or launch attacks. Places could vary in size and mean different things—from whole industrial towns near Paris, to "fortress zones" in Milan, to sports clubs in Leeds and mosques in London and Hamburg. All of these city haunts held one central feature in common: they were reconstituted environments connected to their surroundings, but also separate from them.

From City Haunts to Global Nodes

One of the more important functions of place is support and supply. City haunts are eminently well suited for terrorist logistics. Their tight-knit fabric allows for a "clustering" of opportunities so that "bunches of guys" can be in frequent communication with each other and work in collaboration. The clustering of activities occurs in a number of proximate places and for a multiplicity of functions. These include recruitment, socialization, bomb making, forging needed documents, safe houses, and finances. City haunts can be turned into factories for assembling an apparatus of urban terror.

As we have seen, recruitment and training can be conducted in local mosques or bookshops. Chemists can be enlisted from local universities and texts borrowed from their libraries to produce explosives. It is easier in these clustered spaces to obtain raw material and supplies for forging documents as well as find the necessary expertise. Much more available in clustered city environments are "safe houses" to keep potential operatives out of sight or hide fugitives. Also, transporting operatives from one place to another is more easily accomplished in crowded rather than open spaces.

Not the least, finances are more readily raised and in greater abundance in clustered city spaces. Cities have larger expatriate and immigrant communities that are valuable sources of support. Higher densities and heterogeneous populations make it much easier to locate patrons. These are often drawn from sympathetic merchants; congregations at mosques; university faculty, staff, or students; and diplomatic missions from supportive governments.

Clustered urban environments are not only better coordinated internally, but better coordinated externally with other cities. In much the same way that international corporations use global cities to coordinate resources, so to do terrorists convert individual cities into a larger network of connecting "global nodes." Sageman brings this point to bear by describing how different cities were used to coordinate terrorism across national boundaries. These cities formed a complex of global nodes made up of Montreal, London, Madrid, Hamburg, and Milan. Each node was used to enlist volunteers and coordinate their travel to training camps.[38] In this way, terrorist cells could remain separate and decentralized, but when necessary could band together and operate as a comprehensive unit. For this to work, efficient transportation and reliable communication are essential.

Only cities possess the assets and infrastructure to complete nodal loops. Metropolitan airports allow for quick and relatively inexpensive travel across continents. Parisian terrorists maintained personal contact with members of the GIA in Algeria. Leeds terrorist entrepreneur Mohammed Siddique Khan frequently traveled to Pakistan. The 9/11 attackers traveled from points far and wide in order to meet in the United States. The Hamburg cell traveled separately in order to avoid suspicion, though once in the United States the two cells operated as a group.[39] When its members were scattered, they maintained contact with one another and bolstered morale by streams of e-mails.

Travel is particularly easy throughout the European Union, either by rail or air. Recall Ahmed Rabei (alias Mohammed the Egyptian), who was apprehended in Milan for the attack in Madrid. Before Rabei arrived in Milan he had spent time in Germany and was regarded by local police as an experienced operative. As Milan prosecutor Armando Spatero put it, "Rabei was some sort of contact person with links to cells all over Europe. We verify his presence in Spain, France and Italy. Besides, he had contacts in Belgium and Holland."[40]

What had emerged earlier as a network of nodes visited by operatives like Rabei was eventually turned into a system of cybernodes. The links across city haunts extended into a virtual world. Cell phones and computers became ubiquitous tools of the trade. Al Qaeda's trademark of synchronized attack was enhanced by the digital age. After the attacks in Madrid and London, investigators found that terrorists had used modern technology to carefully plan attacks, so they could occur within minutes of each other.

For those who later investigated these attacks, computer hard drives provided valuable information. A computer captured in Manila in 1995 furnished detailed information about a plot to blow up aircraft over the Pacific (Bojinka Plot). A most memorable portrait was that of a 9/11 plotter sitting on the floor of a safe house in Karachi, surrounded by three laptops and five cell phones.[41] While globalization and the electronic age made cities vital nodes of the international economy, they also made them havens for urban terror. There is, then, a dark side to globalization facilitated by high technology, permeable boundaries, transnational cooperation, and a "loose corporate" structure. The very tools invented by the West have been turned against it.

Conclusions

Terrorism has a lengthy history running the gamut from anarchists to secular extremists and religious radicals. Its most recent manifestation, "fourth wave" terrorism, is dominated by a religious rationale whose content is Islamist. As distinguished from earlier types of secular terrorism, religiously inspired terrorism is more lethal, causes greater destruction, and its agents are given to self-destruction through suicide. Cities are particularly well suited for this kind of assault and over the past decade or so have been blistered by mega attacks. These have not just included 9/11, 3/11, and 7/7, but large-scale attacks in Mumbai, Bali, Jerusalem, Nairobi, Karachi, Moscow, Istanbul, and Oklahoma City. While some of these are purely local, most mega terror has international linkages of one kind or another. More than just happenstance, there is a connection between a proclivity toward mega terror and the rise of international terrorism. Some of this may be due to the capacity to carry out large-scale attacks, but it is also due to the desire of world jihadists to put their cause on the world stage.

Further, cities are not just the objects of attack but often incubate terrorist cells. Some of the best-known instances revolved around core and satellite cities of Paris, Milan, Leeds, London, and Hamburg-Harburg. In most instances, terrorist haunts have grown up within these cities and reconstituted small communities. Cities provide a clustering function, pluralism, and uncommon tolerance. These qualities enable cells to recruit members, find ready sources of supply, hide operatives within safe houses, and coordinate activities. Universities, mosques, bookstores, local shops, and a housing stock of inexpensive apartments provide both the infrastructure and anonymity for cells to flourish. Last, cities have been linked together in a network of nodes made possible by modern technology. Emerging from this are groups of cybernodes, which have enabled urban terrorists to travel, communicate, and coordinate attacks.

Decontrolling Territory

Territoriality is a form of behavior that uses bounded space, a territory, as the instrument for securing a particular outcome.

—Peter J. Taylor

City Territory

We begin this chapter with some fundamental premises. Cities are located in bounded territories where different uses are created, mixed, and continually enhanced. Within this bounded territory, cities allow for the production of things and the conduct of social life. Human mobility, interaction, and information flow are keys to sustaining its dynamic; so too is the ability to assemble as members of one kind of community or another. Cities give meaning to anonymous spaces by converting them into what one writer calls "remembered landscapes."[1] *Civitas*, the polis, the agora, the neighborhood, the central business district, and the skyscraper—all sustained by a tapestry of infrastructure—endow the city with immense capacity. Because of this capacity, cities are able to continually reinvent their territories and adapt to challenges.[2]

These conceptions have been communicated in different ways by scholars with vastly differing perspectives. Lewis Mumford wrote about the "crystallization of the city," Louis Wirth referred to "a mosaic of social worlds," Henri Lefebvre described the "rhythm of the city," and Jane Jacobs defined it all as a "settlement that consistently generates its own economic growth."[3] Despite their different perspectives, these writers expounded that cities are alive, they grow and recede, and they are filled with movement between their diverse parts. Without that movement, cities can become paralyzed and whither.[4]

Two aspects of this discussion warrant further amplification. One is that cities actually *make space* and the second is that they exercise a certain *mastery* over that space. To begin with the first, cities make space by adding value to territory through infrastructure, by assigning different legal designations to property, and by connecting different terrains. The production of space also means that territory has become a commodity—an object of value that can be invested with wealth, traded, exchanged, and speculated upon for profit. While treating territory as a commodity typifies liberal, capitalist cities, it is not entirely unique to them and in a modified manner applies to cities in command or socialist economies.[5]

Modern cities also make space by adding new dimensions to territory. City territory has a four-dimensional capacity—on land, underneath it, above it, and across different territories. On land, cities build residential neighborhoods, factories, and central business districts. Underneath land, cities construct metro systems, underground pathways, and subterranean commercial centers. Above land, cities build skyscrapers, skyways, and elevated transit lines. Finally, across different terrains, cities set up electronic transmitters, uplink stations, and streets laden with copper or fiber-optic lines that conduct billions of information bites through cyberspace.

Turning to the second point, cities work because they can *master their spaces.* They do this by exercising political control over their territory through zoning, environmental regulation, licenses, permits, prohibited uses, municipal ownership, public investment, and the like. That control stimulates, facilitates, and regulates relations between a city's multitudinous parts. Nor is this a matter of passively adhering to a set of rules. Cities can be enormously active in raising massive amounts of money for transportation, convention halls, sports stadiums, or parks and educational facilities.[6]

Mastery allows for movement across spaces. The routine acts of municipal administration permit countless commuters to travel to millions of destinations, stop and go, speed up and slow down, arrive and depart. The mastery over city spaces transpires each day, often twenty-four hours a day, seven days a week and fifty-two weeks a year, year after year. More often than not, it is exercised with minimum interference and under the protective care of throngs of municipal workers. In democratic, liberal societies this mastery is continuing, encompassing, and usually exercised by benevolently controlling territory. We take this control for granted, except when it stops.

Decontrolling Territory

If in the normal course of events, cities make and master space, the tactic of terrorism is to undo that supremacy by decontrolling urban territory. The immediate or medium-range objective of the terrorist is to put a halt to city function—preventing it from "crystallizing" its creative energies (Mumford), breaking down its rich "mosaic" (Wirth), upsetting its natural "rhythms" (Lefebvre), and sabotaging its "economic generation" (Jacobs). Urban terrorism draws on low-intensity warfare in order to destabilize cities by upsetting their routines and undoing their productive capacity. Boiled down, where cities seek to make space, urban terrorism seeks to despoil it; where cities seek to facilitate movement, urban terrorism seeks to paralyze it.

Urban terrorism aims at all four dimensions of city space by blowing up people in cafés, crashing planes into skyscrapers, releasing poison gas in metro systems, and, at least potentially, sabotaging cyberspace. Terrorism is not just about a message, but about raw destruction and through it chaos, confusion, and demoralization. Its purpose is to show that once safe areas can become dangerous, that daily life can become unpredictable, and that assurance of protection can become hollow. Terrorist warfare emphasizes "mass disruption" so that people are separated from place, from each other, and find themselves in a condition of protracted disassociation.

Recall that terrorism is not static. It changes and adapts to circumstance through many mutations. Part of this evolution entails changing the weaponry used to intimidate populations. During the 1970s and 1980s, kidnappings and rapid-fire guns were the weapons of choice. Later, more commonly used weapons included bombs planted in parked vehicles, rail stations, pubs, or crowded thoroughfares. More recently we see an increase in high-risk attacks (where terrorists might expect to be killed by others) and suicide attacks (where terrorists purposely kill themselves). Suicide terror had been a Hezbollah trademark. Today it is employed by al Qaeda and Hamas and used widely in Iraq and Afghanistan by different groups.

Table 5.1 draws data from twenty-five of the hardest-struck cities examined in this study between 1968 and 2005. It displays the types of weaponry used for attack, the percentage of incidents employed, attacked sites, the impact of attack, and cities in which the event occurred.[7] The cities are chosen for prevalence of attack and for illustrative purposes.

Among more than 1,000 cities examined for this study, the instances are rare in which pirated planes were successfully employed as missiles, there have been just a few chemical or biological attacks, and we know of no instances of cyber, radiological, or nuclear terrorism (CBRN). At the same time, we should recognize that CBRN weapons hold a disproportionate and multidimensional impact. Frequency does not necessarily equate with impact. The effect of one attack combining catalytic, mega, or smart terror can far outweigh scores of shootings or planted bombs. There are good reasons why just one sarin gas attack in Tokyo or crashing three planes into the New York's Twin Towers and Washington's Pentagon aroused the world. As we shall see, high-impact weaponry has a disproportionate effect and this accounts for its prevalence in carefully planned attacks against what we call *targets of calculation*. Suicide terror is one way of assuring the successful application of high-impact weaponry, and while it accounts for just 2.9 percent of incidents from our sample, its effects are frightful.

Interestingly, the most numerous types of attack are planted bombs, followed by shootings. Planted bombs are often set within enclosed spaces in order to maximize human casualties. Placing them within an enclosed space like a bus or in a tunnel magnifies the actual blast and not only increases casualties but brings about greater economic disruption. Shootings, stabbings, stone throwing, and kidnappings are geared toward individual casualties and conducted in relatively open surroundings. These are likely to be executed randomly, wherever a conceived enemy arises or where there exist what can be called *targets of opportunity*.

Concentration, Repetition, and Penetration

Not all terror is directed against targets of calculation, but when terror is well planned, a number of means can be used to reach tactical objectives.[8] The prime

Table 5.1

Urban Terrorism's Weaponry, Site, and Impact in Twenty-Five Nations and Regions

Weaponry	Percentage	Site	Impact	City
Shootings (firearms)	19.17	Tourist attractions, airports, restaurants, and cafés	Casualties	Tel Aviv, Jerusalem, Karachi, Cairo, Istanbul, Paris, Lima
Stabbings/stones thrown	0.36	Tourist attractions, pedestrian streets, businesses	Casualties (light to serious)	Jerusalem, Istanbul
Kidnappings/hostage taking	2.28	Diplomats, businesses, mass media, stadiums, theaters	Casualties, insecurity, intimidation, fear	Moscow, Bogotá, Munich, Algiers
Arson	2.16	Businesses, diplomatic missions, houses, automobiles	Property destruction	Athens, Frankfurt, Paris, Rome, Istanbul
Biochemical (sarin gas, anthrax)	0.68	Public transit, government buildings	Disruption of transit, stoppage of government	Tokyo, New York, Washington, DC, Karachi
Planted bombs	72.33	Businesses, diplomatic missions, government buildings, public transit, cafés, restaurants, schools, markets	Casualties, property damage, public shock, economic destruction	Jerusalem, Tel Aviv, Madrid, Paris, Athens, Mumbai, Nairobi, Moscow, New Delhi, Paris, Haifa, Lima, Istanbul, Karachi
Suicide bombings	2.93	Hotels, restaurants, public transit, cafés, concerts, religious institutions	Casualties, property damage, public shock, economic disruption	Bali, Jerusalem, Tel Aviv, Moscow, London, New York, Haifa, Istanbul, Jakarta, Riyadh, Cairo, Islamabad, Karachi, Casablanca, Mombassa
Pirated planes as missiles	0.12	Skyscrapers, military headquarters	Casualties, property damage, economic disruption	New York, Washington, DC
Cyber/radiological/nuclear	Not known	Not known	Not known	Not known

Source: Adapted from RAND database, available at www.tkb.org. Type 1 data.

ingredients for calculated attacks consist of *concentrating* and *repeating* attacks at strategic sites, demonstrating over time that those sites can be *penetrated*.

Concentrating an attack at a strategic center is important because it allows smart terror to do optimal damage. The highest choice sites are banks, hotels, entertainment centers, and public transit. Concentration conveys the notion that attacks are geographically circumscribed within a particular area and are often synchronized in a timed series of multiple assaults. A well-known tactic of al Qaeda and Hamas is to launch simultaneous, high-combustion attacks within a confined area. *Concentration* is also important because it optimizes casualties as well as shock. In fact, it is usually the force of the blast, rather than shrapnel, that brings about human and property damage. Tall buildings, diplomatic missions, and especially enclosed public transit like buses and metro tunnels magnify explosions.

Repeating strikes on the same particular space over and over again reinforces conditions for chaos. A substantial amount of urban terror consists of a first strike and a series of subsequent assaults. The repetition can take place over short time intervals (Jerusalem's Ben Yehuda Mall) or over long time intervals (New York's World Trade Center) or in cycles that cluster attacks (London's square mile). Repeated attacks are audacious demonstrations that the violence is unstoppable, security is unattainable, and mayhem can break out at any moment. Terrorists have been able to construct mental maps of an area and use that knowledge to find and conduct subsequent attacks on an urban "soft spot" (defined as frequently habituated by crowds or as possessing high material or symbolic value).

The *penetration* of an area is essential for terrorist success, and this is why camouflaged attack is so intimately tied to the exercise of urban terror. Urban terror functions through the ability of operatives to blend into a civilian population and attack from within. Over the last ten years, terrorists have depended upon young men willing to strap on explosive-laden vests and destroy themselves. Once personal searches were put into effect and young men were stopped as suspects, terrorists turned to young women to slip past guards. In Moscow, women were used to penetrate a rock concert and set off suicide vests. Women and adolescents have also been used to penetrate Israeli checkpoints—sometimes prepared to blow themselves up and at other times serving as couriers for explosives.[9]

Penetration is made easier by establishing proximity to the target, so that intelligence can be gathered and weaponry or explosives can be set at a decisive point. Proximity can be achieved in different ways. Often, national, ethnic, or co-religionist communities can be found adjacent to potential targets. These communities might provide logistical support, but they also enable terrorists to blend into a larger population. In Londonderry and Belfast, local neighborhoods served as launching pads for terrorists who, after committing an assault, frequented a local pub. East Jerusalem and villages in the West Bank serve a similar purpose, and attackers have used the homes of acquaintances to set up shop or conceal themselves. In Amman, neighborhood anonymity not only shielded some terrorists from detection, but enabled them to store tons of explosives in underground caverns located behind their residence.

Another way of achieving proximity is to find a "safe house" within enemy territory where operatives can hide and explosives can be manufactured or stored. Turkish Hezbollah availed itself of a network of safe houses used both as hideouts and to imprison kidnapped victims. As we have seen in the previous chapter, both the Leeds and Hamburg cells sought out nondescript, inexpensive housing in transient neighborhoods to minimize detection. Once in the throes of an operation, Islamist terrorists will shave their beards and wear Western clothing so as not to stand out. Sometimes they are instructed to stay away from mosques. Al Qaeda's manual tells operatives to adopt the ways of the host country and embed themselves in the population.[10] The greatest obstacles to penetrating the enemy consist of travel to another county and the absence of safe houses. These obstacles did not stop the 9/11 terrorists, though since that time restrictions on foreign travel and surveillance have increased.

As a general rule, the more proximate the demographic support for a possible attack, the more frequent the terror. Examining this from a domestic perspective, Moscow, whose terrorism far exceeds that of St. Petersburg, is half the distance from Chechnya; Belfast, whose attacks are far more frequent than London's, lies in the IRA's heartland; and Jerusalem's frequency of attacks as compared to Tel Aviv can also be attributed to terrorist support from nearby neighborhoods. Looked at from an international perspective, the issue of proximity is equally significant. Communities that might harbor terrorists are farther from and fewer in New York than Moscow. Those same communities are farther from and fewer in Moscow than London. And they are farther from and fewer in London than Jerusalem.

Last, cities will experience very different frequencies of urban terror. Attacks may be continuous, sporadic, or occur in intense cycles. Jerusalem best exemplifies a high-frequency, continual pattern of attack. New York demonstrates an irregular or sporadic pattern. London falls somewhere in between and has tended toward cyclical occurrences. As treated in the next section, each of these patterns takes account of concentrated, repetitive attacks and terrorist penetration.

Patterns of Attack in Jerusalem, New York, and London

Jerusalem's Continual Attacks

Israel's experience with urban terror is all too familiar and much too costly. Along with a handful of nations on the Indian subcontinent, Israeli cities register some of the highest per capita tolls in the world. During the period between 1968 and 2005, the country encountered over 700 attacks and more than 7,000 casualties. Smaller attacks against individuals may be more frequent in rural areas or settlements, but those of significant size have occurred in cities. As with any terrorist venture, noncombatants have been the targets of choice, and in Israel a large plurality of victims consists of women, persons over fifty years old, and children.[11]

Jerusalem holds the dubious distinction of having suffered more attacks and incurred more casualties than the combined total of its two largest sister cities—Tel Aviv and Haifa. During more than three decades the city accounted for 40 percent of terrorist-inflicted casualties within Israel. This should be understood relative to the larger metropolitan populations of Tel Aviv and Haifa.[12]

For all the notoriety that a surfeit of terrorism has brought to Jerusalem, most attacks are small. Between 1998 and 2005, the city incurred 148 incidents and averaged 11 casualties per incident. Most easily targeted for frequent attacks are restaurants, shopping centers, and buses. The Old City is especially prone to attacks on individuals because its labyrinthine streets are filled with hideouts for those who choose to wield knives. While there are significant exceptions, terrorism has crept up on Jerusalem rather than having pounded the city in one fell swoop. Its shock derives not from the big mega attack but from the cumulative impact of assaults that are more likely to resemble catalytic and smart terrorism.

Terror's friction is made tenable by an assortment of weaponry including abductions, stabbings, shootings, thrown grenades, and planted bombs. These attacks accounted for a little more than half of the incidents during Jerusalem's most severe wave of terror. The remaining assaults were conducted through suicide bombings.[13] Depending upon what and how incidents are counted, suicide attacks generate between four and six times the casualties of other terrorist methods.[14] In Israel as a whole, the rate of suicide attacks has leapt from 9 percent in the early 1990s to 58 percent since the year 2000.[15] Just as important, suicide attackers have the highest rate of success. Almost half the planted bombs are discovered before detonation, and individuals hurling grenades or shooting into crowds are also likely to be stopped at an early stage of attack by security forces.

Thus far, the year 2002 has been the most severe in Jerusalem's modern history. Attacks occurred on an average of nearly four per month. During the first four months of that year, Jerusalem was struck by continuous waves of terror in which nine assaults killed or maimed hundreds of people. "It was horrendous," one woman said. "No one went out for coffee. No one went to restaurants. We went as a group of people to one another's houses only."[16]

Jerusalem's "City Center" is the pivotal hub for Israelis. This neighborhood is located immediately to the west and within walking distance of the Old City. Its major thoroughfares and meeting places are along King George and Jaffa streets with the Ben Yehuda outdoor mall nestled between them. Buses, taxis, private automobiles, and a prospective light rail system converge at their most prominent intersections. The neighborhood's mixed uses embrace daytime commercial life as well as a vibrant nightlife. All this is made possible by the close interface of retail shops, cafés, restaurants, office towers, banks, and government buildings. Just a short walk from the King George/Jaffa/Ben Yehuda complex is the Mehane Yehuda market. Bustling enterprises along this route have been severely struck, especially on Friday mornings or Saturday evenings when last-minute shoppers, strollers, or partygoers flock into this area.

Figure 5.1 displays a map showing the concentration and repetition of attacks

Figure 5.1 **Jerusalem Terror Attacks, 1998–2005**

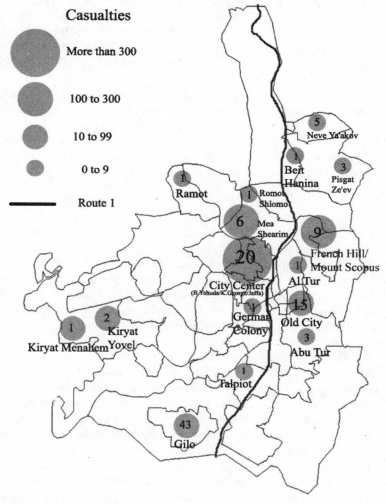

Note: Numbers in the circles represent total incidents for the years indicated.

in Jerusalem. Neighborhoods in which the attacks occurred are listed, along with casualties (designated by the size of the circle) and frequency of incidents (designated by the number in the circle). Also displayed is Route 1, or the "seam line," which once separated West Jerusalem from East Jerusalem, and where today Arab and Jewish neighborhoods are in close proximity.

Note the tight clustering of attacks in the City Center. The municipality of Jerusalem holds a territorial surface of 50.4 square miles (130.5 square kilometers).

By comparison, the City Center is just 0.4 of a square mile (one square kilometer). Yet this tiny area incurred 20 attacks and over 900 casualties and had come to be called Israel's "ground zero." Put another way, for the period noted in the figure, 15 percent of the attacks and 57 percent of the casualties were absorbed on just 2 percent of Jerusalem's territorial surface (see Appendix, Table A10).[17] Other nearby neighborhoods such as Mea Shearim, the Old City, and French Hill–Mount Scopus are also target prone.

While some locations, like Gilo, Neve Ya'akov, and Pisgat Ze'ev, have experienced numerous shooting incidents, the casualties in these neighborhoods are relatively low. The correlation between intensity of attack and urban densities is well established and has been mapped by other scholars.[18] As one moves farther from the center toward lower densities, terrorism markedly declines. This is particularly true for neighborhoods farther west.

Concentrated and Repetitive Attacks

A common practice is to concentrate on and strike at the same site over and over again. In Jerusalem the practice has historical precedent, with much of it aimed at the King George/Jaffa/Ben Yehuda complex. As Israel was about to declare its statehood in 1948, three truckloads of bombs driven by Arab oppositionists exploded at the site. The attack left 52 dead and over 32 injured. Terrorists struck again at this same site in 1975, when they packed a refrigerator with five kilograms of explosives and unloaded it onto the street. The event, known as the "refrigerator bombing," left 15 dead and 77 injured.

Repeating attacks at key locations is intended to induce semi-paralysis. Entertainment districts are particularly prone to attack because of their crowds, festivities, and celebratory air. Ben Yehuda is often saturated with pedestrians, open-air diners, street entertainers, and people hawking anything from children's toys to political pamphlets. Its remarkable ambiance has been upset on numerous occasions. In 1997, three suicide attackers struck. One of the attackers, disguised as a woman, was stationed at a café while two others took positions 20 meters down the street. Within half a minute, all three human bombs had exploded, leaving 8 Israelis dead and 208 injured.[19] To date, the most severe attack occurred in late 2001, carried out by two suicide terrorists. As ambulances and emergency medical workers rushed toward the victims and crowds tried to escape, they were met by a third explosion, detonated within a nearby automobile. The explosive-laden automobile also contained mortars that were set off and splayed through the downtown area. This particular attack took place on a Saturday evening, when Ben Yehuda was filled with young men and women. Ten people—all between the ages of 14 and 20—were killed in the blasts and another 19 were critically injured, while 150 incurred moderate to light wounds.

A similar modus operandi can be seen along other parts of King George and Jaffa streets, near Zion Square, as well as at Mehane Yehuda market. Zion Square is the city's major center for banking and professional services. Mehane Yehuda's fresh food market is staffed by Sephardic vendors who cater to Jerusalem's blue-collar families as well as middle-class adventurers out for a shopping jaunt. Assaults at these sites also bear the markings of organized terrorism. These are tightly coordinated, multiple, synchronized strikes that are executed by trained operatives who make sure to inflict maximum injury or death. Suicide attackers have worn a variety of inventive disguises to move into the midst of unsuspecting crowds, dressing as Israeli soldiers, Orthodox Jews, and middle-aged women. And just as security officials began to believe that only young men would be chosen as human bombs, terrorist organizations began to recruit young women.

Bus stops and terminals at King George/Jaffa are easily exploited by attackers. Their tactic is to turn the gas-filled fuel tank of a bus into a fireball that will spread into adjoining traffic and waiting crowds. Once attacked, vehicles, commuters, and emergency medical personnel are then trapped within a massive traffic jam. Similarly, the Mehane Yehuda market contains all the elements of urban congestion. While workers occupy its maze of stalls and delivery trucks stand outside, terrorists have set off explosions that caused mayhem in the area.

One of the more notorious attacks occurred in August 2001 at a pizza restaurant located at the corner of King George and Jaffa streets. The Sbarro Pizzeria was a favorite for teenagers, schoolchildren, and young families seeking an inexpensive meal. The suicide bomber set off the charge when the restaurant was packed with summer vacationers, killing 15 people and wounding 90. Attacks at the Yehuda Mehane market also bear a familiar emblem. In July 1997, two suicide terrorists entered the marketplace, took positions among the crowd, and set off their charge, killing 16 and injuring 178.

Not all attacks are so well planned, and some assaults are directed against *targets of opportunity*. These targets are attacked because they offer quick access to terrorists or enable them to move undetected. One of these sites is the Old City of Jerusalem, another is in the French Hill neighborhood, and others are scattered sites in East Jerusalem. All of these locations are either predominantly Arab or close to Palestinian populations. The Old City has experienced a rash of gunshot and knife assaults, often carried out by unaffiliated individuals. Given the fact that a majority of Old City residents are Arab, uncontrolled explosions are relatively rare. On the other hand, predominantly Jewish French Hill has seen a spate of buses exploded by suicide bombers. French Hill's vulnerability can also be attributed to its location on the road to Ramallah. One bus junction on French Hill has been struck over and over again by suicide attackers. Many bus attacks are carried out on Sunday mornings—the first day of the workweek for daily commuters and students and the end of the weekend for visitors and returning soldiers.

Also on French Hill, the Hebrew University (Mount Scopus Campus) suffered an attack in which 9 students were killed and over 80 injured. The university is an oasis of tolerance, liberalism, and fellowship between Arabs and Jews, and few thought it would be targeted. The belief among many academics that "neutral ground" would be immune to attack proved to be mistaken because it overlooked a fundamental component of urban terror—its shock value undertaken without regard to whether the area might be a friendly venue or not.

Finally, it may very well be that high-frequency attacks enabled Jerusalem's first responders to act with greater efficiency. Once the dreaded sirens sound, police, firefighters, ambulance drivers, rescue workers, and internal security patrols converge on the scene, quickly cordoning it off and tending to the victims. Israel's Magen David (equivalent of the Red Cross) provides a variety of emergency and ambulance services. During the worst of the years its response improved.[20] Four major hospitals serve the Jerusalem area, and their emergency physicians are among the best in the world. Israel even enlists religious volunteers (called the Zaka) to conduct the grisly task of collecting body parts, while other specialists are trained in identifying the wounded and counting the dead.

In the immediate aftermath of attack, stray mobile phones ordinarily are piled in a corner of the site. One is struck by the continued ringing emanating from that mound of phones as desperate friends and relatives continue to search for the missing. An able corps of social workers also assists victims through convalescence. Jerusalem still faces problems in coping with terrorist attacks, especially as crowds gather around the site of an attack and block access. But its long experience with continual and often smaller attacks better enables the city to deal with traumatic situations.

Penetration by Proximity

For some, Jerusalem appears to be two very different cities whose Arab and Jewish populations live in different worlds.[21] For the most part, Jews and Arabs live in separate neighborhoods, with Jewish communities concentrated in western portions of the city, while pockets of Arab and Jewish neighborhoods are interspersed farther east. But Jerusalem is also a complex, whole city—a multifaceted mosaic of neighborhoods, villages, urban centers, parks, and commercial streets that is open and easily traversed. It is filled with grand vistas and dotted by an abundance of hills and valleys. Fluid pathways allow travelers to move from one neighborhood to another. While few Israelis venture into Arab neighborhoods these days, it is natural and easy for people to travel to any part of the city—either by bus, automobile, taxi, or on foot. Some interaction between the two populations is bound to occur.

While not ordinarily reported in the Western media, many terrorists initially cross from the territories and enter Jerusalem without arms or explosives, only to pick up lethal cargo at safe houses. Over the years, the number of East Jerusalem Arabs involved in attacks has increased, and as of the current period over 120 individuals have been implicated in acts of terrorism.[22] A handful of Jerusalem Arabs have been convicted of assisting attackers by gathering intelligence, moving explosive material, transporting attackers, or carrying out assaults. Neighborhoods in and around Bethlehem often provide easy access to Israel, and attackers are known to have walked directly into Israel. During the height of al Aqsa terror, dozens of attempts were foiled each week. At least 15 suicide bombers have traveled fewer than 10 miles from their own homes to begin the deadly carnage.[23] These attacks often grow outward from the seam line along Route 1, where Arabs and Jews live in proximity to each other.

Easy penetration allows for feasible logistics. Urban terrorism is not a simple matter of sending off someone with explosives or weaponry, but entails extensive cooperation across different territories. The list of operatives used to complete the logistical chain can be elaborate. These include *recruiters*, who locate volunteers for high-risk or suicide attacks; *weapons specialists*, who concoct the explosive charge and pack suicide vests with nuts, bolts, and metal shards in order to augment the human toll; *handlers*, who instill spiritual or ideological zeal and make sure that attackers will not lose nerve; *reconnoiters*, who locate high-value targets; *spokesmen*, who take videos and record statements from the recruit so they can be communicated to the public; and *transporters*, who deliver an attacker to the target. Some of these roles overlap, but they all involve organization, a division of labor, and coordination.

Proximity allows for penetration and facilitates terrorist logistics. This explains why some cities will experience a greater frequency of attack. The opportunity to launch persistent attacks may also encourage lower-impact assaults. The nature of the targets also influences the nature of the attack. Jerusalem is a small city, and grand targets are sparse compared to those in global cities like New York and London.

New York's Sporadic Attacks

The first bombing of the Wall Street area did not occur on September 11, 2001, when planes hijacked by al Qaeda smashed into the Twin Towers. Nor did it occur on February 26, 1993, when a truck bomb went off in the underground parking area of the World Trade Center. Rather, it occurred more than eighty years before these events, when a horse-drawn cart exploded at noon on September 16, 1920, at Wall and Broad streets, just as swarms of pedestrian were about to start their lunchtime break.[24] The blast caused the deaths of forty people and was set off by anarchists intent on destroying the seat of American capitalism. The attackers left behind pink leaflets entitled "Plain Words," which read: "There will have to be bloodshed; we will not dodge; there will have to be murder; we will kill because it is necessary; there will have to be destruction; we will destroy to rid the world of your tyrannical institutions."[25]

Other bombings had occurred in American cities during this period, mostly attacks by anarchists and labor radicals. Collective violence of this sort is hardly new to America. Despite this history, however, American cities have been spared the systematic terrorism that spread through Western Europe in the 1960s, 1970s, and 1980s. New York had relatively little experience with assaults upon its territory until the advent of "fourth wave" terrorism. Besides the two attacks on the World

Trade Center, at least five other assaults were planned or carried out by "fourth wave" terrorists. In 1993, al Qaeda agents aimed their sights on a quintet of major targets—the Holland and Lincoln tunnels, the George Washington Bridge, the United Nations, and Federal Plaza. A year later, a Palestinian gunman standing on the Brooklyn Bridge opened fire on a van carrying five Hassidic students, killing one of them. In 1997, another Palestinian chose the Empire State Building to conduct a shooting spree. The man proceeded to the building's observation deck on the 86th floor and shot seven bystanders, killing one of them. That same year, the city's police department uncovered a scheme to blow up a subway complex in downtown Brooklyn. Police intervention occurred at the eleventh hour, just as the potential attackers were assembling the explosives.

Since 9/11 more than a dozen significant threats have been discovered. These incidents include mailing anthrax to major news media, "plots" to blow up the stock exchange and headquarters of major corporations, "plans" to bomb a subway station at Herald Square in anticipation of the 2004 Republican National Convention, and a "plot" to flood mass transit tunnels. As of this writing, other nascent threats have been discovered—one of these arose farther from the city, in Fort Dix, New Jersey, while the other occurred closer by at Kennedy International Airport. The Fort Dix plot involved six young men who were intent on randomly shooting down military personnel. The men already possessed automatic weapons and had trained at locations in Pennsylvania. The threat on Kennedy involved four men and was not as advanced. That plan called for blowing up the airport's fuel tanks and causing a chain of conflagration throughout the area. At least one member took steps to case the fuel tanks, make video recordings, and gather satellite photos of airport facilities.

New York is a global city with a cosmopolitan spirit and this makes it difficult to see threats as coming from a unique brand of "homegrown" terrorism. In many instances domestic roots mix with foreign ones. Some of the Fort Dix conspirators were brought to the United States illegally and now were said to be "inspired" by al Qaeda. The Kennedy conspirators were based in the New York area but came from Trinidad, Tobago, and Guyana. They, too, were inspired by Islamist doctrine and sought to enlist Islamic groups in the Caribbean or South America. Taken in the larger scheme of terrorism, some of these events might be seen as inconsequential, though politicians and the media have made the most of FBI findings.

Notwithstanding the flurry of FBI announcements, New York has been a city of the mega attack. It was 9/11 and not a long series of attacks that accounts for New York's lopsided ratio of nearly 11,000 casualties per attack. We should also understand that there is great variation in what is considered to be a "plot" or "planned" attack. Some may be rather minimal and amount to little more than talking, others may be more of an aspiration involving some initial reconnaissance, and a few may have matured to identifying agents and developing logistics.[26] With this caveat underscored, these threats are significant because they tell us something about the mental maps used to select targets.

Figure 5.2 **New York Terror Attacks, 1993–2005**

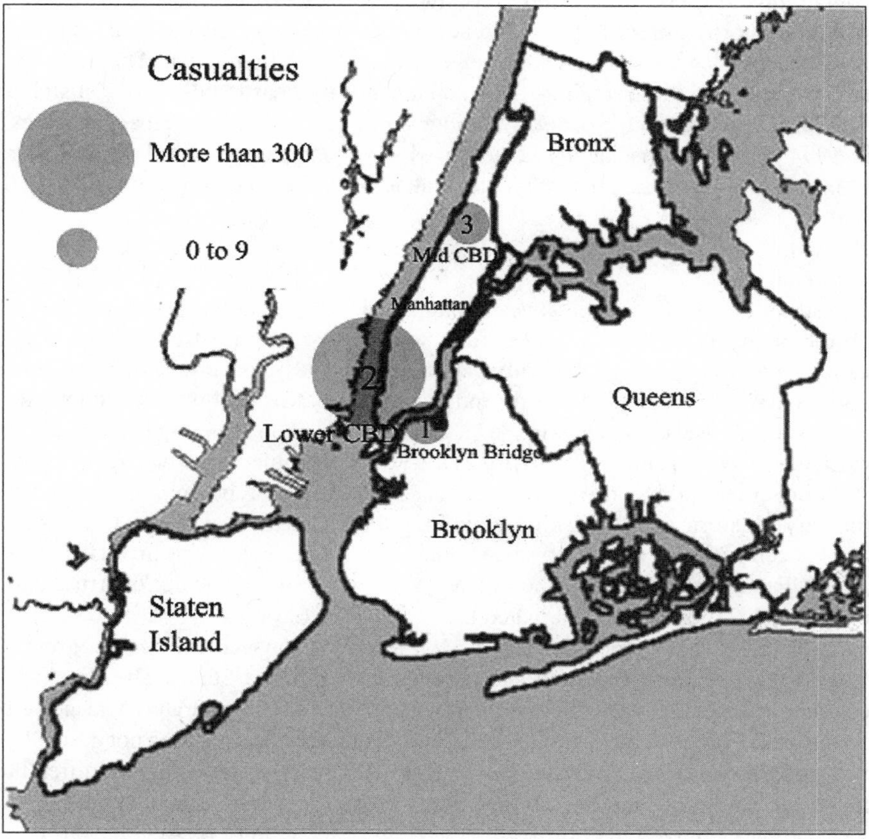

Note: Numbers in the circles represent total incidents for the years indicated.

Concentrated and Repetitive Attacks

Most threats have been concentrated in New York's two central business districts. One of these was sited for lower Manhattan in the vicinity of Wall Street while another was supposed to take place in midtown Manhattan, immediately north or south of Times Square. Major targets like the Brooklyn Bridge and Holland Tunnel are located in lower Manhattan, while the United Nations and Empire State buildings as well as Herald Square are within the midtown central business district.

Figure 5.2 displays a map of actual attacks launched in New York City. All five of the city's boroughs are represented. The map contains the location of attacks, casualties inflicted (designated by the size of the circle), and total incidents (designated by the number in the circle).

To put matters in perspective, New York City's territorial area is quite extensive, containing over 300 square miles (780 square kilometers) of surface. Yet the overwhelming portion of anticipated and actual assaults repeatedly focused on just a few square miles of the city within midtown and lower Manhattan. The midtown area experienced three small assaults and a handful of casualties. Terrorist sights were also twice set on the Brooklyn Bridge—one plot in 1993 and an actual attack in 1994. The most spectacular occurrences were planned or carried out in lower Manhattan. No less than five attempts or attacks were aimed at that area.

Penetration from a Distance

The attack of 9/11 sent shockwaves through the United States because it combined all the elements of catalytic, mega, and smart terror. It was also the arch mega attack—carefully planned, centrally placed, purposefully concentrated, and shockingly massive. The irony of this profoundly anti-urban assault was that among its major designers was a student in the Department of Urban Planning at the Technical University of Hamburg-Harburg (TUHH). Mohammed Atta had spent years studying cities and had traveled to Aleppo, Syria, to research a master's thesis on that city's historic quarter. Taking a cue from their acquaintance with TUHH, Atta and his cell assigned the targets code names. The Twin Towers was given the code name "Faculty of Planning," the Pentagon was called the "Faculty of Arts," and the Capitol Building was designated the "Faculty of Law."

Penetration was complicated. Nineteen terrorists traveled in separate groups from distant points abroad and had no base in the United States. The Hamburg cell planned their arrival as a contingent while others did so separately and arrived from various points in the Middle East. The "twentieth hijacker" was not granted a visa and never did arrive. Those who "piloted" the planes took lessons at different locations, while the "muscle" trained abroad. After arriving in the United States, most of the men lived in cities across the country including Los Angeles, Miami, New York, and Las Vegas. Being rootless, they adapted poorly to their new environments. Some of the terrorists argued with their landlords or flight instructors, others were seen as rude, and many of them were viewed by Americans as very peculiar. Life in a foreign country was complicated by constantly transferring funds from abroad. Despite the obstacles, the hijackers went undetected and aroused few suspicions—perhaps because attacking New York and Washington with passenger airplanes was unfathomable.

Minimizing Logistical Obstacles by Imploding the City

The 9/11 attackers saved themselves the trouble of transporting weaponry by converting commercial airlines into guided missiles. They also minimized logistical obstacles by using the power of the enemy against itself. The selection of lower Manhattan was an act of quintessential urban terrorism. The site is a highly clustered,

Figure 5.3 **Schematic: Attack on the World Trade Center, September 11, 2001**

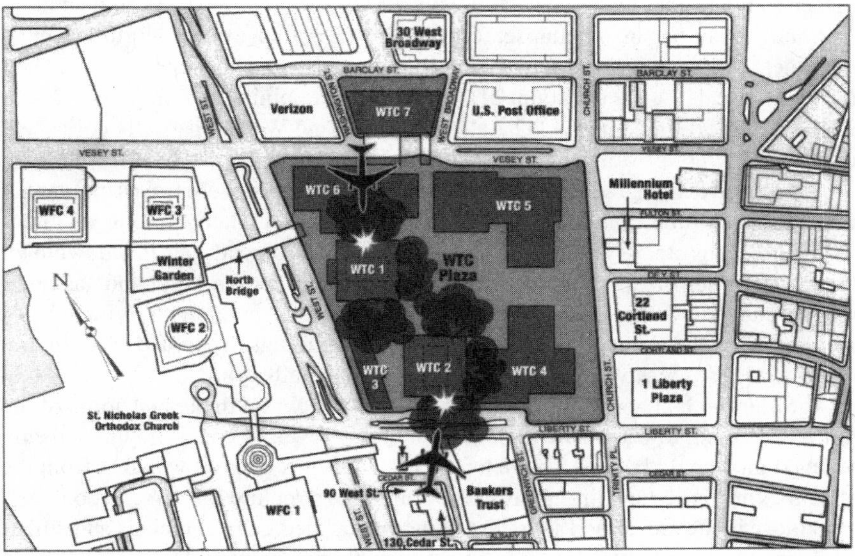

Source: Federal Emergency Management Agency. *World Trade Center Building Performance Study,* FEMA, Region II, New York.

intricately woven business district with very high-density workday populations whose operations contribute heavily to world finance. The World Trade Center (WTC) is actually a large complex of seven buildings, with the Twin Towers serving as its flagship. The complex is ringed by four buildings of the World Financial Center (home to American Express and Merrill Lynch) and a bevy of banks, insurance companies, hotels, a post office, and a cultural center (the Winter Garden). The New York Stock Exchange is just three short blocks to the southeast. Some commuters travel by bus, automobile, or foot, while the largest number are funneled to their offices by a network of underground mass transit. During the day the neighborhood population swells to 58,000 workers.

Figure 5.3 presents a schematic of the area. Seven buildings of the WTC are designated, as are four buildings of the World Financial Center (WFC). Also shown are the Winter Garden and other surrounding structures.

It was as if the entire neighborhood had been designed for urban terrorism. Its thousands of incoming commuters would be the fodder for mass pandemonium. The preeminence of the Twin Towers coupled to clusters of satellites made the site vulnerable to a contagion of firestorms. The impact of an explosion could be telegraphed onto adjacent buildings, streets, underground subways, contaminating the air with a swill of fumes, asbestos, and fragments for miles around. At 8:46 in the morning, the first pirated plane struck WTC 1 (North Tower), followed just sixteen minutes later by a strike at 9:02 on WTC 2 (South Tower). Within an hour, the South Tower began to collapse, followed by the collapse of the North Tower an hour later. The seismic vibration of each collapse measured between 2.1 and 2.3 on the Richter scale. A huge amount of debris fell on adjoining buildings WTC 3, 5, 6, and 7. A short time later WTC 7 also collapsed and WTC 3 partially collapsed. Meanwhile, fires spread throughout the remaining buildings.[27]

The sudden disintegration of these buildings produced pressure waves that spread more than a million tons of pulverized glass, asbestos, and concrete in all directions. Enormous clouds of these substances rumbled through the narrow downtown streets. Their density and pressure lifted small vehicles, broke water and gas lines, and smashed windows. Because rescue workers were taken up with trying to save lives, most of the damage was left to simmer. Buildings continued to burn and spouting water mains were left unattended for hours afterward.

Aboveground, chaos reigned. Office workers caught on the upper floors of the North and South towers made their way to higher levels because they mistakenly believed they could be saved by helicopters. On the ground, crowds fled from the site, blocking police and firefighters. The command structure for "first responders," from those in the uniformed services to emergency medical technicians and ambulance drivers, just about collapsed. Emergency phone operators were left helpless, unable to provide escape routes or give sound advice to those trapped inside the towers. Amid the tumult, communications were plagued by mechanical failures. Phone lines failed to operate, and computers did "crazy things."[28]

The response was extremely upsetting for people who sought information about casualties. The numbers of dead and injured continually changed, and at one point estimates went as high as 5,000 dead and more than twice that number injured. Trying to locate missing victims was especially disheartening. Relatives and friends of the missing were forced to take matters into their own hands and walked around the site for days carrying and posting photographs. A makeshift wall on the site was inundated with posted photos, earning a morose place in 9/11 memorabilia.

One might suppose that 9/11 was the first such experience and that the performance of first responders could be improved. While reforming emergency procedures will bring benefits, the fact remains that global cities are difficult places to defend. Tightly coupled massive environments are built to transmit and magnify terror. The story is by now known that prior to the 1993 bombing of the World Trade Center, Ramsi Yousef was inspired by Aum Shinrikyo's chemical attack in Tokyo and wanted to emulate it. The idea was to construct a *mubtakkar*, Arabic for "invention." The *mubtakkar* is a bulky device that holds sodium cyanide in one chamber and hydrogen in another. A *mubtakkar* can be moved and set off by a remote cell phone, which ignites the fuse, breaks the chamber seal, and creates hydrogen cyanide gas. This deadly gas works by poisoning human cells, stopping the flow of oxygen, and bringing about an agonizing death.[29]

Chilling as the thought may be, the *mubtakkar* is very real. Used in a confined space like an office building, bus, or metro station, the monstrous potential of the *mubtakkar* would be augmented. By one plausible account, agents from al Qaeda had planned to set off the device in New York subway cars. Cell members were said to have arrived in the city from North Africa and were readying themselves. The White House and Central Intelligence Agency were in anguish about a portable and conceal-able chemical weapon slipping into a packed metro system. Al Qaeda was about to realize its threat to bring about a sequel to 9/11, but for some reason it called off the attack. Exactly why the *mubtakkar* was not used is not known, but security officials entertain the notion that al Qaeda felt such an attack would not be big enough.[30]

London's Cycles of Terror

Attacks in London have neither been as frequent as those in Jerusalem nor as sporadic as those in New York. Between 1998 and 2005, London sustained 20 attacks, with the events of 7/7 boosting casualties to 38 per incident.[31] This is no small amount and they make London extremely target prone. The frequency with which the city has been struck also shows that assaults have been clustered within particular periods.

Not all terror has been related to the dispute over Northern Ireland. On occasion, attacks by the IRA or its different factions took place along with assaults by other radical groups.[32] Most of the violence can be counted in chronological cycles—during the early 1970s, for short periods in the 1980s, during an intense cycle in the first half of the 1990s, and again at the turn of the millennium. At times, damage to property has been substantial and casualties have varied considerably; sometimes few if any people were hurt, while at other times dozens or most recently hundreds were left dead or needed hospitalization.

The British-Irish conflict goes back many years, but the most severe attack on London reaches back to the thirties when the IRA targeted it. More systematic at-tacks began in 1972, when a faction of the IRA, the Provisional Irish Republican Army (PIRA), decided to launch a campaign against the British economy. The attacks began throughout the country, killing nearly fifty people, and soon focused on London.[33] In 1973, bombs went off at a courthouse and a government building, killing one person and injuring 150 others.[34] During that same year, two planted bombs went off in mainline transit stations. The first explosion, at King's Cross, was powerful enough to create a hail of shattered glass and hurl a baggage trolley into the air. The second explosion went off at Euston Station minutes after a warning call was made. The blast sent passengers into a panic and knocked the station out of commission. These attacks were synchronized, occurring within fifty minutes of each other and causing thirteen casualties. One year later, a twenty-pound bomb exploded at Westminster Hall.[35] The last attack in this cycle occurred in the summer of 1975, when banks and hotels in central London were targeted.[36]

For a while London was quiet, but by 1982 and 1983 the metropolis burst asunder and the relative peace was punctuated by two infamous attacks. IRA bombs went off in Hyde Park and Regent's Park, killing 11 people and wounding more than 40. Another more spectacular attack occurred when a car bomb exploded just outside Harrods department store. That assault killed 6 people and wounded 100.

Concentrated and Repetitive Attacks

While most of the attacks mentioned above took place in what would be called "central London," subsequent attacks were even more concentrated within London's financial district, known as The City. Consisting of just one square mile, The City serves as a nerve center for global finance and is located at the epicenter of Greater London. This space is both the historic symbol and economic soul of London. Of the nearly 3 million commuters who travel to London each day, 46 percent of them are destined for the square mile.[37]

Within a span of just four years, PIRA launched a string of attacks, all of which concentrated on The City. The attacks hit the London Stock Exchange (1990), Furnival Street (1992), St. Mary Axe (1992), Coleman Street (1992), Bishopsgate (1993), and Wormwood Street (1993). Most of these sites are within 500 meters of each other, and all of the attacks were carried out through planted bombs.[38] Just a few miles away, the PIRA launched a mortar from the roof of a parked white van and its shell exploded in the garden of 10 Downing Street (1991). The blast blew out all the windows of the Cabinet room. At the time, Prime Minister John Major was leading a session of the Cabinet, though no one was hurt. These are all instances of smart and catalytic terror that had some resonance. Though the attacks within The City produced relatively few casualties and the assault at 10 Downing Street caused none, alarm bells sounded in financial quarters and the government soon installed a "ring of steel" around the area (barriers, checkpoints, cameras). The prime minister also took note of the government's vulnerability, as did the rest of the world. Meanwhile, the British were stunned at the audacity of the attacks.[39]

Just as the conflict in Northern Ireland began to dissipate, London was beset by "fourth wave" terrorism. While July 7, 2005, marks the beginning of this most recent cycle, there were ample indications that new sources of terrorism were gestating. Radical Islam had already gained a small but significant foothold within London's community of 600,000 Muslims. By this time, London had become a hub for violence-prone Islamists, most of whom preached their doctrine in a few mosques.

The pieces gradually fit together. The al Qaeda assault on 9/11, Great Britain's friendship and support for the United States, foreign policy choices in Afghanistan and Iraq, and the proximity of radical Islamists made a terrorist attack on London likely. July 7 was a surprise that was fully expected. Indeed, prior to 7/7 at least nine suspected terror attacks had been thwarted over a previous six-year period.[40] The British intelligence service, known as MI5, alerted the public that it was not so much a question of *whether* terrorism would strike but *when* and *where* it would strike.[41] While MI5 recognized the imminence of an attack, it had not fully appreciated that

Figure 5.4 **London Terror Attacks, 1998–2005**

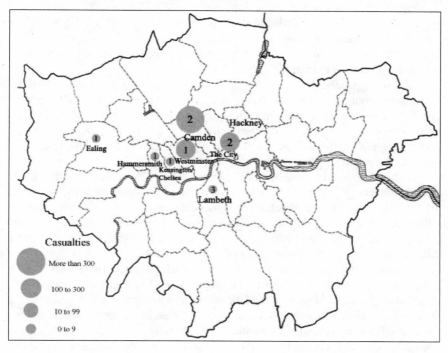

Note: Numbers in the circles represent total incidents for the years indicated.

homegrown terrorists would launch an assault. Since 7/7, Britain's intelligence has identified thirty terrorists plots with international roots in al Qaeda.[42]

Given London's earlier experience with terror, its central neighborhoods were logical targets. Most were close to immigrant communities, radical mosques, bookshops, and Islamic centers. Prospective attackers came to know the lay of the land and construct mental maps of vulnerable sites. Inner London was a great crossroads of diversity, packed with people and valuable assets—a premier choice for fringe elements seeking to send a message.

Figure 5.4 shows some of Greater London's central neighborhoods. As with previous figures, the map designates the location of attacks, the casualties inflicted (designated by the size of the circle), and the total incidents (designated by the number in the circle).

Greater London's 32 boroughs plus The City constitute nearly 610 square miles (1,580 square kilometers) of a richly built urban environment. London's central business district, located immediately to the west of The City, holds approximately 9 square miles of territorial surface. These nine square miles in and around The City absorbed the bulk of attacks; foremost was the terror of July 7, 2005, in London's Underground. In that attack, explosions that wrought 179 casualties were set off in tunnels underneath The City. Similar explosions occurred in Camden and above ground in Westminster, bringing more than 500 casualties (see Appendix, Table A12). By the end of the day, London had its most dramatic experience with mega terror. July 7 left more than 700 casualties.

The timing around 7/7 was particularly significant. Just a day before, the International Olympic Committee had announced that London would be the site for the 2012 games. Paris had been favored, and upon hearing the news Londoners were completely buoyed. On the very same day, the G8 (group of big industrial nations) met in Scotland to discuss the global policies. Great Britain and its capital were on the world stage.

Much like the suicide bombings at Jerusalem's Ben Yehuda Mall and the pirated planes that were steered into New York's World Trade Center, London's terrorists understood that concentrated attacks augmented shock. Four explosions were set off during the morning rush hour around three core locations. The first three occurred in the Underground within three minutes of each other; the fourth ignited little more than one hour later on one of London's double-decker buses.

July 7 was executed ad seriatim and the attacks could be counted in minutes. At 8:49 A.M., somewhere between Liverpool and Aldgate East (The City), a train was blown apart; at 8:51 A.M. at Edgewar Road (Westminster) another train exploded; this was followed at approximately 8:53 A.M. by a series of train blasts between King's Cross and Russell Square (Camden). Later that same morning, at 9:47 A.M., an attacker at Tavistock Square (Camden) blew himself up on a bus's upper deck, shearing off its rooftop. More than four thousand people were directly caught up in the conflagration, exacerbating the confusion.[43] Figure 5.5 displays the locations of each blast. Shown are the train lines as well as tube stations. Hyde Park lies southwest of the sites.

The scenes at each of these sites were filled with carnage. Belowground, portions of the city's extraordinary transit system turned into death traps. The blast within the trains created small fireballs, and as the lights went out everything turned black. Smoke filled the air and as passengers began to choke, they tried to exit the trains, but the doors locked. Some of the panicked passengers used their bare hands to break windows, only to discover there was not enough room to squeeze out of the tunnel. All this time, drivers or conductors were unable to communicate with passengers and a deathly silence ensued. As one survivor described the attack:

> Splintered and broken glass flew through the air towards me and other passengers. I was pushed sideways as the train came to a sudden halt. I thought I was going to die. Horrific loud cries and screams filled the air, together with smoke, bits and chemicals. Large and small pieces of stuff hit me and covered me. . . . I was hit on the head by a piece of metal and covered with splinters and broken glass from the window behind me. . . . I could not breath, my lungs were burning because of the smoke and dust. I crashed my head between my knees to get some air. There followed a silence.[44]

Figure 5.5 **The 7/7 Attacks: Underground and Bus Locations**

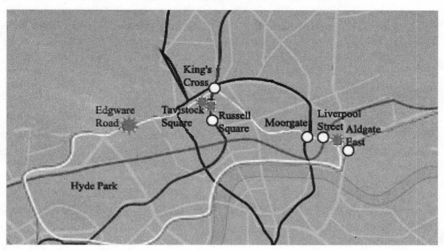

Pandemonium filled the streets. Passengers poured out of the stations dazed, some weeping, and others shouting for help. Initial reports indicated that London's Underground had incurred a "power surge," and officials brought the entire system to a halt. First responders often filed multiple, conflicting reports, and it was unclear what had happened, whether an accident had occurred, or where the emergencies were located.[45]

London's Fire Brigade was unable to coordinate its response with the Ambulance Service. The police were also confused about the extent of the explosions.[46] For some time afterward, hospitals were unaware of what had occurred and unprepared for the onslaught of emergency patients. Communications broke down and ambulances reported to incorrect sites. Other calls were delayed and first responders were unable to reach those most desperate for help.[47]

Victims and their families suffered from the havoc. During much of the day, neither the extent nor the identity of the casualties could be ascertained. Friends and family trundled through the areas searching for suspected victims. In desperation, photos of missing persons were hung on nearby lampposts. Scenes like this are not uncommon for a mega attack, and they demonstrate its capacity for contagious disruption.

Exactly two weeks later, on July 21, London confronted another set of attacks. This time the attackers were unsuccessful. Once again the target was central London's public transit. Four men attempted to set off bombs at the Oval Station (Lambeth), at Warren Street Station (Camden), at Shepherd's Bush (Hammersmith), and Hackney Road (Hackney). By pure fortune, the bombs either failed to detonate or detonated with no effect. Their choice of targets, three tube stations and a bus, matched those of the 7/7 attackers. Whether this was a coincidental or an intentional choice is unclear. More apparent is the inspiration generated by the 7/7 attackers and an attempt to mimic their acts. While the scale was considerably smaller than New York's, the London assaults demonstrated the power that can obtain from such inspiration as well as efforts to combine mega, catalytic, and smart terror.

Penetration and Logistics from Within

London has been confronted by two major groups operating at somewhat different periods of time. Both groups had relatively easy access. Operatives from the IRA or its splintered offshoots could easily travel from Northern Ireland or reside anywhere in England. Their physical features also permitted easy travel throughout the United Kingdom, and they made the most of this with a major attack in Manchester (1996) and a continuous stream of violence in Belfast and Londonderry.

Secular violence was replaced by another stream of terrorism stemming from Islamic radicalism. Recruitment came largely from immigrants who arrived from Pakistan, Bangladesh, Kashmir, and parts of North Africa. London's Finsbury and other smaller mosques became recruiting stations for terrorists who went abroad to carry out their work. London's "graduates" attained notoriety and included a convert from South London's Brixton Mosque named Richard Reid, who tried to explode an airplane with a "shoe bomb"; Zacarias Moussaoui, who was implicated in the 9/11 attack; Ahmed Ressam, who was arrested for attempting to bomb Los Angeles Airport; and Abu Doha, who recruited terrorists in and around Paris.[48]

While the seeds took years to be sown, London eventually harvested a subculture conducive to radical violence. It was not long before a "Londonistan" mentality would inspire a generation of homegrown terrorists that included Omar Khan Sharif and Asif Mohammed Hanif, who participated in a bloody attack in Tel Aviv. And not long before, that subculture would turn against London on 7/7 and 7/21. The capture of potential attackers during Operation Crevice shows how radical these young men had become. Exploding gas utilities or poisoning London's water supply was regarded as a "beautiful plan." Blowing up "slags" (women) in a nightclub seemed altogether justified because they considered women who frequented dancing clubs to be morally wanting. Killing kuffars (non-Muslims) was legitimate because God "hates the Kufs."[49]

Logistics were relatively uncomplicated. Those apprehended in Operation Crevice used nearby West London to store explosives. The 7/7 attackers set up shop in a local neighborhood, while the 7/21 attackers were much sloppier. This most recent cycle of terrorism demonstrates that penetration need not be from a distance (New York) nor arise through populations in an adjoining territory (Jerusalem), but can be grown from within. If opinion polls are to be believed, over 100,000 British citizens consider the 7/7 attacks to be justified, and it is not a far leap to imagine that homegrown terrorists could draw support from some of these sympathizers.[50] Herein lies the greatest risk.

Conclusions: Parallels Across Cities

Three different cities whose terrorists are also different show similar patterns of targeting designed to bring about chaos, paralyze urban life, and decontrol the city. Striking Jerusalem were secular terrorists from the Palestinian Liberation Organization and al Aqsa Martyrs' Brigade as well as religious terrorists from Hamas and Islamic Jihad. In the early days, those groups hitting New York were anarchists; more recently they were religiously motivated terrorists. London saw attacks from secular nationalists and more recently Islamists. For all the variety of experience, terrorism struck at the same general sites, with similar repetition and like concentration.

The transfer of successful tactics from one situation to another goes beyond cities like Jerusalem, New York, and London. Another city crystallizes the lessons learned and helps us understand general aspects of the pattern. Istanbul, Turkey, joins East and West, and while the Turks have no conspicuous quarrel with al Qaeda, they do have a problem with the Kurdish minority.

By the criterion of severity of attack, Istanbul resembles Jerusalem more than New York or London. During the last decade, Istanbul incurred frequent attacks, amounting to 352 incidents, though just three casualties per incident. This is closer to Jerusalem's 11 casualties per incident than to New York's extraordinary ratio of nearly 11,000 casualties or London's substantial 760 casualties. Rather than a mega attack, Istanbul has been the target of continual smaller assaults designed to elicit the effects of catalytic or smart terror. As in Jerusalem, terrorism in Istanbul operates through continual pinpricks designed to disrupt or collapse ordinary life.

Major targets are often at busy commercial centers on the "European" side of the city in what is called the New City. Located just across from the historic Old City, this space lies on the western side of the Bosporous and is less than 0.8 of a square mile (2 square kilometers). Istanbul's New City is filled with financial institutions, businesses, hotels, and shopping centers. Foreign embassies and consulates have also settled in this area. By day, business and government executives fill its streets and by night tourists patronize its restaurants and shops. *Mutatis mutandis*, Istanbul's central business district has much in common with those in Jerusalem, New York, and London.

By the criteria of concentration and repetition, all of these cities share the same terrorist tactics. Figure 5.6 provides a glimpse of terror strikes in the neighborhoods of Istanbul. Shown in the figure are neighborhoods that have been attacked along with casualties (designated by the size of the circle) and incidents (designated by the number in the circle).

As with our other cities, attacks have been concentrated in the commercial heart—in the case of Istanbul, its New City. The size and number of incidents both diminish as we move farther from this critical center.[51] Attacks have occurred at the Swiss Hotel (1994), a main square (2001), a shopping center (2001), and serial assaults have been launched on the British consulate and HSBC bank. The serial

Figure 5.6   **Istanbul Terror Attacks, 1998–2005**

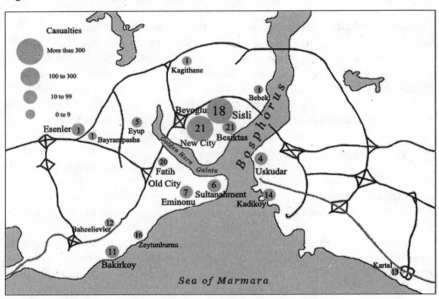

Note: Numbers in the circles represent total incidents for the years indicated.

attacks were especially traumatic. Using trucks filled with explosives, terrorists detonated their cargo within two minutes of each other, killing 27 people and injuring 400. As if to openly mock conventional authority and demonstrate that nothing was beyond their reach, the bombers struck while President George Bush and Prime Minister Tony Blair were holding a joint appearance. Reports described the city as in chaos and the general scene as follows:

> There is collapsed masonry, shattered windows, burned out cars and general scenes of confusion at the two sites. Much of the city's phone network has been cut. Hospitals are inundated with hundreds of wounded people, traffic is block-ing the roads and crisis officials are asking people to leave the center to clear the way for ambulances.[52]

The elements of political timing as well as concentrated, repetitive attacks to produce chaos have a familiar ring. Change a few nouns and the above paragraphs could have been written for other cities. The fact of the matter is that terrorists not only learn from each other, but also imitate the details of attack and the symbols of success. One of Turkey's most notorious groups, Turkish Hezbollah, bears no relationship to its counterpart in Lebanon. It has, though, adopted its nomenclature and copies its style.

What might account for the similarity of attack? For one, simple logic might be the answer. Terrorists strike where people congregate and assets accumulate. Concentration and repetition may then be a reflexive action, so terrorists gravitate to particular locales. A second explanation is that because the sites are central, they are also easily accessible. Many targets are proximate to communities in which terrorists find safe harbor, and most are easy to enter or exit.

While these explanations have some plausibility, a third possibility is the most compelling, simply because terrorist tactics across so many different cities are too similar to be explained by coincidence. The strongest explanation can be found in the rudiments of organizational behavior and the empirics of urban terror. Organizations seek to improve their efficiency and terrorists are no different. Terrorists do learn from each other, from their success and by exchanging know-how. Information can be obtained informally and nonsystematically, or it can be shared systemically through established networks. Like any circuit of information, what works best is often communicated, adopted by the groups, and adapted to the circumstances. For all their differences, Irish and Arab terrorists were in communication during the 1970 and 1980s. Today the al Qaeda network stretches across the Middle East into Chechnya, the Balkans, and the rest of Europe. Its electronic sites and operatives provide a ready supply of information about tactics and a résumé of methods on how best to strike the enemy. A variety of other organizations like Hezbollah and freelance terrorists throughout the world also perform the same function.

Tactical transfer is very much part of urban terror. This is a phenomenon that has certain commonalities. It stands to reason that if tactical transfer is viable, so too is tactical defense. To this issue we now turn.

_____ Part 3

Policy Responses and Local Resilience

Surveillance and Shrinkage

The mark of genius is knowing where to look.

—Albert Einstein

Walls and Barriers

Through antiquity and into the Middle Ages, cities were defined by their walls. These barriers encased the city and set its outer boundaries. Settlements outside the walls were known as *faubourgs*. As the city grew outward, old walls were taken down and replaced by new ones to encompass the *faubourgs*, which by this time were joined to the city. And so it went; like a tree sprouting new layers of outward growth with each new age, additional settlements were incorporated into the city and walls laid out their contours.

Most great cities were protected by walls, and a few have lasted into the modern era. Paris, London, Moscow, Quebec, and Istanbul began as walled cities. Throughout its history, Jerusalem has been walled, unwalled, and rewalled. Like Beijing's Great Wall and Moscow's Kremlin, the wall around Jerusalem's Old City still stands, attracting tourists from around the world. Even the relatively new cities of the United States were defined by their walls. Eleven American cities had walls during the early years of their colonial development. These included Boston, Charlestown, Savannah, Albany, New Orleans, Detroit, and St. Louis. New York was the most prominent among the colonial cities to have a barrier, and today its Wall Street marks the site.[1]

Walls were built to defend cities against invading armies and hostile intruders. They furnished a sense of security to inhabitants of the medieval city. Those living outside its walls, in the *faubourg*, sought the city's protection in the face of invaders. Lewis Mumford's classic work *The Culture of Cities* begins with a chapter entitled "Protection and the Medieval Town." Mumford recounts that "in terror of invaders," the inhabitants of Mainz restored the old Roman Wall and the surrounding moat to keep attackers out.[2] Another writer points out that in China, the most commonly used words for the early city related to "walls and gates," and barriers of all kinds were used extensively to protect Oriental cities.[3] The Belgian historian Henri Pirenne describes the city wall as taking the "shape of a rectangle surrounded by ramparts flanked by towers and communicating with the outside by gates."[4]

In our modern age, walls have usually been used to stop illegal border crossings, impede military forces, or imprison people. More recently, some have been built to combat terrorists, though the definition of a wall has been loosely applied to any barrier that cuts off open space. The best-known use of a "wall" to impede terrorism is the extensive barrier begun by Israel in 2002 during the height of al Aqsa violence. While referred to by its detractors as the "apartheid wall" and by its supporters as the "anti-terrorist fence," it is neither entirely a "wall" nor entirely a "fence," but a combination of concrete, wire mesh, ditches, roadways, sand paths, and electronic detectors. Though the media continue to photograph its more dramatic concrete slabs, the walled portions of the Israeli barrier make up less than 5 percent of the total.[5] Israel's barrier stretches for 430 miles (687 kilometers) along its eastern peripheries that mark off Palestinian areas.[6]

Less-known walls have been built in Kashmir and Northern Ireland. On the Indian subcontinent a "line of control" separates Indian from Pakistani Kashmir. This particular "wall" rises to 12 feet high and spreads another 12 feet in width. It is constructed from coils of concertina wire layered between rows of pickets. Sharp-edged metal tape, electrification, scanning equipment, and border guards prevent unauthorized persons from crossing. This "line of control" is being built along 460 miles (736 kilometers) of territory. Like the Israeli barrier, Kashmir's wall divides former neighbors and breaks up land. A series of gates permit farmers and animals to cross into grazing lands.

In another side of the world, Belfast's "peace wall" was built to prevent violence between Catholics and Protestants. In sheer mass the wall in Belfast rivals its Israeli and Kashmiri counterparts. It is constructed in an array of brick, iron, steel, and concrete, topped off by barbed wire and interspersed with observation towers. Belfast's wall is relatively short, covering just thirteen miles. In North Belfast's parish of Holy Cross, a thirty-foot wall stands as a sectarian divide between "green" and "orange" partisans. Paramilitary gangs roam the streets on either side of this divide, enforcing their own rules of conduct.

Walls have been built to separate Greek from Turkish Cyprus, Morocco from Western Sahara, Botswana from Zimbabwe, Saudi Arabia from Yemen, North from South Korea, and the United States from Mexico. Many walls have significant social detriments, create power differentials, and scar the landscape. Other walls have succeeded in designating respective turfs between warring factions and temporarily pulling them apart. At least some walls have saved lives and brought a measure of safety to areas. The wall in Belfast has contributed to a period of tranquility between Catholics and Protestants, and walls surrounding Jerusalem and Kashmir have contributed to a marked reduction in terror attacks.[7] "Walls" are best judged by their intended purpose and use, not by stereotypes. When fully considered, some may be good while others may not. Most should not be confused with the notorious Berlin Wall, which was built to keep civilians from escaping a one-party state.

Also considered as being walled in are "gated communities," where spaces are separated by concrete, gates, fencing, hedges, and booms. The separation can be complete, as when whole communities are set off from the surrounding environment,

Figure 6.1 **Part of Belfast's Wall**

The photo shows one of the main gates in Belfast's "peace line." This gate is used to block a road between Catholic Falls Road and Protestant Shankhill. (*Courtesy of* Conflict and Politics in Northern Ireland (CAIN), *Belfast, Northern Ireland. For more information see cain.ulst.ac.uk/photographs.*)

or partial, as in the case of "alley gating," where the sides or rears of individual houses are closed off. Alley gating is particularly prevalent in Liverpool, and both wealthy and poor neighborhoods use it to prevent loiterers and burglars from accessing neighborhood housing.[8]

Gated communities have been used for a variety of purposes that include social segregation, crime prevention, and efforts to attain privacy. As of late they have been employed to ward off terrorism—most notably in Northern Ireland and Israel. Gated communities are common in the United States (Jacksonville, Miami), the United Kingdom (London, Manchester), Brazil (São Paulo), South Africa (Johannesburg, Cape Town), and Nigeria (Lagos). Scholars have few kind words for gated communities and view them as bastions of privilege that feed social tensions.[9]

Indeed, any kind of barrier is viewed with suspicion and assigned the fuzzy, if not pejorative, connotation of being a "wall." Notwithstanding their negative effects, walls come in many different forms. Society has come a long way from the simple wall guarded by someone standing on its ramparts. The most modern are outfitted with sophisticated devices for observation, detection, and tracking.

Today's walls are not just solid barriers, but allow for an enormous range of surveillance and protection. In a manner of speaking, modern walls are amalgams of human patrols, elaborate lighting, automated observation, complex detectors, and scanning devices. People may or may not like them, but their use grows. I interpret surveillance broadly to include all types of "walls" and devices that permit public supervision. Also, because barriers are central to conducting surveillance, I consider them in all their manifestations (fences, gates, booms, and the like). As the availability and types of regulatory devices have grown, so too has their application to surveillance. A widely received report on surveillance in the United Kingdom includes all types of regulation—from low-tech Breathalyzer tests to monitoring of financial transactions and advanced DNA sampling.[10] The issues are how can we best understand surveillance and what does it portend for the regulation of city space?

Surveillance to Date

Among other things, surveillance can be seen as a way to regulate public space.[11] As applied here, surveillance denotes intense scrutiny and various means of control in order to deter, mitigate, preempt, or halt terrorist attack. Rather than an absolute, black-and-white, descriptive noun, surveillance is better seen as activities that occurr on a continuum ranging from the least to the most physically obstructive. The measure of obstruction is the extent to which human movement is blocked or prevented. Beginning with the least obstructive, the generic categories include (1) *the animated presence of the citizenry or street watchers*; (2) *panoptic devices* that facilitate observation; (3) *advanced technological detection* that identifies biological, chemical, or other traits; (4) *moveable barriers*, *guards*, *and police patrols* that regulate human behavior, and, the most obstructive; (5) *fortress construction* that permanently restricts movement by shielding or blocking people.[12] All of these measures define or shape the urban landscape. In many ways they often reconfigure the urban landscape—narrowing pathways, closing off others, and ultimately channeling pedestrians and vehicles into predictable patterns of movement. The result: a shrunken urban setting beset by stultified and rigidified social relations.

Animated presence of the citizenry and street watchers use the presence of community residents, workers, and pedestrians to ensure public safety. They are the "eyes on the street"—shopkeepers who greet customers, neighbors who peer out of windows, shoppers who stroll around stores, or building guards and traffic controllers who stand at critical junctures. These are the most natural ways of deterring attack because the best awareness emanates from indigenous forces: from people carrying on everyday functions who belong in the neighborhood. The idea here is to take advantage of the natural properties of buildings and their inherent connection to streets. Some buildings have an osmotic relationship to what occurs around them.[13] They constantly absorb and release energy into their environments as people enter, remain, and exit, making surveillance normal and easy.

In her classic *The Death and Life of Great American Cities*, Jane Jacobs recounts how urban osmosis worked to prevent a child from being lured away by a stranger:

> As I watched from our second-floor window, making up my mind how to intervene if it seemed advisable, I saw it was not going to be necessary. From the butcher beneath the tenement had emerged the woman who, with her husband runs the shop; she was standing within earshot of the man, her arms folded, a look of determination on her face. Joe Cornaccchia, who with his sons-in-law keeps the delicatessen, emerged about the same moment and stood solidly to the other side. Several heads poked out of the tenement windows above, one was withdrawn quickly and its owner reappeared a moment later in the doorway. Two men from the bar next to the butcher shop came to the doorway and waited. On my side of the street, I saw that the locksmith, the fruit man and the laundry proprietor had all come out of their shops and that the scene was also being surveyed from a number of windows besides ours.[14]

Granted, Jacobs is writing about a unique neighborhood in Manhattan and one that had a very special sense of community. But many city neighborhoods lend themselves to "eyes on the street." London, Istanbul, Jerusalem, Mumbai (Bombay), and most other traditional cities are filled with such communities. The strength of animated presence lies in harnessing the attributes of a community and a sense of territoriality to build safety.[15]

Moreover, animated presence may not just prevent an imminent action, but is meant to supply long-term intelligence so that terrorists trying to use a neighborhood to plan an attack might be spotted. It was not by accident that the Leeds and Hamburg cells planned their attacks in largely rootless neighborhoods with highly transient populations. There were very few eyes on these neighborhoods, and those eyes that were present were largely averted from suspicious behavior.

For all its value, animated presence will not prevent small-scale spontaneous attacks. Terrorists who are determined to hit a target are very difficult to stop. In 1981, French fascists struck a tightly knit Jewish neighborhood in the heart of Paris. The attack was carried out from a speeding automobile whose inhabitants fired automatic weapons at patrons of a well-known restaurant. There is very little in the arsenal of protections, and certainly not in animated presence, that could have prevented this incident.

Next, we consider *panoptic devices* such as cameras, closed-circuit television cameras (CCTV), and one-way mirrors. The notion of a panopticon goes back to the early writing of Jeremy Bentham, who believed that watching people could be used for the public good. Bentham offered an architectural design for prisons that featured a circular building housing inmates in cells located on a radius around the perimeter. Inspectors would be posted in a guardhouse at the center to observe the conduct of prisoners, without the prisoners seeing those who were watching them.[16] Bentham saw this in the starkest terms as enlightened reform—or as he put it, "morals reformed, health preserved, industry invigorated, instruction diffused, public burdens lightened, and economy seated, as it were, upon a rock by a simple idea in architecture."[17] So appealing did panoptic architecture seem at the time, that it was proposed for schools, factories, and other institutions.

The nineteenth-century panopticon has since taken on modern usage through sophisticated forms of video surveillance. Today, CCTV is employed throughout Europe, North America, and other parts of the world. France, Spain, the Netherlands, Germany, the United States, and Israel have used it extensively, especially in monitoring government buildings, public spaces, and borders. In Germany, video surveillance came into vogue during the 1980s to protect officials against kidnappings by the Red Army Faction. Cameras have also been used in Spain to detect possible attacks in Basque cities, and France employed video surveillance decades ago to guard against Algerian terrorists in Paris. Shortly after the 9/11 attacks, the federal government set up dozens of cameras in sensitive locales. The Statue of Liberty was outfitted with surveillance apparatus, and anyone who wanted to take the extra climb into its crown passed through additional screening. Israel has set up extensive video surveillance in Jerusalem's Old City to prevent knifings and assaults on civilians.

Great Britain is far ahead of other nations in applying panoptic technology. One study estimates there may be as many as 4.2 million CCTV cameras, or nearly one for every fourteen citizens.[18] Over 500 town centers rely on CCTV to combat crime, terror, or other unwanted behavior.[19] London's financial district alone contains over 1,500 cameras that monitor pedestrians. As of this writing, London's transportation system uses over 6,000 CCTV units across the network, nearly a third of which are dedicated to trains. Additional cameras are planned over the next three years, bringing London's total to more than 9,000 cameras. It is commonly thought that the average Briton crosses the line of sight of video surveillance 300 times each day.[20]

Soon after the 7/7 attack, videos of the terrorists preparing for the event were shown on home television screens. Viewers could see terrorists wearing backpacks, passing through turnstiles, racing through the underground, or searching seats on a bus. Yet the fact that the London bombers chose the most heavily watched city in the world reminds us that suicide attackers risk very little when being taped. Some studies indicate that video surveillance is not likely to reduce terrorism, and others claim that it only displaces crime to other, unobserved locations.[21] Nevertheless, the British experience also shows that panoptic devices do provide authorities with valuable information about terrorist behavior and suggests ways in which similar attacks might be deterred. Video surveillance also furnishes clues about logistics and connections between terrorist networks.

A related category consists of *advanced technological detection*, which ties advanced panoptics to elaborate databases. Technological detection also embraces motion or thermal sensors, biometric devices, and scanning for entry and exit. While these are mostly used at airports or border fences, they are applicable to urban environments. Public mass transit is a favored target and all manner of devices can be used to identify people and packages as they enter a station or board

Figure 6.2   **Video Camera in Jerusalem**

The camera is located on the ceiling of one of the Old City's labyrinthine streets. Pedestrians and shoppers walk through this area with some frequency. *(Photo by H.V. Savitch)*

a train. These range from CAT scanners that can inspect the interior of luggage, to electronic devices that can "sniff out" explosives, to a host of biometrics that identify people by their organic properties (irises, retinas, hand geometry, vein patterns). Recently, security agencies have begun to emphasize "behavior detection" by using sequential photography to identify facial expressions that reveal anger, fear, and deceit. Another type of behavior detection tracks the pathways taken by an individual and constructs a composite of a person's movement over a period of time. This allows authorities to spot suspicious patterns and detain a suspect for investigation. While highly effective, many of these technologies are bulky and slow because they screen people one at a time.

Some types of entry–exit detection, however, can be employed in a collective manner by separating trusted individuals from suspicious ones. This sometimes takes place on the entry side by requiring advanced clearance before individuals can enter a building or by exacting a fee before someone can use a highway. London's system of Automatic Number Plate Recording (ANPR) is intended to discourage single drivers from entering crowded portions of the city by applying steep user charges. ANPR utilizes digital imaging to read vehicle license plates and automatically charges their owners an entry fee.

Singapore has implemented a system that allows motorists to use a "smart card" in order to travel on a highway. While ANPR and "smart cards" are designed to expedite traffic, they can be put to multiple uses and applied toward civil, criminal, or terrorist surveillance. Once cars enter a thoroughfare, electronic devices tie the identification of the vehicle to a database that can flag other characteristics. The data can run all the way from listing the personal characteristics and habits of vehicle owners to identifying vehicles by size, color, and shape, to tracking vehicular patterns. Vehicles in the vicinity of a terror attack could be put on a watch list and subsequent driving patterns checked. London and Singapore could be the forerunners for converting ordinary traffic control into large-scale surveillance.[22] By 2006, London had read over 25 million vehicles and begun tracking them for crime, terrorism, and tax evasion. If much of this sounds alarmingly Orwellian, take note of the following five steps designed for collective entry–exit screening.

> First you project electromagnetic waves across a wide range of frequencies, from radar, millimeter-waves, and infrared heat through visible light and x-rays. There are other alternatives, too—magnetic pulses and acoustic waves, for example. Second, you carefully look for what gets through or bounces back. Third, you intensely analyze the same, crunching the numbers to turn the massive stream of return data into a coherent image. Fourth, you make sense of it, generally by another massive round of number crunching for pattern recognition, comparing the image at hand with a huge database of images, previously stored. Fifth, you don't like what you see, then you kill it, disable it or at the very least shunt it aside for closer and more leisurely scrutiny. If you see anthrax, say, kill it with a burst of gamma rays or an electromagnetic pulse intense enough to shatter DNA.[23]

Setting aside the objection that these devices might constitute an invisible intrusion into people's lives, most of the public is not likely to feel or even see their physical effects—at least not initially. Put to its ultimate use, however, high-tech detection can signal the most dangerous intrusion. Certainly, zapping a person or a commodity with deadly rays is not something to be easily countenanced. Ultimately, advanced detection can build a virtual wall of discrimination around a city.

More apparently obstructive are *moveable barriers, guards, and police patrols*. These measures are commonly used in emergencies when police set up stanchions or wooden barriers to restrict the use of space. As urban terror became more brazen, these measures were quickly adopted. London's experience with terror attacks on The City is a case in point. Soon after the attacks in 1993, the police set up a "ring of steel" to protect financial institutions. As Coaffee describes it, the "ring of steel" was hardly that and more like a "ring of plastic." The regulation consisted of traffic cones that guided automobiles, gates placed around various checkpoints, and an extensive network of cameras.[24] Barriers of this sort provided some security for London's global financial institutions. Soon after 9/11 and in the wake of threats to New York's high finance, Wall Street adopted a downscaled version of London's ring of steel. Wall Street's regulatory measures were more like a ring of barriers and police at the New York Stock Exchange.

Jerusalem went through a similar experience in its city center after al Aqsa terror broke out during 2002 and 2003. As suicide attacks took a devastating toll on life and property, troops were placed behind temporary barriers along King George and Jaffa streets. Critical spaces like Zion Square were cordoned off and reinforced by army patrols. Guards stood at entrances to restaurants, cafes, and public establishments. Those establishments not guarded locked their outer doors, allowing customers to enter only after they identified themselves and went through a brief pat-down. A few blocks from the city center at the Mehane Yehuda market, barriers and army troops cordoned off its entrances. This allowed shoppers to be inspected on their way into the market and guided around its open stalls after entering.[25]

Some regulatory measures place greater emphasis on sorting out individuals by direct confrontation. Soon after attacks in Moscow, the once-discarded *propiska* system was revived, whereby citizens were required to carry identity cards and routinely stopped. The checks went beyond a random examination of papers and focused instead on interrogating dark-skinned residents, presumably from the Caucuses. Stop, identify, and search techniques are also common in Istanbul. The city's teeming marketplaces and sinuous streets are difficult to seal off, so authorities have turned to more intensive street patrolling. The norm is to regulate, sometimes with traffic stops coupled to personal searches.

Last, we find various kinds of *fortress construction*, which includes permanent partitions, fences, gates, and solid walls. Any settlement that is wholly or substantially surrounded by a permanent barrier can be considered as protected by fortress construction. Seen in this light, fortress communities have always existed and are today more common than we realize. Not only are residential subdivisions partitioned off from their surrounding environments, but so too are factories, office complexes, holiday resorts, and shopping malls.

The partitioning can be unfinished and unsightly, as when factories put up cyclone fences that demarcate their space. Quite differently, the partitioning can be polished and subtle, as when lavish houses are surrounded by high hedges backed up by spacious lawns that divorce them from street life. Many luxurious communities reinforce their fortresses by prohibiting public parking and hiring guards to keep unwanted guests away. Owners of the palatial houses along the coasts of New England, New York, and the Florida keys have succeeded in building fortresses around precious seashores without much complaint.

Still another variation of fortress construction can be found in "edge city" office complexes that are fronted by large lawns and parking lots.[26] Gates, booms, or a guardhouse are used to allow entry—either by paying a fee or by right of ownership,

Figure 6.3   **Barriering the New York Stock Exchange**

The gates around the New York Stock Exchange can be moved. Less portable are the concrete planters in front of the entrance. The two barriers are respectively designed to keep people away and prevent explosive laden vehicles from reaching the building. Security personnel also patrol the entryway. *(Photo by H.V. Savitch)*

tenancy, worker, or guest status. Malls use milder forms of fortress construction because they are formally open to all entrants. But malls too block off their surrounding environments and privatize their own spaces. Many are also located at a distance from population centers and can be reached only by private automobile. The effect is an unsupervised, systemic selection of clientele.

Rarely are whole communities built to ward off terror. Intended or not, some are built with fortress-like features. Gilo is one such community, located on the southern perimeter of Jerusalem, minutes from the West Bank towns of Bethlehem and Beit Jalla. Over the years it has been subject to streams of gunfire and infiltration from nearby Arab villages. Its defensible space has now mitigated that vulnerability. Gilo's housing consists of clustered, attached units, fronted by open spaces that allow for easy surveillance. Its entrances are fronted by elongated gates or low walls. Its construction is in concrete or stone. Gilo also sits on a hill that affords considerable protection. Additional slabs of concrete have been put up along its most vulnerable sides to shield against gunshots. In recent years, these protections have worked to reduce assaults to near zero.[27]

The prevalence of this kind of scrutiny should not be overstated. Most city spaces are not subject to heavy or extensive surveillance. As of this writing, it can

Figure 6.4 **Gilo's Fortress Construction**

Gilo is on the southern perimeter of Jerusalem and overlooks the West Bank towns of Bethlehem and Beit Jalla. In order to protect against unwanted individuals and assaults, it has erected a permanent fence around its periphery and installed concrete slabs. *(Photo by H.V. Savitch)*

be said of liberal democracies that surveillance is hardly the dominant condition of the urban environment. Still, there are significant exceptions, and select spaces are intensely scrutinized. In these instances, surveillance has changed the immediate environment and the behavior of its users. Almost always, surveillance involves intrusion of one kind or another. Invariably there are costs for this protection and risks for nonprotection. Ultimately, surveillance hinges on whether the intrusion, the costs, and the risks are justified.

Shrinking Urban Space

Despite the fact that many ancient cities were begun on a sheltered landscape, safeguarded by moats and surrounded by walls, there is an incompatibility between surveillance and urban vitality. As often mentioned, cities depend upon the cultivation of an open, diverse, and tolerant environment. The imposition of panoptic, high-tech detection, barriers, patrols, and fortress construction suffocates a city's countless self-adjusting human transactions. This is true even when surveillance is intended to be as unobtrusive as possible, say by converting what would normally be seen as obstacles into attractive planters and street furniture or by attempting to

Figure 6.5   **Shrinking Urban Space in Lower Manhattan**

Shriveled space in the vicinity of Wall Street. Note the unused space on the street and the planters that block space on the opposite side of the road. These barriers shape human behavior. *(Photo by H.V. Savitch)*

camouflage a device or blend it into its surrounding environment. Even the most benign surveillance can be problematic. Thus, when brought to excess, street watching can cast a pall of suspicion over neighborhoods and upset social relations.

Space is the oxygen of the city, and surveillance reduces the room in which it can circulate. The most serious shrinkage occurs with the most obstructive protections such as moveable barriers, patrols, and longer-term fortress construction. Stanchions, gates, and sidewalk barricades funnel mixed crowds into seemingly uniform queues. With these protections, once pulsating throngs of people are converted into compliant subjects, gathered along narrow passages for personal inspection or collective surveillance. As a result, parts of the streetscape remain empty and unused while other parts overflow in awkward processions of harried citizens. Examine, for example, the photos of New York's lower Manhattan in Figures 6.5 and 6.6.

Notice, in Figure 6.5, the "disappearance" of the left sidewalk and the constriction of the crowd onto a narrow path on the right side. Before 9/11, both right and left sidewalks teemed with people who often spilled onto a street once intended for horse-drawn carriages. After 9/11, that same space has shrunk by about two-thirds. Concrete planters intended to prevent a truck bombing now restrict the passageway on the left sidewalk. Portable gates and security patrols block the street vista, centered at the end of the pathway by the Greek Revivalist Customs House.

Figure 6.6 **Slowing Movement in Lower Manhattan**

Shriveled space near the New York Stock Exchange. A post–9/11 scene where obstacles dressed up as street art slow pedestrian movement and make conversation awkward. *(Photo by H.V. Savitch)*

The photo in Figure 6.6 also provides a view of how movement can either be halted or radically reduced by street protections. Here, a number of polyhedron sculpted forms are awkwardly situated at a building front—apparently to thwart an attacking truck or automobile. What this does to human traffic is quite another matter. Pedestrians have either stopped in the middle of the sidewalk or meandered around the objects. Notice the makeshift guard station fronted by a portable gate on the far right corner, which blocks off a portion of the sidewalk.

We should remember that pedestrians using this space are not queuing or gathering for a Broadway show, but are workers who are supposed to be going about their normal midday schedules. To be sure, people adapt and nonchalantly bypass the obstacles. But the obstacles have nonetheless reduced available space and shaped the behavior of those who seek to use it.

These are *shriveled spaces.*[28] As defined here, shriveled spaces are areas that once amply accommodated large numbers of pedestrians and now have been converted to scarcer spaces. These spaces channel people in predictable directions. Predictability lies at the heart of surveillance and entails inducing people into knowable patterns of movement, so they can be controlled and inspected. To a very real extent, these barriers have accomplished that, though questions remain about whether it is good for the city.

Figure 6.7   **A Ring of Concrete in Washington, DC**

Prickly spaces at the U.S. Treasury Building. Movable concrete barriers and a guardhouse block entryways. These obstacles make it inconvenient for automobile passengers to be dropped off and for pedestrians to use the area. *(Photo by H.V. Savitch)*

There are other ways in which fortress construction and regulations have the effect of discouraging and shrinking the use of urban space. After 9/11, a national commission recommended that Washington, DC, be fortified and aggressively regulated. Six contextual zones were chosen for special protection.[29] New buildings were supposed to be built with setbacks of at least 100 feet, further divorcing them from street life and compromising their osmotic potential. All buildings were hardened with barriers of various kinds. While genuinely trying to make these obstacles attractive, there were limits to how bleak-looking walls and gates could be disguised as "street furniture." The changes amounted to the installation of "rings of concrete and steel" around high-profile institutions. Placed at the likely targets were delta barriers, jersey barriers, bollards, and concrete benches that jut into the street like daggers. Aside from marring some precious architecture, the protections produce social vacuums. This has become all too apparent in post–9/11 Washington. Examine, for instance, the site of the U.S. Treasury building shown in Figures 6.7 and 6.8.

These barriers deaden the streets, ridding them of pedestrians and anybody seeking to be let out of an automobile. Even the most valiant attempts to treat these obstacles as natural parts of the landscape falter in the face of their position, mass, and bleakness. While the benches situated in front of the building may be able to

Figure 6.8   **"Street Furniture" in Washington, DC**

More prickly spaces at the U.S. Treasury Building. While seeming to provide seating for pedestrians, these are really camouflaged spaces intended for protection. The benches are neither comfortable nor do they offer much to watch. *(Photo by H.V. Savitch)*

jut into an oncoming truck bomb and stop it cold, they have little civilian use or aesthetic value. For the most part, people are likely to shy away from the hard, uninviting surfaces of the concrete benches. Those who do choose to take a seat will have a difficult time finding something that is interesting to observe.

These are *prickly spaces.*[30] By virtue of either placement or construction, prickly spaces are difficult to comfortably occupy. They can include backless benches, seats that are too high, too hard, steeply sloped, or laden with spikes. We might doubt whether these spaces were genuinely intended for occupation. Certainly their primary function appears to keep people away, without individuals having to notice that the spaces are unusually uncomfortable.

In other spaces the need for surveillance has led to a coarsening of the urban texture. What was once a fine-grained built environment that facilitated stopping, watching, chatting, or taking a detour via an open gate, is today a flat, monotonous expanse. These spaces are not so much created by filling them with barriers, but by the presence of forbidding conditions that have a tendency to empty the streets. The best illustration of this can be found at 1600 Pennsylvania Avenue. Take note, for instance, of Figures 6.9 and 6.10, which show the front entrances of the White House as well closures at the end of Pennsylvania Avenue.

We should recognize that placing gates around the White House is not brand-new.

Figure 6.9   **Field of Vision at the White House**

Hostile space at the center of Pennsylvania Avenue. Note one of many guards at the gates of the White House. Intensive surveillance can substitute for barriers and bring about the nonusage of space. *(Photo by H.V. Savitch)*

Prior to 9/11, gates demarcated pedestrian areas from the White House and adjoining buildings. But rather than serving as a barrier, these gates identified a particular place, and pedestrians passed through their entrances with minimal inspection. Before 9/11, Pennsylvania Avenue was a busy thoroughfare, not just for tourists anxious to visit the White House, but for surrounding businesses, strollers, and busy officials. Its gates were used to lead and invite people into its interior spaces.

All this changed after 9/11. Pennsylvania Avenue was closed to traffic, blocked off at each end, and reinforced by patrols and guardhouses. The avenue was converted into a super-block, which today serves as a field of surveillance. Police guard it on foot and patrol it on bicycle. Hidden from view are sharpshooters, guards with automatic weapons, armored trucks, CBRN (chemical, biological, radiation, and nuclear) units, and more. The avenue of presidents has been turned into a concrete moat. This radical change illustrates that it is not only barriers that shrink urban space, but intensified surveillance that renders them useless by eliminating anything that makes them remotely interesting.

These are *hostile spaces.* This term is meant to convey an expanse of land or the creation of a super-block, watched and guarded by uniformed patrols, lacking in detail for passers-by, and often laborious to traverse. There are few opportunities here for unintended stops, chance encounters, or impromptu detours. Pedestrians

Figure 6.10 **Blocking Off and Patrolling the White House**

Hostile space at the middle and end of Pennsylvania Avenue. Vehicular traffic is now closed off to a formerly thriving street. Note the bicycle patrol as well as the barely visible barriers and guardhouse at the end of the avenue. While one can see small clusters of people in front of the gates, the environment does not invite lingering for any length of time. *(Photo by H.V. Savitch)*

are encouraged to move quickly from point A to point B. While not explicit, the effect on passers-by is to discourage activity that is unplanned or unofficial.

All in all, we can understand the effects of barriers, patrols, fortification, and intensified surveillance. These protections are meant to control, investigate, and possibly apprehend those who would harm the city and its people. They are also intended to reduce the visibility and exposure of potential targets. Nonetheless, they have created spaces that have either shriveled in size, become prickly for users, or lapsed into a hostile environment. In sum, they have shrunk urban space and their paradoxical effect is to drain the city of the very vibrancy they are supposed to safeguard.

Surveillance and Preemption

When asked about the physical changes made for protecting Jerusalem, the city's former chief engineer, Uri Shetreet, shrugged off the question. "Terror," he said, "cannot be dealt with at the point of contact or at the moment of detonation." Shetreet continued, explaining that "Any real protection has to stop terrorists in their tracks, when they're preparing or well before, and that takes a lot of hard work. It's not easy to be proactive . . . anybody in this business has to be a desperate optimist."[31]

Shetreet was talking about preempting terrorism by killing, capturing, or interdicting attackers before they had a chance to strike. If anything, he had understated the challenges that make any kind of preemption feasible. Effective preemption requires extensive surveillance whose range can include direct infiltration of terrorist cells to less direct scrutiny of money trails used to support terrorism. Preemption depends upon mounds of intelligence and grounded intimacy with an enemy's habits and movement.

This is a tall and complicated order and it begins with information gathering. At base is the capacity to find and block sources of finance. Terrorists generate their own funds, acquired through voluntary donations, copyright theft, drugs, smuggling, kidnapping, and shakedowns of Arab expatriates. In South America, al Qaeda and Hezbollah have amassed funds by selling pirated films and recordings.[32] In Detroit, terrorist operatives have made use of millions of dollars in fraudulent cashier's checks; in Boston they have exploited credit card and social security numbers; and in North Carolina and Michigan they have resorted to cigarette smuggling.[33]

The institutional sources of terrorist finance are extensive and involve transactions to send and receive money, "loans" from conventional banks, and donations to charitable fronts. Conventional banks serve as financial intermediaries in laundering and funneling money. The United States and several other nations identified the Bank al-Taqwa as serving the needs of a conglomerate of radical Islamists including the Muslim Brotherhood (Egypt), Hamas (Palestinian territories), and the Armed Islamic Group (Algeria).[34] The Al Rashid Trust is closely linked to al Qaeda (worldwide) and Ja'ish Muhammad (Indian subcontinent). The Arab Bank is known to have funneled money to al Aqsa Martyrs' Brigade and al Qaeda (Spain, Pakistan, and Yemen).[35]

Enlisted in the effort to dry up funds are the European Union (EU), the G8, and a host of other nations, led in part by the United States. The EU keeps a list of terrorist organizations and is actively engaged in tracking funds and shutting down illicit banking transactions. The G8 has also compiled a list of terrorist groups and frozen their assets.[36]

The United States has taken the most vigorous action through a Brussels-based consortium of banks formally called the Society for Worldwide Inter Bank Financial Telecommunication, dubbed SWIFT. Up until recently, the SWIFT program was a covert operation conducted by the FBI, the CIA, and the U.S. Treasury Department. Working in concert, these agencies were able to monitor more than 6 trillion daily transactions conducted among nearly 8,000 financial institutions. SWIFT provided the technology to siphon off those that looked suspicious. Counted among its successes was the capture of a leading Jemaah Islamiya terrorist responsible for the bombing in Bali and others who plotted attacks in New York and Los Angeles.[37]

Charitable giving is a mainstay of Islamic culture. Some terrorist groups maintain a network of social services, and this makes the line between charity and violence very permeable. The financial trail has often led to Saudi Arabia, which has funded charities and charitable fronts throughout the world. Among its major beneficiaries have been al Qaeda, Abu Sayyaf (Phillipines), and Hamas. Some of the more notorious charities include al Wafa (weapons smuggling into Afghanistan), the Islamic Relief Organization (embassy bombings in Africa), and the Holy Land Foundation (suicide attacks in Israel). At least some of these fronts have been raided and their offices shut down in the United States or Canada.[38]

Preemption is normally associated with more frontal operations that track down terrorists and interdict them. Interpol serves as a clearinghouse for police forces around the world, and it coordinates the activities of more than 100 members. Its Fusion Task Force maintains a rogue's gallery of over 300 terrorist suspects and holds more than 7,000 profiles. Much of this is complemented by national counterterrorist agencies around the world whose major prongs include a complex of American agencies (FBI, CIA, Department of Defense, Homeland Security) as well as Great Britain's MI5 and its Home Office and France's Direction de la Surveillance du Territoire, or DST, and its special courts. Other nations' counterterrorism agencies are no less formidable and include Russia's Federal Security Service (FSB), Israel's Shin Bet, and India's National Security Guards (NSG). All of these agencies maintain massive databases that denote areas of terrorist concentration, trajectories of action, and probable logistical paths. Anybody able to visit these agencies would see mountains of digital information, photo galleries, video tapes, audio recordings, organizational charts, network matrices, briefing books, intelligence reports, and old-fashioned paper files. One would also spot small surveillance gear like mini cameras and high-end bugging devices for listening, dubbing, and taping, as well as banks of secure telephones and a television tuned to al Jazeera.

Anti-terrorist surveillance is labor intensive. During Operation Crevice, MI5 consumed 34,000 hours of intelligence and police work. Listening devices and cameras were installed in the homes and cars of the plotters, and undercover agents tracked their movements by day and night. The sheer cost and consumption of time required MI5 to limit its priorities, thus preventing it from extending the same surveillance to the Leeds cell.

At a local level, New York's lead is unchallenged. NYPD, the city's 37,000-member police force, has more than 1,000 officers devoted to counter-terrorism, some of whom speak Arabic, Pashto, Farsi, and Urdu. Its Counter Terrorism Bureau conducts surveillance, investigates, and is prepared for any preemptive action. The bureau's work begins at the micro level. Within its offices, maps can be found that display neighborhoods, with some tagged as containing concentrations of Pakistanis, Palestinians, or other groups.[39]

NYPD has a significant network of intelligence gatherers that work locally and internationally. The bureau's contacts reach into the sinews of the commercial world with over 25,000 contacts that cover the city and some major states.[40] At an international level, bureau personnel have been stationed in London, Hamburg, Tel

Aviv, Toronto, Lyon, Amman, and Singapore.[41] They have visited Istanbul, Madrid, and Moscow after those cities were attacked. And they made special efforts to be on hand after suicide attacks in Jerusalem and the massacre of schoolchildren in Beslan.

There is also a good deal of brawn connected to NYPD's brains. Specially trained "Hercules teams" of heavily armed police, riding in armor-plated automobiles might make sudden appearances in city hot spots. The Empire State Building, Brooklyn Bridge, Times Square, and New York Stock Exchange are likely places in which terrorists might be interdicted. The city's subway system is given the most careful scrutiny, and all seven of its underwater tunnels are subject to constant surveillance. Much of this is a show of force—an effort to demonstrate that the city can strike terrorists with devastating effect and can do so preemptively.

By at least the bureau's own accounts, interdiction has paid off. Its undercover agents spent more than a year tracking a Pakistani immigrant and his accomplice who, in 2004, were planning to blow up a subway station at Herald Square. A year before, the bureau traced an al Qaeda operative named Lyman Farris as he sought out possibilities for destroying the Brooklyn Bridge. After months of searching the target, Farris called off the attack by signaling to his handlers that "the weather is too hot."[42] Another well-known plot was alleged to have occurred in 2001 when an al Qaeda operative named Issa al Hindi was discovered to have searched out for destruction the New York Stock Exchange as well as large buildings in Jersey City and Washington, DC. NYPD's bureau has been given credit for interdicting other plots in or around the city.[43]

Having lived through one of the worst terror attacks in history, New York City may be in a state of unusual readiness. By the same token, New York is much like other megaglobal cities. London or Tokyo, Mumbai or Cairo contain extensive public transit, large buildings, huge agglomerations of people, and complex infrastructures. The New York experience could inform us about the costs and benefits of this kind of surveillance.

Surveillance on the Horns of a Dilemma

There are those who despair of surveillance preventing or deterring an attack. Experts admit that little can be done to truly stop a determined terrorist from reaching some kind of target. They reason that once targets are "hardened" and put out of reach, terrorists can simply turn to "softer" targets. Threats are then displaced from less vulnerable to more vulnerable sites. Others argue that surveillance and terrorism are in a race without end, where one side escalates its defenses only to find the other side has discovered ways to evade those defenses. And so on it goes, in a race to the bottom where each side finds a way to outwit the other. In the course of running that race, surveillance exacts social penalties and most importantly costs to fundamental rights. David Lyon is particularly skeptical about any possible gains stemming from surveillance and admonishes policymakers to "beware of high-technology surveillance systems that cannot achieve what their proponents claim but which may all too well curtail cherished and hard won civil liberties."[44]

There is something to be said about the dangers of sliding into a surveillance mentality, where people come to believe that protection can only be benign. The day-to-day infringements of surveillance are incremental, but the long-term political costs are cumulative. Ironically, the overuse of surveillance can evoke fear, generating the very insecurity it is supposed to prevent. What has come to be called "surveillance creep" embodies snowballing costs, and its risks stem from new technologies that are gradually incorporated into society.[45] As the term suggests, surveillance creep sneaks up on a society without much notice. Sometimes the mere discovery of detection equipment is enough to bring it to public acceptance. Surveillance creep can also be encouraged by rival cities that are seen by local elites as being on the "cutting edge" of civic protection. The immediate response is to copy them, lest a city be accused of lagging behind the times.

Continuing, gradually escalating surveillance is also thought to evoke distrust among the citizenry. Scanning people and examining their everyday movements produces an atmosphere where suspicion becomes the norm, and this is bound to redound on those conducting the surveillance. Thus, it may not be by chance that police and police supervisors have become less trusted and are sometimes faced with hostility. The curious irony is that while many British applaud the police for pursuing terrorists, public confidence in law enforcement officers has fallen by 15 percent since 2003. This is particularly acute among minorities, where trust in the police is much lower. In London's Whitechapel, bearded young men hand out pamphlets warning their compatriots not to talk to investigators, while in New York's Harlem and Paris's northern suburbs, black or Maghrebian teenagers openly mock police surveillance.

Sometimes surveillance creep will be superseded by "surveillance surge." This occurs when traumatic assaults suddenly generate a demand to find a deterrent or protective shield.[46] Events present opportunities for technological innovation, a perceived need to use it, and a "must have it" attitude. The onset of terrorism in Jerusalem, New York, and London brought an avalanche of new businesses dedicated to security. Among the hottest items sold to cities were cameras that featured algorithmic surveillance, new methods of facial detection, and black boxes that tested for contraband material.

Both surveillance creep and surveillance surge are made possible by the habits of power holders. Government is a slippery slope along which increased surveillance can travel. Once security agencies intrude into peoples' lives, they rarely let go. What was once a pilot becomes a long-term fixture. Power has a voracious appetite, and smaller groups of officialdom can all too easily exploit it.

Besides this, it is much safer for politicians and bureaucrats to aggressively adopt surveillance than resist it. After alarm bells ring, officials are inclined to inoculate themselves against charges that they are failing to take adequate precautions. Officialdom is always on guard about allegations that it was negligent in not putting up barriers against a truck bomb or did not adequately patrol the corridors of a shopping center or did not purchase suitable detection equipment. A sense of being exposed to risk prompts authorities to do more surveillance rather than less. Nor is public overreaction helped by the media, which may rail against surveillance before an attack, but after an attack will be the first to point out what was not done to thwart it.

Rather than treating surveillance as an absolute liability to be resisted, we might appreciate the dilemma associated with any choice.[47] On the one hand, surveillance violates privacy, but its absence also puts peoples' lives at risk. Either way, we pay a price—either for surveillance or for the lack of it. Exactly how this dilemma is resolved or who resolves it is not clear. Certainly if we consult public opinion, surveillance is fairly well supported in both the United States and Western Europe. Americans are somewhat less enthusiastic about surveillance than Europeans, but both publics generally endorse it. When asked if they were in favor of video cameras, 78 percent of Americans and 71 percent of Europeans expressed a positive view. Similarly, equal percentages of Americans and Europeans (54 percent) favored the monitoring of Internet communications. Monitoring of bank transactions was less popular, with only a minority of Americans supporting it (39 percent) and more Europeans favoring it (50 percent).[48]

On a more practical but less scientific level, security experts claim the public actually feels reassured with more surveillance. Public spaces that are visually monitored or patrolled or hold entry searches are more likely to attract clientele than those with few or no precautions. In Jerusalem, real estate agents were quick to point out that enclosed malls and guarded apartment complexes were more likely to please buyers than unprotected sites.[49] Hebrew University officials were surprised to learn that its multiple layers of surveillance actually enticed students to enroll.[50] And ordinary citizens were more apt to attend public spectacles that were enclosed by temporary partitions and regularly patrolled. It may be that over a period of time, the public will grow weary of surveillance and reject it. But for the foreseeable future, citizens will be quick to express their satisfaction with aggressive surveillance.

Surveillance on Balance

Does this mean that efforts to combat terrorism are bound to severely compromise local democracy or pave the way for a repressive state? By some accounts, the United States has already reached that dismal condition. Writing about American reactions to 9/11, David Harvey claims that "Dissident views were condemned outright and freedoms of speech were threatened. There were more than a few signs of U.S. versions of fanaticism and zealotry, initially directed against Muslims."[51] Harvey does not indicate where, when, or how often free speech was threatened. Nor are we ever informed about the identity of the alleged repressors. This leaves the allegation in doubt, but even if true, these are crude generalizations. There is a crucial difference between repressions that are sanctioned by government or repressive statements that are promulgated by a mass media and repressive acts by a few hatemongers.

Taking Harvey's accusation a step further, another writer asserts: "Systematic state repression and mass incarceration have thus been brought to bear on Arab American neighbourhoods like Dearbon [sic] in Detroit. . . . Thousands of U.S. citizens have also effectively been stripped of any notion of value, to be thrown into extra or intra-territorial camps as suspect terrorists. . . ."[52] Exactly how many thousands have been incarcerated or thrown into camps is never stated, neither is the figure corroborated. Indeed, the estimates of post–9/11 incarcerations in the United States are substantially different than anything suggested by these sentences.[53] Further, in a nation of 300 million people stretching across a continent, one is bound to find abuses; trying to create the impression of governmental or popular rampage against Arab Americans strains credibility.[54]

The question of surveillance is best treated by avoiding hyperbole, and many accounts do bring a sober analysis to the issue. These express real concerns about slippage in American democracy, and phrase it as a danger to be watched by everyone and evaluated by the facts at hand. Editors and collaborators at *Urban Affairs Review* (UAR) write about a post–9/11 tendency where "public safety can overwhelm values emphasizing civil liberties, civic discourse and human dignity."[55] Another UAR writer legitimately points out that "the main threat to cities comes not from terrorism, but from the policy responses to terrorism. . . ."[56]

These are serious warnings about overreacting to threats and the need to put them in democratic perspective. Any answer to these concerns can only be tentative and extrapolate from experience. To date, the evidence would suggest cautious optimism. India, the world's largest democracy, and Israel, one of the world's smallest democracies, have retained the essentials of their democratic institutions. This has occurred while Srinagar and Mumbai, Jerusalem and Tel Aviv, experienced withering assaults. The United Kingdom, Spain, and France also have held to their democratic institutions in the wake of attacks. When London, Madrid, and Paris faced waves of terrorism, all of these nations responded with large-scale surveillance and extraordinary measures for law enforcement.

Spain and France have imposed a system of administrative deportation for radical Islamists found to be exhorting others to commit acts of terrorism. Citizenship can also be revoked in some instances. In both countries, legislators, the courts, and civil rights groups have acted to counter possible abuses. Great Britain passed the Terrorism Act of 2006, which among other newly designated illegalities, makes it a crime to glorify terrorism or issue statements that lead to terrorist acts. This legislation goes quite far in regulating the exercise of free speech. For all the allegations about being excessive, the legislation has been scrutinized in the House of Commons, criticized in the House of Lords, and held in check by British courts.

Similar responses occurred in the United States. There, a free press reported on possible excesses from Operation SWIFT and an auditing firm verified that data searches were connected to proper intelligence leads; Congress continued to oversee the Patriot Act and the courts have freed persons accused of violating anti-terror laws.[57] Civil liberties organizations have sprung to life in the judicial arena by working for defendant rights; coalitions have emerged to lobby legislators on behalf of aliens; and cities have refused to enforce federal laws restricting immigration, choosing instead to become "immigrant sanctuaries."[58] During 2006, the Democratic opposition made impressive gains at the polls—its members, rightly or wrongly, have been fulsome critics of the Justice Department, the FBI, and the CIA. Political, legal, and social checks on authority have held, despite 9/11 and charges of terrorist plots.

People may complain that government has gone too far and that more needs to be done, but this is a far cry from a repressive state. Democracies are dynamic, constantly evolving, and subject to abuse. They are filled with flaws, but warts and all, they are remarkably resilient. This is because they contain self-corrective institutions and habits. The institutions of democratic accountability provide a clue about how we might balance the threat of terrorism against the costs of surveillance.

With the exception of ensuring constitutional protections, no hard-and-fast rules can be put on highly mutable and unpredictable conditions. Rather, democratic institutions should be brought to bear—incrementally, with proper safeguards, and as the situation warrants. This balance can be achieved by using standard incremental techniques—frequently matching means to ends, often making adjustments, and, most of all, invoking constant comparisons between one situation another.[59] Depending upon the circumstances, the balance will frequently shift, require a high degree of judgment, and should be weighed by type of surveillance and effects on city space. An alert citizenry, a vigilant, honest, and consistent press, a vigorous legislature, and an independent judiciary are the only ways to balance competing ends. These institutions should be matched by energetic local government and strong neighborhood involvement. A net of democratic institutions, coupled with citizen involvement, can then be used to thicken public oversight of bureaucratic police powers. This combination of incremental adjustment and institutional thickness can work to put surveillance within a framework of democratic accountability.[60] This is more easily said than done, but it remains the best available choice.

Conclusions

Surveillance of one kind or another has always been a part of city life. Throughout the Middle Ages, walls served this function, and up through modern time they have become more elaborate. While modern walls are unsightly from a functional point of view, they are neither necessarily good nor necessarily bad. Rather, they should be judged by their purpose, their use, and whether they are necessary. Some walls have reduced terrorism, separated warring factions and establishing boundaries, while others have created carceral cities.

Walls are just one way of maintaining surveillance, which can best be viewed as a continuum that ranges from less to greater obstruction. The least obstructive are *animated presence, panoptic devices*, and *advanced detection*; more obstructive are *moveable barriers and patrols*; and the most obstructive is *fortress construction*. Almost all surveillance shrinks space, though some types of surveillance are more deleterious to city space than others. Excessive street-watching and panoptic devices can create unwarranted suspicion and stultify social relations. Advanced detection can become alarmingly Orwellian. Barriers have been known to narrow city space, and fortress construction can completely block off space. Intensive surveillance coupled with forbidden space can deaden street life. The paradoxical effect of surveillance is that it drains the city of the very vibrancy it is supposed to safeguard.

A final component of surveillance is preemption, and experts point out that terrorism cannot be stopped at the point of detonation but should be interdicted well before. This requires extensive, on-the-ground intelligence as well as a strong capacity to apply force. New York has shown itself to be well ahead of most cities and could be setting a pattern for other global or mega cities.

For all its drawbacks, surveillance has become necessary. In fact, urban populations have demanded protection, and surveys show that most citizens favor surveillance of one kind or another. The challenge is to resolve particular tensions—between the need for a modicum of surveillance and a maximum of local democracy as well as the need to minimize target vulnerability and to maximize the open qualities of city space.

Sustaining Local Resilience

You know, I really miss September 10th.

—Doonesbury

9/11 Dystopia

September 11 will best be remembered because it came to symbolize a new con-sciousness and brought about a new era. For all the rightful recognition that day brought, it also drew an extremely dismal picture of the urban future—or, as it is called here, 9/11 dystopia. The elements of 9/11 dystopia were manifested in dif-ferent responses to the attack. One was an emotional response reflecting a deep pessimism that saw cities falling into stifling fear and dark repression. Another had more to do with a strategic response, and saw the path to national survival in movement away from cities and toward a "defensive dispersal" of people, housing, and industry. The last was burrowed in a belief that cities had gone astray because of their infatuation with "tall buildings." According to this creed, skyscrapers not only compromised the values of sound planning but made cities vulnerable to at-tack. Each of these responses is taken up.

The most emotional responses were drawn in the days immediately following 9/11 and denoted a new world of darkness. Often heard were predictions about growing repression by armed police, bounty hunters, and authoritarian rulers. Image makers produced a frightful picture. Brought into vogue again were films like Fritz Lang's *Metropolis*, an expressionist work made in 1920s Germany, and Ridley Scott's *Blade Runner*, an American cult classic released during the 1980s. While separated by more than half a century, both films show the city at its worst—lorded over by technology gone mad, ridden by social divisions, and headed for self-destruction.

At a scholarly level, Harold Lasswell's 1941 classic, "The Garrison State," was brought back to life to show the political temper of 9/11 dystopia. The article presaged an equally bleak urban future.[1] Lasswell wanted to "consider the possibil-ity" that we would face a world where "specialists in violence" would become the most powerful group. He went on to write that "internal violence would be directed principally against unskilled manual workers and counter-elite elements, who have come under suspicion."[2] As he saw it, society was there to be ruled by those who could manipulate appealing symbols and dominate mass opinion through public relations. Lasswell's "garrison state" went far beyond Madison Avenue manipulation and took the coercive form of military control coupled with modern technology. Its cardinal rule was obedience, service, and work. In many ways, the idea of a "garrison state" was influenced by the rising fascism of the 1930s, but to some it seemed applicable to the days following 9/11 when the FBI launched large-scale searches and police swarmed downtown streets.

This was dystopia's emotional mindset, and it was filled by the speculation of newspaper columnists, popular writers, and academics. Little more than a month after 9/11, Mike Davis referred to "military and security firms rushing to exploit the nation's nervous breakdown." They would "grow rich," he wrote, "amidst the general famine." Davis predicted that "Americans will be expected to express gratitude as they are scanned, frisked, imaged, tapped and interrogated. . . . Security will become a full-fledged urban utility like water and power."[3] Davis was no less ominous about the economy as he declared that the coming days

> may likely be the worst recession since 1938 and will produce major mutations in the American city. There is little doubt, for instance, that bin Laden et al. have put a silver stake in the heart of the "downtown revival" in New York and elsewhere. The traditional city where buildings and land values soar toward the sky is not yet dead but the pulse is weakening.[4]

While Davis was at an extreme end of dystopia, others in the planning profession joined him. One professional voiced concern that "the war against terrorism threatens to become a war against the livability of American cities."[5] At about the same time, Columbia University planner Peter Marcuse flatly predicted of 9/11 that "the results are likely to be a further downgrading of the quality of life in cities, visible changes in urban form, the loss of public use of public space, restrictions on free movement within and to cities, particularly for members of darker skinned groups, and the decline of open popular participation in the governmental planning and decision-making process."[6] These were not isolated commentaries, and similar diagnoses were published along with Marcuse's article in the *International Journal of Urban and Regional Research.*[7]

In the midst of this, another group of writers took a different tack, arguing instead for a change in urban strategy. Their watchword was "defensive dispersal," and the idea was to find a path that would ensure safety. As mentioned in Chapter 3, "defensive dispersal" dates back to the 1950s, when interstate highways were lauded because they produced low-density suburbs that would elude a single devastating bomb. The Housing Act of 1954 had reinforced defensive dispersal by promoting low-density peripheral development. Other advocates of dispersal laid out a scheme to build "a dispersed pattern of small, efficient cities" with radiating expressways in order to thwart an enemy attack.[8] Once 9/11 hit, the idea of defensive dispersal was revised and linked to the digital age and a broader movement toward decentralization. As the theory went, compact cities had outlived their usefulness and were not as efficient as planners might have thought. Building density by vertically storing people and industry was outmoded, and modern industry would operate far more efficiently on an expanded horizontal scale. Even air pollution would be better controlled by dispersing population across wide-open spaces rather than confining people to compact cities. The digital age had rendered compact cities unnecessary by permitting people to communicate across vast distances.[9] Besides, since we were already a suburban nation, why not push this trend further and gain a defensive edge?

The theory of defensive dispersal was promoted by editorialists from the *Wall Street Journal*, who saw an advantage in sprawled cities, and by journalists at the *Detroit News*, who noted that "in the wake of September 11, the constituency for density had probably thinned out."[10] Other writers began to think aloud about the dangers of density and saw a trend in the making. In an article titled, "The De-Clustering of America," Joel Kotkin wrote, "the dispersion of talent and technology to various parts of the country and the world has altered the once fixed geographies of talent."[11] By this thinking, countering terror also coincided with low-density and unstructured patterns of settlement where anything could be done anywhere. As Kotkin saw it:

> This dispersion trend has been further accelerated by the fallout from September 11. Already, many major securities companies have moved operations out of Manhattan. . . . Many of them have signed long-term leases and aren't coming back. Financial and other business service firms are migrating to the Hudson Valley, New Jersey, and Connecticut.[12]

Finally, 9/11 dystopia was reinforced by a belief about the declining quality of urban life. This was a testimony about values that needed to be restored and it was based on an aversion to tall buildings. Far from being an effort to abandon the city, these writers wanted to reinstate a more traditional European-styled city, whose human scale would facilitate closer identity within a meaningful community. For these value-oriented theoreticians, tall buildings had not only robbed the city of its humanity, but brought suffocating congestion to its streets and overloaded its fragile infrastructure. Packing people into floor upon floor of skyscraper was intolerable, and it created an abysmal condition, which they labeled "urban hypertrophy."[13] Having discredited tall buildings because of their seeming threat to humanity, it was not a far step to point up the risks of inhabiting them and predicting their demise. Two urban writers mounted the campaign against tall buildings, writing shortly after 9/11 that "We are convinced that the age of skyscrapers is at an end. It must now be considered an experimental building typology that has failed. We predict that no new megatowers will be built, and existing ones are destined to be dismantled."[14]

To say the least, 9/11 dystopia was stark. It either saw little future for cities or argued for their complete reconception. It was predicated on some narrow possibilities. Either society had rotted from the inside and the attacks were to be expected, or cities had left themselves exposed to September 11 by misplaced development and they should be abandoned or revamped. Taken as a whole, the 9/11 disillusion was a reaction to recent decades of urban development and its remedies left little room for leeway.

The Resilient City

Understanding Resilience

At best, 9/11 dystopia missed the mark and at worst it ignored a city's capacity for resilience. Before exploring this proposition, we might ask how people who had observed and studied the city for so long could have been so mistaken. Any number of explanations is plausible. Among the more apparent reasons for the miscalculation was that lower Manhattan's devastation was so extensive that it distorted individual perspectives. A single stroke of so great a magnitude had so stunned the public, and created so dark a cloud, that it was to difficult to spot a silver lining much less see sunlight. Amid the gloom one could only portend additional gloom. Another explanation for the distortions of 9/11 dystopia is less generous. This rests on the ideology of its analysts—from both the political left and the political right. As this explanation goes, some commentators were so convinced about the righteousness of their belief that they saw its vindication in any act or circumstance. Their predictions were couched in a polemic that sought to justify its premises. A final explanation would deny that 9/11 dystopia was entirely wrong. It might go on to argue that most of the analyses and predictions were basically correct. Dystopia's defenders might cite the growth of surveillance and the shrinkage of urban space to convince an audience that their prognosis was correct. Those who held a dim view of the city might also point to the continuing flight to the suburbs. While this has some plausibility, the facts about what happened to New York (and other cities) after being attacked do not quite fit.

Any assessment of resilience works best when guided by the historic or empirical record, most particularly by other cities that underwent warfare, terror, or endemic violence.[15] While this is a complicated matter, the majority of findings point in a similar direction. The salient conclusion is that most cities have a remarkable capacity for resilience. Cities may well experience short-term negative effects from an attack, but under varying conditions and over varying periods of time they do recover. Moreover, recoveries are not accompanied by a period that gives to a rise a "garrison state" or repressive politics.[16] To the contrary, cities in free societies retain the fundamentals of local democracy, and while citizens may feel pangs of anxiety, their day-to-day habits are unchanged:[17]

To get a better idea of how resilience works, we can think of cities as large agglomerations of human settlement, social relations, and factors of production—held together and made dynamic by an extensive infrastructure. What makes cities dynamic is circular causation, where fortuitous circumstances trigger positive effects, which in turn feed those circumstances again to produce still more positive effects. Lying at the heart of this repetitive process is the magnitude of the city and its dynamic agglomeration. Generally speaking, the larger and more dynamic the city, the more difficult to set it in reverse. Any attack would have to be massive in order to permanently halt these self-generating processes. Even when subject to enormous shocks, cities seem to regenerate and spring back to life.

The most complete picture on the effects of violent shock to urban society can be found in studies of conventional warfare. Research on select cities examines their experience with intense periods of incessant bombing, firestorms, or even atomic warfare, and shows them to be remarkably resilient. In the United Kingdom and France, London and Paris experienced years of air bombing, close combat, or military occupation. In Germany, cities like Cologne, Hamburg, Berlin, and Dresden were subject to heavy aerial bombardment. In Japan, the devastation in Tokyo and especially Hiroshima and Nagasaki was much greater. Large sections of Japanese cities were destroyed and hundreds of thousands of people killed. Yet all of these cities in Europe and Asia recovered, and most went on to a period of unprecedented prosperity.[18]

A somewhat more complicated picture emerges from cities under terrorist attack. As we know, urban terror is a different type of warfare that emphasizes longer assaults on civilians, persistent attacks geared toward the decontrol of territory, and sustained efforts to paralyze normal life. Rather than extensive and abrupt shock, most terror consists of low-intensity warfare that is supposed to wear the enemy down through protracted friction.[19] It stands to reason that urban terror might affect cities in different ways than conventional military action. In these cases, the evidence points to varying degrees of recovery over varying periods of time. While the findings are qualified, they still are reasonably optimistic. Studies of American cities indicate that they are "highly unlikely to decline in the face of even a sustained terrorist campaign."[20] Other research on Italian cities demonstrates short-lived economic effects lasting for about a year after attack.[21] Another line of work on Israeli and Basque cities shows longer-term effects from terrorism, though in the absence of continued attacks these effects do wear off.[22]

We should understand that resilience is not an absolute or a matter of either being resilient or not. Cities are resilient to different extents, in different ways, and have different periods of recovery. Much depends on the size of the city, the strength of its economy, and its social coherence. These factors can then be coupled to the frequency and severity of attack to obtain a more nuanced picture of recovery. From all indications, the resilience of New York and London are different from that of Jerusalem.

How might we know whether resilience has been achieved? While it is normally difficult to precisely sort out the effects of one variable upon another, assessing resilience involves the simpler task of determining the extent to which a previous condition has been reinstated.[23] Simply put, the threshold for resilience can be satisfied by establishing whether a city has bounced back after sustaining an attack or wave of terror. For example, after a city experienced mega terror we would want to know whether the population has returned, or after a city incurred smart terror whether an infrastructure has been rebuilt. Measurable results should then tell us whether an area has recovered, the extent of that recovery, or whether any recovery took place. Resilience might also be achieved if an attack had not changed fundamental conditions or had no significant effect on normal life. This would mean a city had seen no adverse change and withstood an intended shock. A city meeting these criteria could be seen as resilient.

Different Cities/Different Resilience

As we know, New York's terrorism has been sporadic and marked by one enormous blow. With over 3.5 million jobs and a gross product of $400 billion, New York possesses one of the largest local economies in the world.[24] Almost 64 percent of the city's agglomeration is located in Manhattan, and most of that is concentrated in its midtown or downtown business districts.[25] High finance undergirds this great financial edifice, and its geographic concentration makes it vulnerable to attack. September 11 showed just how smart terror could pinpoint critical assets.

London's terrorism has been less murderous, though more frequent, and has occurred in cyclical patterns since the 1970s. Its economy is similar in size to New York's, with an employment base of close to 4 million jobs and a gross product of over $250 billion.[26] London's central business district is concentrated in The City and in the central boroughs of Westminster and Kensington, lying to the west. Much like New York's business cores, these areas are driven by high finance.[27] While the cycle of attacks in the 1990s targeted The City, the attack of 7/7 was somewhat more dispersed, occurring in Westminster and The City, but also just astride these boroughs.

By comparison with its two giant counterparts, Jerusalem's socioeconomic profile is quite modest and its pattern of continued terror differs. Jerusalem's 180,000 jobs and its gross product of $14 billion are a fraction of its giant counterparts.[28] Also, unlike the other two cities, Jerusalem is a not an economic capital but a political and religious one. Its central business district consists of moderately priced retail shops, restaurants, and a few important banks. Government buildings and cultural institutions are scattered throughout the city.

One asset that all three cities have in common is an important tourist industry, though this too greatly varies in size. London is one of the foremost tourist destinations of the world, and its tourism reached a zenith in 2005 with 14.9 million foreign visitors. New York's tourism is less than half that much, having reached its height in 2005 with 6.8 million international tourists. Tourism is one of Jerusalem's major industries, and its tourism reached a pinnacle in 2000 with 953,000 visitors. Unlike more stable industries, the elasticity of tourism relative to terror is a useful a barometer of local resilience.

Under the circumstances, we would expect the resilience of these cities to be markedly different from one another, and it is. Among the factors used to assess recovery in New York, London, and Jerusalem are employment, tourism, and office markets (see Appendix, Tables A13 and A14).

Resilience in New York, London, and Jerusalem

In the immediate period after 9/11, New York employment fell sharply and the city lost more than 100,000 jobs.[29] The drop was precipitous, linked directly to the collapse in lower Manhattan, and it occurred in the few months after September. The bulk of the lost employment occurred in the area around the World Trade Center, though it also spread to other parts of Manhattan and the rest of the city. For a time, the job situation was bleak, but by 2004 the city's employment began to move upward; by the end of 2005 the city's job base had reached 3.6 million.[30]

London's cyclical violence burst out again between 1990 and 1993, when financial institutions were targeted by the IRA. By comparison to New York, these attacks were pinpricks, though they engendered a huge psychological response, which eventually led to the "ring of steel." While it is not possible to attribute the subsequent drop in London's employment to these attacks, the falloff was significant. Once the cycle of terror had ceased, London was down by about 450,000 jobs from the previous period.[31] As in New York, the number crept up in subsequent years, and by the turn of the century employment reached a high that hovered around the 4 million mark.

For Jerusalem, the key period of terror occurred in the fall of 2000 through 2002. Here, too, the City Center was targeted, though neighborhoods within a short distance were also struck. Unlike London, the targets were people, rather than financial institutions. While businesses were severely affected and many closed, others waited out the storm. The Israeli government also stepped in to bolster the local economy.[32] Apparently, government programs made up for private business failures and through these years jobs remained at about 180,000. By 2003, terrorism subsided and employment rose to 183,000; it has since modestly continued on that trajectory.[33]

Table 7.1 summarizes these observations. Note the periods in which terrorism began to rise, reach a plateau, and wind down. As we can see, there are instances when employment falls after an attack and gradually rises as terrorism subsides. There is also variability in each city and instances where an attack had no discernible effect on employment. The first attack on New York's World Trade Center (1993) left no imprint. To the contrary, employment continued to rise through the 1990s. The second, much bigger attack (2001) left a deep imprint, but by 2004 the city showed signs of recovery. London fell into a trough just as the IRA struck in the early 1990s, but its employment dramatically accelerated through time. Jerusalem fared somewhat worse and also somewhat better. Its drop-off was not as steep, but its recovery was slower and more modest.

Table 7.1

Employment and Terrorism in New York, London, and Jerusalem (in thousands)

City	1989	1990	1991	1992	1993	1994	1995	1996	1997	1998	1999	2000	2001	2002	2003	2004
New York	3,550	3,600	3,380	3,260	3,220	3,250	3,280	3,270	3,480	3,550	3,650	3,821	3,630	3,510	3,500	3,580
					WTC first attack								WTC second attack			
London	3,810	3,720	3,540	3,410	3,340	3,360	3,400	3,460	3,610	3,750	3,856	4,060	4,014	3,921	3,928	3,953
			IRA terror campaign													
Jerusalem		148.7	155.0	161.4	166.0	171.0	177.0	180.2	181.6	180.6	180.6	180.1	181.0	183.0	183.5
											al Aqsa terror campaign					

Source: U.S. Department of Labor, Bureau of Labor Statistics, *Current Employment Survey*, 2006; "City Research Focus," available at www.cityoflondon.gov.uk/Corporation/business_city/research_statistics/Research+periodicals.htm#focus. Jerusalem Institute for Israel Studies, 2001, 2002, 2003 *Statistical Yearbook of Jerusalem*; data were estimated for Jerusalem 2003 and 2004.

Might all this be coincidence and tied to other factors? No doubt exogenous factors played a role, though we can see the same fall and rise in other sectors of the local economy, particularly tourism. Foreign tourism is a useful gauge of resilience because of its sensitivity to large-scale, highly publicized violence. If a city were resilient, we would expect foreign visitors to return within a reasonable period of time. Indeed, in the immediate years after 9/11, New York's tourist traffic plummeted. A year after the attack, tourism had dropped by 25 percent compared to its pre-attack level, and by the second year it had fallen by more than 29 percent from its pre-attack level.[34] For a while it appeared the tourist industry would fade, but by 2004 it was back up and by 2005 the industry had fully recovered to its pre-disaster level of 6.8 million foreign visitors annually.

London's tourism was hardly touched by the attacks of 1990–93 and tourism actually increased. By 1995, London's tourism had grown to more than 13 million foreign visitors each year. Following some erratic years, London tourism continued to rise until the attacks of July 7, 2005.[35] The attacks of that summer changed everything, wreaking also a short-term effect on tourism. During the month after 7/7, tourism fell by 18 percent from the previous year and the decline persisted into August.[36] Not until September did tourism begin to revive, and it has now climbed to an all-time high. A possible explanation for the difference between the pre– and post–7/7 tourist reaction was the human toll of the latest attacks. London demonstrated again that mega terror aimed at people is more damaging to the tourist industry than smart terror aimed at things.

Jerusalem, where attacks have been especially aimed at people, bears out this generalization. Figure 7.1 shows the trajectory of terrorism counted by total casualties as compared to the trajectory for hotel trade, counted by numbers of foreign hotel guests. Observe the clear inverse relationship as the lines rise and fall in opposite directions. During the 1990s, low terror corresponded to high tourist visits and the number of foreign visitors surpassed 950,000 at the turn of the century. By the end of 2000, Jerusalem was in the throes of al Aqsa violence. Terrorism shot up and we can see tourism plummeting during this period. As casualties from terror continued to rise through the years 2001 and 2002, tourism continued to fall. By the end of 2003, terrorism had taken a sharp decline and tourism rose once again. The trend toward lower terrorism and higher tourism continues through 2004 as the lines move again in opposite directions. With the decline of terrorism, Jerusalem began to bounce back, though it is still a distance from record levels.

Office markets also reflect a city's capacity for resilience. They indicate willingness to invest in a city, use clustered environments, and take a chance on tall buildings. Jerusalem has relatively little of this kind of investment and almost no tall buildings, and we put that case in abeyance. But New York and London are the world's corporate office capitals and exemplify the dynamics of urban agglomeration.

Figure 7.1   **Elasticity and Resilience in Jerusalem Tourism, 1998–2004**
(foreign guests shown in thousands)

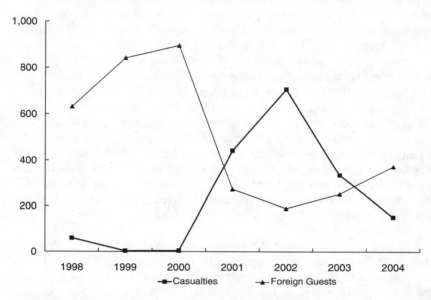

Source: Data derived from Table XII/4—Foreign Guests, Overnight Stays, Average Overnight Stays per Guest, and Occupancy in Tourist Hotels in Jerusalem, 1985–2004. *Statistical Yearbook of Jerusalem,* 2004. Jerusalem Institute for Israel Studies.

New York's rebound is instructive. After the loss and injury to lives, the most devastating effect of 9/11 was the loss of buildings and office space. The city's estimated property and attendant losses reach as high as $83 billion. The figure includes the loss of six buildings of the World Trade Center and the complete destruction of 13.4 million square feet of office space. Putting this in perspective, the destroyed space equaled the entire office stock in the city of Detroit.[37]

Under clouds of distrust for tall buildings, one might have expected the disaster that befell New York to have eliminated its market demand. Indeed, for a while the office market continued to soften, even in the wake of space shortages created by 9/11. In the two years after 9/11, office vacancies rose in Manhattan and elsewhere around the nation. By 2005, however, office markets had turned around. Mid-Manhattan vacancies shrunk to below 8 percent while lower Manhattan fell below 11 percent. Manhattan's office markets were not back to the halcyon days of the late 1990s, but they had considerably improved from the devastation of 9/11 and by 2005 they were the envy of much of the world (see Appendix, Table A14).

The news was good on other fronts as well. Surveys showed that more than half the displaced tenants had returned to lower Manhattan and many other firms had chosen New York locations.[38] Most encouraging, the bulk of those who sought new locations chose tall buildings of twenty stories or higher.[39] Elsewhere in the country, tall buildings were doing quite well. From Boston to Dallas, developers continued to put up skyscrapers and fill them. Among the first to ride the tide was developer Donald Trump, who tried to build Chicago's tallest skyscraper. Trump has also set his sights for a tall hotel and tower in Toronto.

Office markets have been even stronger in London. Vacancy rates in the central boroughs have halved in just two recent years. By 2006, empty office space had fallen to under 5 percent (see Appendix, Table A14). The largest development firms push hard to obtain construction permits for skyscrapers, albeit with great public controversy about their aesthetic desirability. The most fervid rush and the sharpest controversies transpire over who had already built or was about to build the tallest building. As of this writing, permission was granted to build London Bridge Tower, which will rise 1,000 feet (305 meters) above street level and will become Europe's tallest building. London also behaved in an untraditional manner when its plan explicitly endorsed tall buildings, cheered on by the effusive support of its socialist mayor.[40]

As Igal Charney points out, tall buildings have continued to appeal to cities.[41] Sometimes called "trophy" or "designer" buildings, they are now a source of prestige. Moscow and Seoul have already approved buildings that are twice the height of those planned for Chicago, Toronto, and London. Dubai has already granted permission to construct the world's tallest building. These new buildings exceed the height of the former Twin Towers.[42]

Finally, as if to defy the admonition against tall buildings (and possible attackers), skyscrapers are once again springing up at ground zero. The Freedom Tower is now under construction and so, too, is a 2 million square foot office tower not far away. As of this writing banks and financial houses are planning other skyscrapers in the area. While lower Manhattan's central business district had slipped after 9/11, it is now rising again as one of the nation's foremost financial centers.

Tall buildings have persisted against the wishes of dystopian value writers as well as the laws of economics. As commercial ventures, tall buildings are inefficient. Skyscrapers forever fight against their own weight because so much capacity is consumed supporting their upper height. Numerous airshafts, elevators, pillars, and other supports take up 30 percent of potentially rentable space. In the aftermath of 9/11, the idea of constructing still more vulnerable targets seemed inconceivable. One economist expressed his fear that "for at least a decade, the primary real estate issue regarding terrorist attacks will not be 60 versus 100 story buildings . . . but whether any unsubsidized buildings will be built by the private sector at all."[43] On this issue, modern economists have been outpredicted by architectural philosophers of another era. The "tall office building," wrote Louis Sullivan in 1896, "is one of the most stupendous, one of the most magnificent opportunities that the Lord of Nature in His beneficence has ever offered to the proud spirit of man."[44]

Resilience and Other Considerations

A fair assessment of these cities would conclude that they rebounded from disaster because of the strength of their social fabric, the dynamism of their economies, and the optimism of their citizenry. In his review of post–9/11 American cities, Peter Eisinger remarks, "If the texture and pace of city life are clouded somewhat by public anxiety about terror, the actual changes urban dwellers encounter in their daily lives in most places in the country and at most times are small and relatively unobtrusive."[45] With some qualification about *time of recovery*, much the same could be said for other cities around the world. For most other cities struck by terror, *time* is a key element in judging recovery because those cities lack the magnitude of New York or London.

Jerusalem presents the alternative view of a major, mid-sized city. In the midst of wave after wave of attack, the city looked as if it would never recover. This author was in Jerusalem observing the situation during one such wave and wrote in a later article:

> At least for the moment parts of downtown Jerusalem have begun to resemble older American urban cores that were shattered by de-industrialization. [Their] worn look creates a "broken windows" atmosphere that can only discourage business. . . . Once thriving retailers have now left and rental signs hang everywhere. Some rents have dropped by as much as 90 percent. Those properties that have been rented sell cheap, fast-turnover merchandise. Once upscale jewelry shops now offer inexpensive souvenirs for sale. Former clothing shops have been converted into storage facilities. Accessories and trinkets hang in store windows or lie on makeshift stands. The upper floors of some buildings have been turned into gambling rooms, exotic dancing studios and sex clubs. Downtown appears to be struck by the effects of a crime wave (bleak and downgraded) rather than war (complete devastation and rubble).[46]

The passages continue in this article, emphasizing that any pessimism about the city's future should be tempered by a number of caveats about drawing hasty conclusions. Among these was that "Jerusalemites are resilient, and even after a bloody attack they persevere."[47] Since then, the city has continued to recover. Foreign tourists have returned to its hotels, downtown streets are refilled, and restaurants have reopened. Tourism has not yet returned to its peak year of 2000, but it has come close and for a single recent year has now exceeded 850,000 foreign visitors. The city is also experiencing a real estate boom. Housing, retail, and office markets are robust and in many places prices have gone above pre-terrorism levels. While not all sectors have fully recovered, most have made substantial progress. Clearly, if Jerusalem's 700,000 residents show this capacity for resilience, we can say it is not the sole preserve of mega or global cities.

We should also acknowledge that while resilience entails recovery, it does not erase a disaster. Critical events, like terrorism, do leave a mark of one kind or another. Sometimes that mark can germinate into a movement that had been hardly discernible before terror struck; at other times it can accelerate recognized trends. Jerusalem's experience with attacks catalyzed an existing exodus of households from the center into the peripheries. The attack on New York catalyzed an existing movement of business from lower Manhattan to mid Manhattan. London's bout with terrorism took a society that was heavily ridden with surveillance and made it even more so. The final word on urban resilience may never be written, but Tom Wolfe's maxim that "you can't go home again" rings ever so true.[48] The challenge is to make that very different future a more secure one.

Sustaining a Better Future

The National Approach to Sustaining Resilience

Much of a city's resilience stems from its agglomerative nature and what might be called its natural dynamism. But this is hardly the end of the story, because a city's capacity for resilience is neither automatic nor is it unassisted. Rather, local resilience is helped and sustained by government. Government at all levels makes recovery possible and plays a critical role, whether that takes place by building infrastructure, educating the citizenry, stabilizing the social order, protecting society, or taking responsibility for a host of functions. For some, the laissez-faire state might have appeal, but it does not exist. Even private insurance is publicly regulated, publicly assisted, and often publicly subsidized. When great calamities strike, government is the foremost actor in rescue and reconstruction. Usually government at upper and mid levels takes the lead. At mid levels, states or provinces can play a role in staunching a crisis, but their geographic limitations and their resource constraints are insufficient to the task. Operating from the top down, national government is best able to cast the widest nets and most capable of coordinating local efforts. National government is also best able to enlist private enterprise or nonprofit organizations to work with authorities at all levels. Generally, the greater the breakdown the more it requires national attention.

This was certainly the case in the post–9/11 era, when free markets failed and most insurance companies refused coverage to high-risk clients. In the United States, the biggest and most vulnerable cities found themselves in a dire situation. Terrorism insurance was especially difficult to obtain in New York, Chicago, Los Angeles, and San Francisco. This put property developers in a quandary because lenders required insurance before a project could be financed. The absence of available underwriters went beyond new building construction and affected city debt ratings as well those of other public agencies. Since then, insurance premiums have risen dramatically, increasing the costs for both public and private sectors. On the public side, premiums for New York's transit system rose by 300 percent, and in the private sector, the owners of the Empire State Building paid 900 percent more for a lesser policy.[49]

Some insurance companies began to write "sunset clauses" into their policies that were designed to relieve them of future obligations. Other insurance companies have either refused to underwrite large-scale projects or charged enormous premiums to do so. Shortly after 9/11, more than $15.5 billion in real estate projects were suspended or canceled because developers could not obtain insurance.[50] In San Francisco, insurance for the Golden Gate Bridge doubled. In Baltimore, insurance companies refused to issue coverage for its International Airport and sporting events in Camden Yards. Under pressure from the state government of Maryland, the companies later relented.

America's federal government sought ways to fill the void and hastily strung together a broad safety net. The foremost means of doing this was the Terrorism Risk Insurance Act of 2002, or TRIA. The act was extended in 2005 through the end of 2007, presumably allowing the insurance market to stabilize and resume normal pricing. Only commercial establishments are eligible and only foreign attacks are insured. In the event of an attack, TRIA covers 90 percent of losses, after deductible payments are met. Losses above $100 billion are not covered by the act. TRIA also limits liability by precluding payments for property damages due to a CBRN (chemical, biological, radiological, or nuclear) attack. Overall, the restrictions are intended to spread the risk between the federal government, private insurers, and the insured.

Elsewhere in the world, the part played by national government in providing terrorism insurance varies quite a bit. France, Spain, and Australia make coverage mandatory, and national government has a direct role in making sure that coverage is complete and equitable. France has established common insurance pools with higher premiums for developers who undertake new construction. The United Kingdom allows insurance to be optional. This has posed problems for British theatergoers and other mass audiences. As prospects of a mega attack increased over recent years, so too did insurance premiums, and public events have borne the brunt of the pain. Insurance rates increased by 200 percent or more for highly publicized events. In tangible terms, this meant that the cost for a concert at the National Theater jumped by 250,000 pounds; the cost of an event at the royal Opera House rose by 500,000 pounds. Given the circumstances, the public would have to forego some events or pay more for a ticket. Because many cities depend upon culture and entertainment to drive their economies, the increased prices for a time dampened the revenue capacity of these sectors. Troubled by this turn of events, Londoners referred to the change as the "Bin Laden effect."[51]

Much of the insurance issue involves guessing about the costs of an attack, and a number of models have been used to estimate potential losses. Monetary estimates greatly vary, beginning at a low of $50 billion and rising to as much as $250 billion per attack.[52] Judging from past attacks, analysts seem to be anticipating significant increases in the cost of terrorism.

Table 7.2 displays a list of attacks and insurance losses for different countries between 1970 and 2001. Also shown are fatalities per attack. As we can see, the amount of insured losses has steadily climbed. The ascension started at a low of

Table 7.2

Largest Insured Losses Due to Terrorism, 1970–2001
(insured losses in millions)

Event	Country	Fatalities	Insured loss ($)
Attack on the World Trade Center (2001)	U.S.	2,749	47,000
Bombing in the city of London (1993)	UK	1	907
Bombing in Manchester (1996)	UK	0	744
First World Trade Center bombing (1993)	U.S.	6	725
Bomb explodes in London's financial district (1992)	UK	3	671
Suicide bombing in Colombo Airport (2001)	Sri Lanka	20	398
Bombing at London's South Key Docklands (1996)	UK	2	259
Oklahoma City bombing (1995)	U.S.	166	145
PanAm Boeing 747 explosion at Lockerbie (1988)	UK	270	138
Three hijacked airplanes dynamited in Zerga (1970)	Jordan	0	127

Source: Hartwig (2002a); Partnership for New York City (2001); and Saxton (2002).

$127 million in 1970 for airplane hijackings in Jordan, rose to over $700 million because of attacks on London's financial district, and culminated in a $47 billion payment in 2001 because of the attack on New York's downtown.[53]

The most positive view of terrorism insurance would acknowledge that it establishes a net below which victims should not fall. More tenuously, the net can be broken by excessive damages (above $100 billion) or by attacks that are not covered. Terrorism insurance is a retroactive way of ensuring a degree of economic security. While post-disaster relief is important, proactive measures are just as important. These, however, are not quite as clear cut; they involve an amorphous array of actions and are conducted by governments and private actors at multiple levels.

Multi-Governance Approaches to Sustaining Resilience

Grand policies can be proclaimed from high political posts and ambitious goals can be announced by presidents, prime ministers, and cabinet members. When all is said and done, however, the action is accomplished at the local level. City politics is the politics of the trenches, where mayors and local officials take matters in hand, do the actual implementation, and face constituents. This is particularly true of the United States, where local police are responsible for public safety and exercise considerable autonomy over policy choices.

Referring to the American situation, Susan Clarke points out that the greater the national security threat, the more important the local role.[54] Clarke is correct, and it could be added that threats do not rest at a single level but in a skein of multiple governments at all levels. There is something about imminent crises that creates a need to pull together different levels of government, even when the immediate challenge is to clarify results in an incomprehensible tangle of relationships. Lyndon Johnson's War on Poverty invigorated intergovernmental relations just as George W. Bush's War on Terror has given intergovernmental relations a new twist. Slogan-eering aside, the agenda of each "war" has been considerably different. Johnson's war converted cities into centers of development and income redistribution, while Bush's war has brought to cities an agenda of security and watchfulness.

The attention paid to terrorism at a local level is far reaching. A recent poll of Americans showed that terrorism was at the very top of the agenda. Fully 79 per-cent of the American public believed terrorism was "very important" (compared to 66 percent for Europeans).[55] At the local level, nearly three-quarters of American municipalities have invested in some type of emergency preparedness (technol-ogy, security, disaster preparedness). Cities have conducted mock drills, closed off buildings, rerouted traffic, and added police and have begun to reorient their emergency medical services.[56] While homeland security no longer tops the list of local priorities, it does appear within the top thirty-eight issues that public officials consider most important to address.[57]

The jumble of intergovernmental cooperation is bound together by federal funding. The major distributor of this largesse is the U.S. Department of Home-land Security (DHS). Since 9/11, that department had dispensed over $18 billion in assistance to states and localities.[58] Because the Patriot Act requires a minimum distribution of assistance, all fifty states plus Washington, DC, and U.S. territories received some amount. Within the DHS money pot, the largest program pertaining to cities is the Urban Areas Security Initiative, or UASI, whose total funding in 2006 was approximately $711 million. UASI funding is based on a formula that assesses three basic risk factors—namely, *threat*, *vulnerability*, and *consequences*. In theory, this should gear funding toward cities facing the greatest probability of attack and potential damages. Realities are different, though, and UASI funding has now been distributed to over 50 localities; central cities ranging in size from New York's 8 million to Sacramento's 445,000 are included.

Table 7.3 lists UASI funding for 2006. Shown in the table are thirty of the heaviest recipients, their funding in absolute amounts, and their per capita funding. Allocations per capita are based on metropolitan area population.

We can see the variation in amounts from a high of 124 million for America's largest city to the lesser amount of 7 million for smaller cities. The per capita amounts are revealing. Taking two high-risk examples, New York City and Wash-ington, DC, were among the highest recipients in both absolute and per capita expenditures. Each city also received a handsome proportion of the total budget. New York City garnered 18 percent while Washington, DC, received 7 percent. Relative to the previous year, however, both of these high-risk cities were down by 40 percent. New York's mayor, Michael Bloomberg, and Washington's mayor, Anthony Williams, protested the cuts. As their reasoning went, each city had already incurred much higher expenses than other localities and each would continue to be an exceptionally sought-after target.[59] Homeland Security was not persuaded and

Table 7.3

Urban Area Security Initiative Funding for 2006 (30 cities)

Urban area	Allocation ($)	Allocation per capita ($)
NY—New York City	124,450,000	13.15
CA—Los Angeles/Long Beach area	80,610,000	8.18
IL—Chicago area	52,260,000	6.16
DC—Washington, national capital region	46,470,000	8.89
NJ—Jersey City/Newark area	34,330,000	12.82
CA—Bay area	28,320,000	4.86
PA—Philadelphia area	19,520,000	3.78
GA—Atlanta area	18,660,000	4.12
MI—Detroit	18,630,000	4.17
MA—Boston area	18,210,000	5.32
TX—Houston area	16,670,000	3.71
FL—Miami area	15,980,000	6.84
TX—Dallas/Fort Worth/Arlington area	13,830,000	2.45
CA—Anaheim/Santa Ana area	11,980,000	8.49
FL—Ft. Lauderdale area	9,980,000	5.77
MD—Baltimore	9,670,000	3.68
FL—Orlando area	9,440,000	5.24
OR—Portland area	9,360,000	4.61
FL—Jacksonville area	9,270,000	7.90
MO—Kansas City area	9,240,000	5.00
MO—St. Louis area	9,200,000	3.46
WA—Seattle area	9,150,000	3.69
NC—Charlotte area	8,970,000	5.56
FL—Tampa area	8,800,000	3.48
WI—Milwaukee area	8,570,000	5.67
KY—Louisville area	8,520,000	8.16
NE—Omaha area	8,330,000	11.24
CA—San Diego area	7,990,000	2.46
NV—Las Vegas area	7,750,000	4.35
CA—Sacramento area	7,390,000	4.12

Source: U.S. Department of Homeland Security, FY 2006, UASI by Urban Areas (Washington, DC, 2006); State of the Cities Data Systems (SOCDS), available at http://socds.huduser.org.

instead awarded increases to smaller cities. Sacramento's allocation increased by 17 percent while Jacksonville's funding rose by 26 percent.[60]

For New York and Washington, DC, as well as other cities police protection and its costs are critical. In addition to heightened protection in densely packed, built-up areas, the new War on Terror mandates that airports and other forms of interstate transportation be covered with additional local police. Yet legislation pertaining to homeland security often prevents federal support for police overtime or hiring new personnel.[61]

While the costs for protection flow to cities, not all the reimbursements follow.

More often than not, states receive funding and pass it down to cities with instructions for the application of that funding. There are times when state priorities differ from those of their cities, widening the gap between response and need. Judgments about priorities are very subjective, and invariably political consideration will enter the mix, thereby shifting the emphasis from protecting targets to distributing rewards.

The conversion from a pinpointed policy measure to a more amorphous monetary benefit is hardly new to Washington.[62] Beneath the surface, a political pageant has been played out. In this pageant, allocations are spread to cities that can offer the rosiest presentation and summon the best rationales. What was once an initiative to concentrate funding in seven high-risk urban areas has been turned into pork-barrel legislation that distributes funding to a larger list of low-risk recipients. The allocations may very well be put to public use, but they are not well connected to the likelihood of attack. Policy analysts might say that a measure to ensure security has been turned into a distributive policy to reward friends and placate opponents.[63]

Inefficient spending may be the least of the obstacles confronting homeland security. The real problem lies in how to sustain the capacity for resilience over a lengthy period of time. At bottom, the objectives of homeland security are riddled by questions of how cooperation can be mustered across diverse metropolitan boundaries and how any momentum can be kept up. Individual metropolitan areas differ by size, number of jurisdictions, socioeconomic composition, political demands, and local culture. Ensuring security within any single area requires working with a great many parties—mayors, legislators, bureaucrats, and private contractors—where motivations differ, problems vary, and rewards are asymmetrical.[64] It is difficult enough to concert collective action among like-minded actors, but how to sustain a common objective amid this political cacophony is a challenge.

The challenge is magnified by the inherent inertia of public protection. Both *time* and *place* are critical but unknown elements. Given the perspective of time, we know that even the most frequently struck cities experience long periods of calm. Typically, assaults occur at the end of extended intervals and those periods can stretch into months or years. This is true even for one of the most incessantly struck cities—Jerusalem. That city experienced intermittent peace in the 1990s and has enjoyed another period of calm during the last three years. Taking New York as another example, more than seven years elapsed between the first and second attacks in lower Manhattan. Since 9/11, more than five years have gone by without an attack, and there is no telling when or if another such event will occur in New York. From the perspective of place, attacks could occur almost anywhere. Big, global cities have seemingly limitless targets. Is a transit system that stretches for miles most likely to be hit? Or is any one of the sixty-plus skyscrapers that fill Manhattan at greater risk? Or is a mass-attended concert most susceptible to attack?

It is by now commonplace in security circles to remind people that terrorists can choose both time and place, while defenders must always be on alert. Attackers require just one success, while protectors require a success rate of 100 percent. It is hardly surprising that over a period of time and at varying places, cities fall prey to what can be called asymmetrical reactions that swing between lethargy and hyperactivity. As used here, asymmetrical reactions are either not commensurate with the problem at hand or out of synchrony with the time trajectory of terrorism or not fully cognizant of realities.

The pattern is familiar to airline passengers during heightened periods of alert. It was particularly vivid for those who found themselves in the midst of an alert in August 2006 because of a threat to blow up aircraft flying out of London. The general scenario is something like this: During the first blush of training, security is ready and alert. In the absence of an emergency, alertness gradually fades. As readiness reaches a low point, an attack or threat catches personnel off guard. Having realized they were unprepared, security officials enter a period of hyperactivity or overvigilance. Picayune rules replace common sense, ordinary actions are viewed with unwarranted suspicion, and authority becomes overbearing. This behavior continues for a while, only to lapse again until the next real emergency.

Asymmetric reaction occurs in most cities around the world. Soon after terror struck Moscow, the militia closed roads, put public transport under intense surveillance, and began implementing strict rules concerning the possession of identification papers. Within a few months the alerts wore off and security forces fell into a state of indifference.

There are no easy answers to the problem of asymmetrical reaction. Any remedy must achieve a steadiness of response that is based on competence and practiced teamwork. The machinery of counterterrorism can be oiled by plans, drills, simulations, and "table-top" exercises. This might not be a substitute for the real thing, but it does enable first responders to be ready for the unexpected. Another remedy is to develop flexible responses that can be raised or lowered in measured steps. The key to achieving this lies in synchronized intergovernmental coordination. Governments can begin that process by clarifying and respecting mutual responsibilities. At the local level, officials should be able to comply with higher-level regulations, while avoiding the trap of goal displacement or becoming lost in mounds of rules. At national and state levels, authorities should exercise oversight while also delegating discretion to local actors, so they can exercise judgment and retain a sense of purpose. The balance between accountability and freedom of action is difficult to achieve, much less maintain over time. Terrorists depend upon surprise, and even modest reductions in uncertainty can mitigate the shock of attack.

Conclusions

The fears arising from 9/11 dystopia underestimated the city's capacity for resilience in the face of war or terrorism. That capacity not only varies by frequency and severity of attack, but also by the size of a city and the dynamics of its agglomeration. The ability of cities to bounce back from violent shock can be seen in the experiences of New York, London, and Jerusalem. In those cities, employment, investment in tall buildings, and tourism often suffered varying degrees of decline.

However, over time, these sectors recovered and some went on to do exceedingly well. Tourism is particularly sensitive to outbreaks of large-scale violence, but this industry too sprang back to life once terrorism abated.

For all the natural resilience attributed to cities, government plays a critical role in their recovery. In Europe, national governments helped establish a better equilibrium between insurance carriers and consumers. In the United States, national policies were instrumental in restoring insurance coverage in high-risk cities. The U.S. federal government also provided a system of aid to localities in order to deal with threats from urban terror. This aid has a tendency to be spread and watered down because of political pressures. Terrorism is still an important concern in North America and Western Europe, and still occupies an important place on the local government agenda. In many instances, local government is responsible for training and furnishing a cadre of first responders. While this has been a positive step, it is not without its problems. The challenges besetting government at all levels lie in bringing about collective action and sustaining long-term commitments. Governments also face problems in maintaining stable levels of performance. High performance is compromised by common patterns of asymmetrical reaction to terrorism, defined as a situation where behavior is not commensurate to an event. This is difficult to remedy, though a beginning can be made by synchronizing intergovernmental coordination and simulating critical events.

London: Surveillance camera used for congestion fees.
(*Photo by Hank V. Savitch*)

London: Underground crowds vulnerable to attack.

(*Photo by Hank V. Savitch*)

London: U.S. Embassy, guarded and blocked off.

(*Photo by Hank V. Savitch*)

Jerusalem: A bus blown up by a suicide terrorist.

(Photo ©2004 Yaakov Garb)

New York: Rescue workers at the World Trade Center.

(Photo courtesey of FEMA)

Part 4

Conclusions

Restoring a Self-Affirming City

Premises arise only as conclusions become manifest.

—John Dewey, "Art as Experience"

Self-Negation versus Self-Affirmation

The premises of urban terrorism are straightforward, and so, too, are the conclusions stemming from them. Terrorists attempt to use the city's own strength against itself, forcing it to implode. A small and determined group can turn a city upside down by exploiting its freedoms, its openness, its interdependencies, and its very magnitude. Catalytic terrorism plays upon the city's concentration of media to attract an audience by stunning it with acts of violence. Mega terrorism uses the city's demographic mass and density as fodder for casualties and to inject fear. Smart terrorism takes advantage of critical assets and infrastructure within a tightly coupled urban territory to promote chaos.

September 11 exemplified this potential for self-implosion by combining catalytic, mega, and smart terrorism. A handful of men turned civilian aircraft into military weapons and used them to ignite skyscrapers. While New York is an extreme case, its experience symbolized a malady that had plagued cities for some time. Over the years, "first cities" of the global, mega, and major variety were used in smaller though similar ways to act against themselves. In Munich, terrorists used an international celebration to create an international calamity, and in Mumbai (Bombay), they turned systems of mass mobility into a stagnant graveyard.

Nor has urban terrorism been confined to a few well-known corners of the earth. Its *scope* has been quite broad and its occurrence widespread. Terrorism's *frequency* can also be traced as reoccurring waves that are largely erratic and skewed by the temper of time. Distinctly ratcheting upward over time is urban terrorism's *severity*, or ability to inflict casualties. The sheer attributes of city life enable terrorists to act with greater efficiency, increasing the lethality per attack. Large cities are likely targets for mega attacks precisely because they hold an abundance of humanity, contain valuable assets, and broadcast an international message. Another reason for the increased casualties lies in the willingness of young men and women to become human bombs—bolstered by a success rate that turns primitive explosives into the ultimate "smart bomb."

The city's penchant to telegraph events to its citizens has also been turned against itself. Messages move quickly and bluntly through urban environments, and this allows terrorists to threaten unrelenting attack. By creating the impression that there is worse to come, terrorists can cast cities into a permanent state of alarm. Proximity magnifies fear. Media reports of terrorists acting in distant places are filled with euphemisms and soft descriptions of terrorists. Once the venue is closer to home, the reports change and so, too, does the descriptive language. A single mega attack leaves a lasting memory that can easily be transmuted into other fears—particularly as the use by terrorists of chemical, biological, radiological, or nuclear weapons no longer seems impossible.

Fear also promotes ambient suspicion and this strikes at the heart of urban life, preventing people from frequenting public spaces or riding on mass transit, making some unwilling to work in tall buildings. New York, London, and Jerusalem demonstrate the enduring effects of stress and anxiety on portions of the public. The consummate effects can be seen as part of the "friction of terror," where the menace of low-level, protracted violence frightens citizens into narrowing civil liberties. The very attributes of a "just society"—trusting, diverse, and tolerant—are brought into question to the point where cities begin to reject the values on which they were founded.

One of the great assets of city life is the anonymity afforded to those who want to disappear or reappear as the occasion warrants. But here, too, a virtue has been inverted. Not only can terrorist cells incubate within particular communities, but those neighborhoods can be used to access nearby sites for attack. Referred to here as terrorist haunts, these neighborhoods are usually located just outside the center city—in gray areas like Harburg or Seine–St. Denis. The initial attack on the World Trade Center in 1993 was inspired in nearby Jersey City; the attacks in Jerusalem between 2000 and 2003 were logistically supported from neighborhoods to the immediate south and east of the city center; and the coordinated blasts that ripped through Mumbai's commuter trains in July 2006 (known as 7/11) were supplied with men and matériel housed in rundown neighborhoods within a short distance of the sites.

The pattern of strikes on strategic spaces acutely shows how city assets can be turned into liabilities. Terrorists have been quick to latch onto this vulnerability by gearing their attacks to decontrolling territory. Their aim is to disrupt, destabilize, and where possible, paralyze civilian movement. Despite the differences in terrorist identity, terrorists do learn from one another. New York, London, Jerusalem, and Istanbul show that attackers share a similar modus operandi. Each of their central business districts accounts for a disproportionate number of incidents and casualties. The same spaces have been struck repeatedly and in concentrated blows. The objective is to eviscerate any semblance of public security and demonstrate that local authorities cannot shield citizens from attack.

Of course, patterns of attack will differ, depending upon the status of the locality. Here again, the cosmopolitan city can be turned against itself. Much depends upon the relationship of a city to the outside world, the ability of cells to establish logistical support, and the nature of the conflict in which the city is enmeshed. These circumstances shape the behavior of international versus local varieties of urban terrorism. International terrorism is likely to be sporadic though launched in larger doses—as mega attacks. Localized terrorism is more frequent and manifested in smaller assaults, often for catalytic effects. The lines between international and local terror, however, are porous, and a great many assaults receive aid from abroad. Even members of "homegrown" cells visit foreign nations for training and have important connections with international sources.

The ultimate irony is that in an effort to defend itself, the city often fulfills terrorist objectives. At a local level, the common defense is to protect citizens and strategic spaces through regulation, partition, and barriers. Obstructive measures like these effectively shrink urban space by making it unavailable or difficult to occupy. Even less obstructive devices like surveillance cameras, metal detectors, and heat sensors discourage the free and open use of urban space. Taken together with other types of surveillance, the results can be self-defeating. All too often, security agencies find themselves on slippery ground by overreacting, acting arbitrarily, or issuing blanket prohibitions—the sum total of which can suffocate the very environment they seek to protect.

Viewing this through a deconstructionist and dialectical lens, philosopher Jacques Derrida likens the Western response to the biology of autoimmunity, "where a living being, in quasi-suicidal fashion, itself works to destroy its own protection."[1] By Derrida's account, the city's reaction to terror has led to a self-inflicted pathology by "immunizing itself against its own autoimmunity."[2] The conclusion is inescapable. Self-negation is much like a disease, but rather than being acquired passively it is purposely and clumsily stumbled onto.

Derrida may well be pointing up a certain excess, but we should keep in mind that reversing an excess does not mean reversing the intended and basic process. Cities should be prudent about heavy-handed surveillance, but that does not mean they need relinquish reasonable uses of it or any other protection. To continue and perhaps embellish Derrida's metaphor, the pathology of "autoimmunity" does not preclude a healthy retention of "immunity."

As we know, cities are far from terror free. While most are not likely to suffer an attack, some will. It may very well be that fear generates its own fear, but fear can also be very real, and an interpretation of social contract theory would suggest that states owe citizens a modicum of protection. Nor does the issue involve a simple bifurcated costless choice of "doing" or "not doing" something to thwart terrorism. One way or another we pay a price—either for surveillance or for the lack of it.

At bottom, cities face two very different and contradictory conditions, each pitted against the other. One condition stresses urban vulnerability—either from unrelenting attack or from overreactions to it and the consequent possibility of self-negation. A second and encouraging condition is the city's capacity for resilience—its continued ability to ward off assaults or bounce back from trauma. As we have seen, cities are not easily stopped. Their economic and social agglomeration enables them to recover from assaults and in some instances barely notice a difference. Despite the hand wringing and dystopian predictions about the city's demise, New York has gone on to prosper. Jerusalem, subject to more persistent and severe attacks than almost any other city, has also gone on to a brighter time. London's social and economic strength was hardly touched by 7/7. Alongside these examples, Madrid, Istanbul, Moscow, and Mumbai continued to thrive in the face of urban terror.

Cities, then, appear to shake off the effects of terrorism. Some of this is attributed to localities growing used to violence. There has been talk about the "banality of terror," and citizens are alleged to have become less sensitive to the brutality of repeated attacks. But this reaction might have more to do with determination than banality. The local response may be an adjustment to a difficult situation and rest on the stubborn belief that people should not be moved by efforts to scare and intimidate them. This, too, is a sample of local resilience that is built into the social fabric.

Local resilience is a long-term and inherent condition of cities. It is nonetheless helped along and sustained by the political order. Without that sustenance, cities would be in a much more tenuous situation. When all is said and done, philosophers may have the last word about cities in a time of terror. Aristotle was among the first to realize that politics made the city possible. For him, the city was the only place where the good life was attainable.[3] It is altogether fitting to end this volume with an affirmation of Aristotle's creed that good politics can reaffirm the urban future.

Appendix

Table A1

Twenty-Five Nations, Regions, and Cities Struck by Terror

Nation	Major cities
Algeria	Algiers
Canada	Montreal, Ottawa
Chechnya	Grozny
Colombia	Bogotá
Egypt	Cairo
France	Paris
Germany	Berlin, Hamburg, Munich
Greece	Athens
India	Mumbai (Bombay), New Delhi, Calcutta
Indonesia	Jakarta, Bali
Israel	Jerusalem, Tel Aviv, Haifa
Italy	Rome, Milan
Japan	Tokyo
Kashmir	Srinagar, Anantnag, Jammu
Kenya	Nairobi
Morocco	Casablanca, Rabat
N. Ireland	Belfast
Pakistan	Islamabad, Karachi, Peshawar
Peru	Lima
Russia	Moscow
Saudi Arabia	Riyadh, Mecca
Spain	Madrid, Barcelona
Turkey	Istanbul, Ankara
United Kingdom	London
United States	Oklahoma City, New York, Washington, DC

Table A2

Global, Mega, and Major Cities: Share of National Population

First cities (global, mega, major)	Share of city population as percentage of the national total	Second cities	Share of city population as percentage of the national total
Algiers	5	Oran	2
Athens	7	Thessalonica	3
Berlin	4	Hamburg	2
Bogotá	15	Munich	2
Cairo	11	Cali	5
Casablanca	10	Alexandria	5
Islamabad	>1	Rabat	6
Istanbul	14	Lahore	4
Jakarta	4	Ankara	5
Jerusalem	11	Surabaya	1
Karachi	7	Haifa	4
Lima	27	Lahore	4
London	12	Arequipa	3
Madrid	7	Birmingham	2
Milan	2	Barcelona	3
Moscow	7	Naples	2
Mumbai (Bombay)	2	St. Petersburg	3
Nairobi	7	Calcutta	1
New York	3	Mombassa	2
Paris	4	Los Angeles	1
Riyadh	18	Marseille	1
Rome	4	Jeddah	12
Srinagar	9	Naples	2
Tel Aviv	5	Jammu	4
Tokyo	7	Haifa	4
		Yokohama	3

Note: Global cities are shown in bold italics; mega cities are shown in bold; major cities are regular type.

Table A3

Terror in Second Cities, 1990–2005

Nations	Second cities	Incidents	Casualties	Incidents: National Share (%)	Casualties: National Share (%)
Algeria	Oran	5	13	7	6
Colombia	Cali	10	3	6	2
Egypt	Alexandria	0	0	0	0
France	Marseille	5	0	5	0
Germany	Hamburg	11	3	6	2
	Munich	15	2	8	1
Greece	Thessalonica	9	0	5	0
India	Calcutta	1	24	3	1
Indonesia	Surabaya	1	0	3	0
Israel	Haifa	9	191	2	4
Italy	Naples	1	0	1	0
Japan	Yokohama	2	0	10	0
Kashmir	Jammu	22	340	2	10
Kenya	Mombassa	4	93	25	2
Morocco	Rabat	1	1	11	>1
Pakistan	Lahore	7	127	8	13
Peru	Arequipa	0	0	0	0
Russia	St. Petersburg	3	0	6	0
Saudi Arabia	Jeddah	5	27	13	3
Spain	Barcelona	8	53	12	3
Turkey	Ankara	17	9	10	1
United Kingdom	Birmingham	0	0	0	0
United States	Los Angeles	1	6	3	1

Source: Adapted from RAND database, available at www.tkb.org. Type 2 data.

Table A4

Terrorist Identity and Incidents in Twenty-Seven Cities, 1968–2005

Cities	Incidents	Anarchist	Secular	Religious	Other/ Unknown
Algiers	39		0	24	15
Athens	300	14	143	1	142
Belfast	N/A				
Berlin	44		7		37
Bogotá	98		49	1	48
Cairo	49	8	15	26	
Casablanca	8		0	4	4
Grozny	N/A				
Islamabad	29		0	3	26
Istanbul	151		46	6	99
Jakarta	17		3	4	10
Jerusalem	306		94	38	174
Karachi	52		15	8	29
Lima	257		175	82	
London	141		58	6	77
Madrid	70		38	5	27
Milan	41	3	13	1	24
Moscow	15		1	2	12
Mumbai	8		5	3	
Nairobi	4		2	1	1
New York	169		72	47	50
Paris	343	1	137	21	184
Riyadh	24		0	6	18
Rome	160		57	2	101
Srinagar	N/A				
Tel Aviv	90		30	14	46
Tokyo	29		9	1	19
TOTAL	2,444	18	962	210	1,254
Percentage	100	0.74	39.1	8.66	51.5

Source: Data from Terrorism Knowledge Base, available at www.tkb.org. Type II database.

Table A5

Terrorist Identity and Casualties in Twenty-Seven Cities, 1968–2005

Cities	Casualties	Secular	Religious	Other/ Unknown
Algiers	84	0	40	44
Athens	200	99	1	100
Belfast	N/A	0		0
Berlin	247	226		21
Bogotá	155	128		27
Cairo	272	41	165	66
Casablanca	134	0	130	4
Grozny	N/A	0		0
Islamabad	1,448	0	79	1,369
Istanbul	1,178	224	812	142
Jakarta	378	0	377	1
Jerusalem	3,019	1,078	1,435	506
Karachi	695	208	44	445
Lima	284	188		96
London	952	76	753	121
Madrid	1,872	79	1,791	2
Milan	10	9	1	0
Moscow	885	0	819	66
Mumbai	1,519	1	1,518	0
Nairobi	5,391	100	5,291	0
New York	10,969	125	10,819	25
Paris	1,256	545	229	482
Riyadh	333	0	249	84
Rome	371	267	2	102
Srinagar	N/A	0		0
Tel Aviv	1,538	683	658	197
Tokyo	5,033	15	5012	6
TOTAL	38,223	4,092	30,225	3,906
Percentage		10.7	79.1	10.2
Casualties per incident	15.6	4.3	144	3.1

Source: Data from Terrorism Knowledge Base, available at www.tkb.org. Type 2 database.

Table A6

Terrorist Identity in Twenty-Two Nations: Comparing 1968–1994 and 1995–2005

Ideology	1968–1994	1995–2005
Anarchist		
Incidents	12	25
Percent of incidents	0.30	2.23
Casualties	78	0
Percent of casualties	0.52	0
Casualties per incident	6.5	0
Secular		
Incidents	1,812	254
Percent of incidents	45.46	22.64
Casualties	5,399	1,665
Percent of casualties	36.08	4.92
Casualties per incident	2.98	6.56
Religious		
Incidents	219	175
Percent of incidents	5.49	15.60
Casualties	1,793	28,966
Percent of casualties	11.98	85.54
Casualties per incident	8.19	165.52
Other/unknown		
Incidents	1,943	668
Percent of incidents	48.75	59.54
Casualties	7,695	3,233
Percent of casualties	51.42	9.55
Casualties per incident	3.96	4.84
TOTAL		
Incidents	3,986	1,122
Casualties	14,965	33,864
Casualties per incident	3.75	30.18

Source: Data from Terrorism Knowledge Base, available at www.tkb.org. Type 2 database.

Table A7

Terrorist Identity in Twenty-Two Nations: Comparing 1968–1994 and 1995–2005 (detailed by group)

Ideology	1968–1994	1995–2005
Anarchist		
Incidents	12	25
Percent of incidents	0.30	2.23
Casualties	78	0
Percent of casualties	0.52	0.07
Casualties per incident	6.5	0
Leftist		
Incidents	828	139
Percent of incidents	20.77	12.39
Casualties	1,780	169
Percent of casualties	11.90	0.50
Casualties per incident	2.15	1.22
Right-Wing		
Incidents	3	0
Percent of incidents	0.08	0
Casualties	1	0
Percent of casualties	0.01	0
Casualties per incident	0.33	0
Nationalist/Separatist		
Incidents	978	115
Percent of incidents	24.54	10.25
Casualties	3,596	1,496
Percent of casualties	24.03	4.42
Casualties per incident	3.70	13.01
Environmental		
Incidents	3	0
Percent of incidents	0.08	0
Casualties	0	0
Percent of casualties	0	
Casualties per incident	0	0
Religious/Christian		
Incidents	1	0
Percent of incidents	0.03	0
Casualties	0	0
Percent of casualties	0	
Casualties per incident	0	0
Religious/Cult		
Incidents	0	1
Percent of incidents	0	0.09
Casualties	0	5012
Percent of casualties	0	14.80
Casualties per incident	0	5,012

(continued)

Table A7 *(continued)*

Ideology	1968–1994	1995–2005
Religious/Islamic		
Incidents	168	173
Percent of incidents	4.21	15.42
Casualties	1,791	23,954
Percent of casualties	11.97	70.74
Casualties per incident	10.66	138.46
Religious/Jewish		
Incidents	47	1
Percent of incidents	1.18	0.09
Casualties	22	0
Percent of casualties	0.15	
Casualties per incident	0.47	0
Religious/Sikh		
Incidents	3	0
Percent of incidents	0.08	0
Casualties	2	0
Percent of casualties	0.01	
Casualties per incident	0.67	0
Other		
Incidents	821	105
Percent of incidents	20.60	9.36
Casualties	3,934	962
Percent of casualties	26.29	2.84
Casualties per incident	4.79	9.16
Unknown		
Incidents	1122	563
Percent of incidents	28.15	50.18
Casualties	3,761	2,271
Percent of casualties	25.14	6.71
Casualties per incident	3.35	4.03
TOTAL		
Incidents	3,986	1,122
Casualties	14,965	33,864
Casualties per incident	3.75	30.18

Source: Data from Terrorism Knowledge Base, available at www.tkb.org. Type 2 database.

Table A8

Terrorist Identity in Twenty-Seven Cities: Comparing 1968–1994 and 1995–2005

Cities	Anarchist		Religious		Secular		Other/Unknown	
	1968–1994	1995–2005	1968–1994	1995–2005	1968–1994	1995–2005	1968–1994	1995–2005
Algiers								
Incidents			18					4
Casualties			29					38
Athens								
Incidents		14	1		115	28	106	36
Casualties			1		97	2	100	0
Belfast	N/A							
Berlin								
Incidents					7		34	3
Casualties					226		21	0
Bogotá								
Incidents			1		47	2	39	9
Casualties			0		54	74	25	2
Cairo								
Incidents			11	4	8		22	4
Casualties			92	73	41		55	11
Casablanca								
Incidents				4			3	1
Casualties				130			0	4
Grozny	N/A							
Istanbul								
Incidents			3	3	37	9	68	31
Casualties			2	810	156	68	120	22

(continued)

Table A8 *(continued)*

Cities	Anarchist 1968–1994	Anarchist 1995–2005	Religious 1968–1994	Religious 1995–2005	Secular 1968–1994	Secular 1995–2005	Other/Unknown 1968–1994	Other/Unknown 1995–2005
Islamabad								
Incidents			2	1			18	8
Casualties			2	77			1304	67
Karachi								
Incidents			4	4	14	1	14	15
Casualties			4	40	152	56	352	91
Jakarta								
Incidents				4	3		1	9
Casualties				377			0	1
Jerusalem								
Incidents			14	24	78	16	88	86
Casualties			87	1,348	675	403	339	167
Lima								
Incidents					172	3	79	3
Casualties					136	52	95	1
London								
Incidents			2	4	54	4	60	17
Casualties			1	752	73	1	120	3
Madrid								
Incidents			1	4	38		24	3
Casualties			100	1,691	79		2	0
Milan		3						
Incidents			1		11	2	17	7
Casualties			1		8	1	0	0
Moscow								
Incidents				2		1		10
Casualties				819				64

Table with 8 unlabeled data columns (column headers not present in this crop). Columns are given here in left-to-right reading order as (1)–(8).

City	Measure	(1)	(2)	(3)	(4)	(5)	(6)	(7)	(8)
Mumbai	Incidents	1						3	0
	Casualties	0				1,519		0	0
Nairobi	Incidents				1	2		1	0
	Casualties				5,291	100		0	0
New York	Incidents			46	1	72		44	6
	Casualties			1,070	9,749	125		20	5
Paris	Incidents			13	8	134	3	166	18
	Casualties			38	191	528	17	306	176
Rome	Incidents			2		56	1	90	11
	Casualties			2		267		102	0
Riyadh	Incidents				6			2	16
	Casualties				249			4	80
Srinagar		N/A							
Tel Aviv	Incidents		17	6	8	22	8	36	10
	Casualties		0	85	573	383	300	133	64
Tokyo	Incidents				1	8	1	18	1
	Casualties				5,012	15	0	6	0
TOTAL	Incidents	1	17	125	85	883	79	946	308
	Percent of incidents	0.05	3.48	6.40	17.38	44.88	16.16	48.67	62.99
	Casualties	0	0	1,514	27,193	4,634	974	3,112	796
	Percent of casualties			16.35	93.89	50.04	3.36	33.61	2.75

Source: Data from Terrorism Knowledge Base, available at www.tkb.org. Type 2 database.

Table A9

Terrorist Identity in Twenty-Seven Cities: Comparing 1968–1994 and 1995–2005 (detailed by group)

Cities	Anarchist		Leftist		Right-Wing		Nationalist/Separatist		Religious Islamist		Religious Non-Islamist		Other/Unknown	
	1968–1994	1995–2005	1968–1994	1995–2005	1968–1994	1995–2005	1968–1994	1995–2005	1968–1994	1995–2005	1968–1994	1995–2005	1968–1994	1995–2005
Algiers														
Incidents									18	6			11	4
Casualties									29	11			6	38
Athens														
Incidents	14	0	95	27			20	1	1				106	36
Casualties			45	2			52	0	1				100	0
Belfast	N/A													
Berlin														
Incidents			4				3						34	3
Casualties			200				26						21	0
Bogotá														
Incidents			42	2	2		3				1		39	9
Casualties			54	74	0		0				0		25	2
Cairo														
Incidents			6				2		11	4			22	4
Casualties			10				31		92	73			55	11
Casablanca														
Incidents										4			3	1
Casualties										130			0	4
Grozny														
Istanbul														
Incidents			22	6			15	3	3	3			68	31
Casualties			5	27			151	41	2	810			120	22

		C1	C2	C3	C4	C5	C6	C7	C8	C9
Islamabad	Incidents	1				1	2		18	8
	Casualties	0				77	2		1,304	67
Karachi	Incidents	1		13	1	4	4		14	15
	Casualties	0		152	56	40	4		352	91
Jakarta	Incidents	3				4			1	9
	Casualties	0				377			0	1
Jerusalem	Incidents	15		63	16	23	13	1	88	86
	Casualties	145		530	403	1,348	87		339	167
Lima	Incidents	169	3	2	1				79	3
	Casualties	135	52	0	1				95	1
London	Incidents	3		51	4	4	2		60	17
	Casualties	0		73	1	752	3		120	3
Madrid	Incidents	9		29	1	4	1		24	3
	Casualties	30		49	1	1,691	100		2	0
Milan	Incidents	5	3	6	1				17	7
	Casualties	3		5	1				0	0
Moscow	Incidents				1	2	1		2	10
	Casualties					819	1		2	64
Mumbai	Incidents	1	1	4					3	0
	Casualties	0		1,519					0	0
Nairobi	Incidents	1		1		1			1	0
	Casualties			100		5,291			0	0

(continued)

Table A9 (continued)

Cities	Anarchist		Leftist		Right-Wing		Nationalist/ Separatist		Religious Islamist		Religious Non-Islamist		Other/Unknown	
	1968–1994	1995–2005	1968–1994	1995–2005	1968–1994	1995–2005	1968–1994	1995–2005	1968–1994	1995–2005	1968–1994	1995–2005	1968–1994	1995–2005
New York														
Incidents			5				67		2	1	44		44	6
Casualties			3				122		1,048	9,749	22		20	5
Paris														
Incidents	1		58				76	3	13	8			166	18
Casualties	0		253				275	17	38	191			306	176
Rome														
Incidents			20				36	1	2				90	11
Casualties			95				172		2				102	0
Riyadh														
Incidents										6			2	16
Casualties										249			4	80
Srinagar	N/A													
Tel Aviv														
Incidents			6				16	8	5	8	1		36	10
Casualties			146				237	300	85	573			133	64
Tokyo														
Incidents			8	1								1	18	1
Casualties			15									5,012	6	0
TOTAL														
Incidents	1	17	473	40	3	1	407	38	78	83	47	2	946	308
Percent of incidents	0.05	3.48	24.23	8.15	0.15	0.20	20.49	7.74	4	16.9	2.44	0.44	48.67	62.99
Casualties	0	0	1,139	155	1	0	3,494	819	1,492	22,181	22	5,012	3,112	796
Percent of casualties	0.00	0.00	12.30	0.55	0.01	0.00	37.73	2.83	16.1	76.58	0.2	17.3	33.61	2.75
Casualties per incident	0.00	0.00	2.41	3.88	0.33	0.00	8.74	21.55	29.6	267.2	0.4	2,506	3.2	2.51

Source: Data from Terrorism Knowledge Base, available at www.tkb.org. Type 2 database.

Table A10

Share of Terror Attacks in Jerusalem Neighborhoods, 1998–2005

Neighborhoods	Incidents	Attempted incidents	Casualties
Talpiot	1	1	0
West Jerusalem	1		47
Gilo	43	1	86
French Hill	9	2	144
Old City	14		12
Al Tur	1		0
Armon Hanatzir promenade	3		4
Beit Hanina	1		1
Center/Downtown	20	3	932
East Jerusalem/Mount Scopus/Hebrew University/Ra's al-'Amud	5		116
German colony	1		0
Kiryat Hayovel	2		35
Mamila	1		6
Mea Shearim	3		2
Musrara	1		2
Neve Yaakov	5		11
Newe Shemu'el	1		1
Pisgat Zeev	3		2
Qiryat Menahem	1		59
Ramat Shlomo	1		1
Ramot	1		1
Shmu'el Hanavi	2		141
Unknown	14	7	27
TOTAL	134	14	1,630

Source: Data from Terrorism Knowledge Base, available at www.tkb.org. Type 3 database.

Table A11

Share of Terror Attacks in New York City's Neighborhoods, 1993–2005

Neighborhoods	Incidents	Attempted	Casualties
British Consulate (Upper Manhattan)	1		0
World Trade Center (Lower Manhattan)	1		1,048
World Trade Center (Lower Manhattan)	1		9,749
Rockefeller Center (Midtown)	1		0
Empire State Building (Midtown)	1		5
Brooklyn Bridge	1		4
New York Stock Exchange (Lower Manhattan)		1	0
Herald Square Station (Midtown)		1	0
PATH Tunnels (Lower Manhattan/NJ)		1	
Unknown		5	4
TOTAL	6	8	10,810

Sources: Terrorism Knowledge Base, available at www.tkb.org. Type 3 database with partial additions from Type 1. U.S. Department of Justice, Press Release, August 28, 2004.

Table A12

Share of Terror Attacks in London's Neighborhoods, 1998–2005

Neighborhoods	Incidents	Attempted	Casualties
Lambeth	3	1	0
The City	2	179	
Westminster	1	170	
Kensington and Chelsea	1	0	
Hammersmith	1	1	0
Ealing	2	7	
Camden	2	1	491
Hackney	1		
Unknown	3	1	2
TOTAL	16	360	493

Sources: Terrorism Knowledge Base, available at www.tkb.org. Type 3 database. U.S. Department of Justice, Press Release, August 28, 2004.

Table A13

Urban Resilience: Tourism in New York, London, and Jerusalem, 1990–2005 (foreign visitors, in thousands)

Cities	1990	1991	1992	1993	1994	1995	1996	1997	1998	1999	2000	2001	2002	2003	2004	2005
New York									6,000	6,600	6,800	5,700	5,100	4,800	6,200	6,800
London	10,300	9,200	9,200	10,200	11,500	13,300	12,300	12,300	12,300	13,200	13,100	11,500	11,600	12,000	13,700	14,900
Jerusalem	N/A	N/A	N/A	N/A	N/A	N/A	N/A	N/A	N/A	N/A	953	296	211	278	414	850

Sources: New York City Official Tourism Web site, available at www.nycvisit.com/content/index.cfm?pagePkey=57 (retrieved on November 9, 2006); UK National Statistics—Focus on London 2003 report, available at www.statistics.gov.uk/downloads/theme_compendia/FOL2003/00Prelims.pdf (retrieved on November 9, 2006); Israel's Central Bureau of Statistics, available at www.cbs.gov.il/tourism_sp/t32.pdf (retrieved on November 9, 2006).

Table A14

Urban Resilience: Office Vacancies in New York and London, 2000–2006
(in percent)

City	2000	2001	2002	2003	2004	2005	2006
New York							
Downtown	3.6	9.5	13.2	13.5	13.7	10.7	
Midtown	3.6	8.2	11.1	11.9	10.1	7.8	
London							
Central London		7.8			10.0	9.6	4.9
The City						10.9	8.4

Sources: James Orr, Research and Statistics Group, "Outlook for the New York Metropolitan Area Economy," Federal Reserve Bank of New York, 2006. Available at www.njmeadowlands.gov/app_forms/NJMC_Econ_Test_30.cfm/James%200rr.ppt?&CFID=513773&CFTOKEN=56831945&jsessionid=72307ed66e1d$B5$A6$5. UK National Statistics Online (2003) "Focus on London." Available at www.statistics.gov.uk/focuson/london/.

Figure A1 Share of Urban and Nonurban Incidents in Twenty-Two Nations and Regions

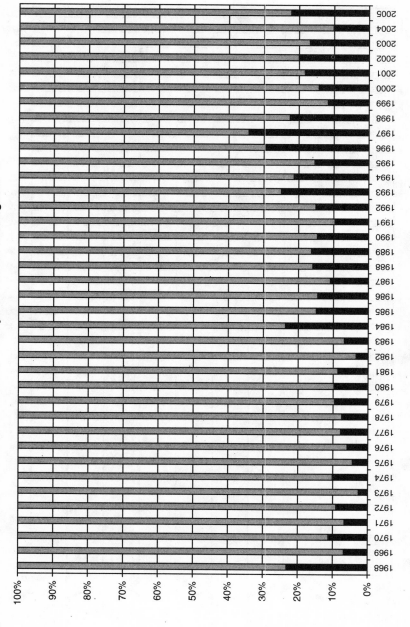

Source: Adapted from RAND database, available at www.tkb.org. Type 2 data.

196

Figure A2 **Share of Urban and Nonurban Casualties, 1968–2005**

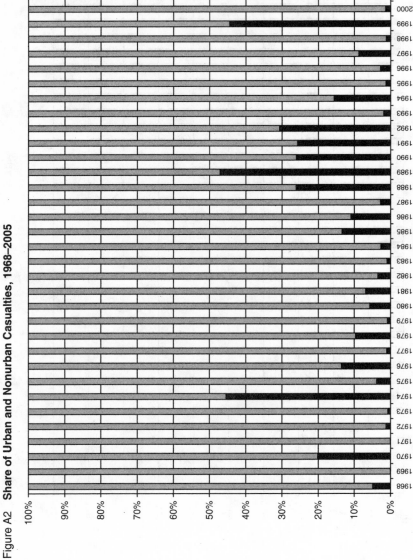

Source: Adapted from RAND database, available at www.tkb.org. Type 2 data.

Notes

Notes to Preface

1. The Rand-MIPT database builds on information from newspapers, information agencies, and radio and television broadcasts. In most cases urban areas are distinguished from nonurban areas. We nonetheless cross-check the locations for their urban designation and investigate areas where the designation is not made (about 10 percent of the incidents). We accept country or regional designations for determining urban versus nonurban locations.

2. Incidents and casualties for each database are as follows: Type 1: 12,741 incidents, 56,589 casualties. Type 2: 5,137 incidents, 46,138 casualties. Type 3: 8,335 incidents, 47,752 casualties.

3. There are a number of reputable sources for data on terrorism. These include the International Institute for Counter-Terrorism (available at http://www.ict.org.il) and the U.S. Department of State (available at http://www.state.gov/s/ct/rls/pgtrpt/). The source used for data in this study is the Rand-MIPT Terrorism Knowledge Base (available at http://www.tkb.org). Because Type 2 data have been consistently collected over more than three decades, it is the type most frequently used. The use of Type 2 data limits the analysis to incidents classified solely as international events. Perforce, cities like Belfast, Algiers, or Srinagar, whose terror is largely "domestic," are undercounted or excluded. Because it is comprehensive, Type 3 is used to confirm propositions that are also established from Type 2 data.

4. See Rand-MIPT at http://www.tkb.org.

5. U.S. Department of Defense, http://www.usip.org/class/guides/terrorism.pdf. U.S. State Department, *U.S. CODE*, Title 22, Section 2656 (f) (n.d.). U.S. Department of State, *Patterns of Global Terrorism* (Washington, DC: U.S. Government Printing Office, 1990), available at http://www.state.gov/s/ct/rls/pgtrpt/; and the EU, Framework Decision on Combating Terrorism (2002), available at http://www.statewatch.org /news/2002/jul/frameterr622en00030007.pdf.

Notes to Chapter 1

1. Figures will vary somewhat according to the database used. Urban incidents account for 76 percent of the total, and urban casualties account for 85 percent of all casualties. Casualties break down as almost 12,000 fatalities and 50,000 injuries, accounting respectively for 71.7 and 88.6 percent of the total. The figures cover only the twenty-five nations and regions used in this study. Adapted from RAND database at www.tkb.org Type 1 data. See also Chapter 2 Table 2.1 for Type 2 data.

2. It might be best to begin with the usage of key terms like terrorism, terror, and terrorist. As defined by *Webster's International Dictionary*, terrorism is best described

as an *act* by which extreme fear is brought about for political purposes. Terrorism is also something that occurs as a result of an action, or more typically as a series of actions. There is, too, an "ism" in terrorism, which allows it to be seen as the adoption of or belief in a set of actions for bringing about a certain result. By comparison, terror is best described as a *state of mind* characterized by extreme fear, which is sought by those committing acts of terror in order to change people's political conduct. A terrorist is a person who commits these acts. Terrorists actively and purposefully use violence against noncombatants. A succinct illustration of these three distinctions could be made by referring to those who have experienced the terror of terrorism brought on by terrorists.

3. One review of the concept of terrorism comes up with 109 definitions of terrorism, and a noted scholar in the field is skeptical about agreement on a single definition. Nevertheless, terrorism does have certain common elements, and even skeptics agree that these include violence against noncombatants designed to threaten and induce fear. See Alex Schmidt and Albert Jongman, *Political Terrorism* (New Brunswick, NJ: Transaction Books, 1988). The notion of common elements of terrorism has yielded historical and conceptual work. See Walter Laquer, *Terrorism* (London: Weidenfeld & Nicolson, 1977); Laquer, "Reflections on Terrorism," *Foreign Affairs* 65: 1 (1986); Laquer, *The Age of Terrorism* (Boston: Little, Brown, 1987).

4. U.S. Department of State, *U.S. Code*, Title 22, Section 2656 (f) (n.d.). U.S. Department of State, *Patterns of Global Terrorism 1990* (Washington, DC: U.S. Government Printing Office, 1990), available at http://www.state.gov/s/ct/rls/pgtrpt/. U.S. Department of State, *Patterns of Global Terrorism 1993–2001*. Released by the Office of the Coordinator for Counterterrorism (2002), Washington, DC.

5. As with any definition, the challenge lies in the accuracy and consistency of its applications. Not all acts of maiming, killing, and so forth of noncombatants will easily fit within this definition, but many will be accommodated by it. Not all situations are pure, and at times they are distinguished by a fine line. This is why the definition is best applied as a continuum with varying degrees of conformity. Much like a court of justice defines and decides various degrees of homicide, so too might we be able to distinguish among types of terrorism and evaluate borderline cases. See Laquer, "Postmodern Terrorism," *Foreign Affairs* 75 (1996): 24; Louise Richardson, "Global Rebels," *Harvard International Review* 20 (1998): 52; and A.T. Turk, "Social Dynamics of Terrorism," *Annals of the American Academy of Political and Social Science* 463 (1982): 119–128.

6. For general treatment of the subject, see Jessica Stern, *The Ultimate Terrorist* (Cambridge, MA: Harvard University Press, 1999); and Bruce Hoffman, *Inside Terrorism* (New York: Columbia University Press, 1998).

7. There are good reasons for these distinctions. Labeling conventional warfare as terrorist would be meaningless because it would be boundless, it would lack precision, and it would be devoid of conceptual signals through which particular kinds of acts could be identified. Put another way, if every violent act can be called terrorist, nothing can be seen as an act of terrorism.

8. Robert Pape argues that for policy reasons it is impractical to include state terrorism within the general category of terrorism. Pape also reasons that the incentives as well as the pressures that shape the behavior for nonstate or group terrorists are quite different. Thus, he defines terrorism as involving "the use of violence by an organization other than a national government to intimidate or frighten a target audience." See Robert Pape, *Dying to Win* (New York: Random House, 2005), pp. 9,

200. Andrew Kydd and Barbara Walter also define terrorism as "the use of violence against civilians by nonstate actors to attain political goals." See Andrew Kydd and Barbara Walter, "The Strategies of Terrorism," *International Security* 31, 1 (2006): 49–80.

9. This is not to say there are no exceptions to these distinctions. These distinctions, however, are reasonably consistent and applicable in a general manner.

10. The more accepted a terrorist organization becomes within a given society, the greater the probability it will develop more complex and hierarchical forms. In fact, as Hezbollah makes greater use of guerrilla warfare, it has become more formal.

11. This is not to say that nonstate terrorists cannot acquire nuclear or chemical or high-tech weapons. But even here, such weapons are likely to be relatively primitive, consisting of "dirty bombs," homemade chemicals, or pilfered nuclear weapons. See Graham Allison, *Nuclear Terrorism* (New York: Henry Holt, 2004).

12. In using terms like *decontrolling territory* or *territorial decontrol*, I mean to describe methods of warfare. It is then possible to distinguish between immediate or medium-range objectives as part of terrorist warfare and what might be termed ultimate political or ideological goals. The immediate objective of terrorists is to decontrol territory, though like all organizations they may ultimately have territorial aspirations. The Basque ETA hoped for secession from Spain and establishment of a territorial state. Jaish-e-Mohammed and Lashkar-e-Taiba also hold as their ultimate objective the incorporation of Kashmir into Pakistan. Hamas and the Palestinian Islamic Jihad hold as their ultimate goal the destruction of Israel and the establishment of an Islamic state in Palestine. Similarly, al Qaeda holds the ultimate goal of establishing a caliphate throughout the Middle East and even extending it to parts of Spain.

13. For a discussion, see Leonard Weinberg and Ami Pedhazur, "The Challenges of Conceptualizing Terrorism" (paper presented at the Annual Meeting of the American Political Science Association, 2003, Philadelphia, Pennsylvania).

14. Comparing a broad and diverse spectrum of terrorist groups can be challenging. There are, however, conceptual features to terrorism that make comparison quite feasible. The first is that terrorism is a type of warfare, and like any other type of warfare it is conducted by an array of very different organizations. In the same way that conventional warfare waged by Communist Russia, Fascist Germany, or the Anglo-American Allies can be examined, so too can terrorist warfare waged by groups as varied as Sri Lanka's Tamil Tigers, Peru's Shining Path, or the global jihadist al Qaeda also be studied. Second, this study places an urban focus on this variation and I examine terrorism as it manifests itself from the unique perspective of the city and its consequences for urban life.

15. To elaborate, internal complexity allows for greater specialization, more detailed divisions of labor, and a need for different sectors of society to collaborate, hence the growth of pluralistic tolerance and the release of creative energy. This conception is very Jacobs-like, but also rooted in the literature. See Jane Jacobs, *The Economy of Cities* (New York: Random House, 1970); and *Cities and the Wealth of Nations* (New York: Random House, 1984). Also consult Peter Hall, *Cities in Civilization* (New York: Random House, 1998); Jay Forrester, *Urban Dynamics* (Cambridge: MA: MIT Press, 1969); and Richard Florida, *Cities and the Creative Class* (New York: Routledge, 2005).

16. For data on this, consult Pape, *Dying to Win.* Another study found that between 2000 and 2003 what could loosely be called "liberal democracies" incurred 51.1 percent of attacks while nondemocracies incurred 26.2 percent and those in an intermediate

category incurred 22.6 percent. Categories for this study were taken from the Freedom House classification consisting of states that are "free" (democratic), "partly free" (intermediate democracy), and "not free" (nondemocracy). See Gregory Gause, "Can Democracy Stop Terrorism?" *Foreign Affairs* 84, 5 (2005): 62–77.

17. This is not to say that cities can be considered as "independent variables" governing the incidence of terrorism. Cities might, however, be "intervening" or "interacting" variables whose presence enables individuals to use terror as a method of warfare. See Morris Rosenberg, *The Logic of Survey Analysis* (New York: Basic Books, 1968).

18. The definition of a city contains a strong territorial component. While cities are internally dynamic, they are identified by land area. Urban terror would not include vehicles like planes and large ships that are attacked outside a city's territorial boundaries. Some writers do see these modes of transportation as urban environments because they are continuations of urban life and considered as being closed, self-contained systems. See Richard Clutterbuck's *Terrorism and Guerrilla Warfare* (London: Routledge Press, 1990).

19. Robert Pape refers to terrorist efforts to gain publicity as "demonstrative terrorism." As distinguished from Papes's notion, catalytic terrorism goes well beyond publicity because it is also intended to shock, frighten, and draw immediate attention. See Robert Pape, "The Logic of Suicide Terrorism," *American Political Science Review* 97, 3 (2003): 343–361.

20. For details, see Nadya Labi, "Jihad 2.0," *The Atlantic Monthly*, July–August 2006: 102–106.

21. See B.L. Nacos, *Mass-Mediated Terrorism* (Lanham, MD: Rowman & Littlefield Publishers, 2002).

22. Quoted in Paul Murphy's *The Wolves of Islam* (Dulles, VA: Brassey Publishers, 2004), p. 179. See also Murphy's description of the Moscow apartment buildings, p. 104.

23. I use the word "essence" to refer to Max Weber's "ideal type." An ideal type is a construct taken from a particular perspective that abstracts a set of specific features. The extrapolated features are not typical, but rather "essential" to the meaning of the phenomenon. As such, an "ideal type" will synthesize a plurality of data and accentuate vital information by incorporating them into an emphatic composite. Terrorism is extrapolated in its pure form, or as the case may warrant, its "extreme" form, as a way to understand its ramifications. See Max Weber, *Theory of Economic and Social Organization*, ed. Talcott Parsons (New York: Oxford University Press, 1947).

24. Barry Rubin and Judith Colp Rubin, eds., *The Middle East* (Oxford, UK: Oxford University Press, 2002), p. 252.

25. See Thomas Hobbes, *Leviathan*, Introduction by A.D. Lindsay (New York: Dutton, 1950); and Daniel Bell, *The Coming of Post-Industrial Society* (New York: Basic Books, 1995).

26. See Todd Swanstrom, "Are Fear and Urbanism at War?" *Urban Affairs Review* 38, 1 (2002): 135–140.

27. See, for example, Dame Eliza Manningham-Buller, Director General of the Security Service, "The International Terrorist Threat," Speech at Queen Mary's College, London, November 9, 2006.

28. See John Mueller, "Is There Still a Terrorist Threat?" *Foreign Affairs* 85, 4 (2006): 1–8.

29. Ibid., p. 8.

30. Just a few representative samples include, Laquer, *Terrorism*; Pape, *Dying to Win*; Stern, *The Ultimate Terrorist*; Hoffman, *Inside Terrorism*; Joseph Lelyveld, "All Suicide Bombers Are Not Alike," *New York Times Magazine* (October 28, 2001); and Jeffrey Goldberg, "The Martyr Strategy," *New Yorker* (July 9, 2001): 34–39. A number of films also appeared in 2005 depicting terrorists, most notably Steven Spielberg's *Munich* and Hany Abu-Assad's *Paradise Now*.

31. BBC World Service, *Newshour 12:00 GMT*, February 14, 2006, available at http://www.bbc.co.uk/worldservice/programmes/newshour/.

32. Ibid.

33. I have identified global cities by their world "connectivity" as expressed by P.J. Taylor, "Global Network Service Connectivities for 315 Cities in 2000," Data Set 12 of the GaWC Study Group and Network publication of inter-city data, available at http://www.lboro.ac.uk/gawc/datasets/da12.html. This data set holds over 300 cities and while the top half-dozen cities are clearly dominant, the amount of world connectivity sharply falls off after that.

34. To simplify and for greater precision I have taken a restricted view of the concepts of global, mega, and major cities. Other writers employ broader definitions of various urban typologies and use ideas like "world cities" to convey their regional primacy. See, for example, John Friedman's "World City Hypothesis," *Development and Change* 17 (1986): 69–83. For useful treatments of this subject see Saskia Sassen, *Cities in a World Economy* (London: Pine Forge Press, 2000); John R. Short, *Global Metropolitan: Globalizing Cities in a Capitalist World* (London: Routledge, 2004); and Peter Taylor, *World City Network: A Global Urban Analysis* (London: Routledge, 2004).

35. The distinction is somewhat arbitrary, but not entirely so. Thus, a metropolitan population of 10 million people or more conveys the notion of a sprawling, unwieldy population that could in the future threaten its security. Metropolitan Paris is quite large, containing populations of 7 or 8 million, but this size can be managed. Once a city's surrounding metropolis exceeds 10 million its manageability is more problematic, especially if it contains large belts of impoverished slums and squatter settlements. See UN-Habitat, *The Challenge of Slums: Global Report on Human Settlement* (2003), available at http://www.unhabitat.org.

36. Thus, some first cities like Istanbul and London hold over 10 percent of the population, account for roughly 20 percent of the national GDP, and monopolize the national media. London has no rival in the UK, and while Ankara is Turkey's capital, Istanbul is Turkey's gateway to the West. In Germany this dominance is shared, so that Frankfurt reigns supreme in economic vitality, Berlin is the political capital, and Hamburg monopolizes the national media.

37. Scores were obtained through a universe of 75 cities, running from 100 as the highest score down to zero. The table displays 30 of these cities, and the lowest score for this selection of cities is 60. The methodology for calculating the severity score is borrowed from Richard Florida's *Rise of the Creative Class* (New York: Basic Books, 2002). To convert Florida's creativity index to a severity index, three equally weighted factors were taken, consisting of (1) number of incidents, (2) number of fatalities, and (3) number of injuries. Seventy-five cities were then ranked by these factors. Cities were given a rank according to each of these factors, and the rank number from each factor was totaled, giving each city a raw score. I am indebted to Anar Valyev for bringing this method to my attention. See Anar Valyev, "Urban Terrorism: Do Terrorists Attack

Cities and Why?" (Ph.D. dissertation, University of Louisville, 2007). Raw scores were standardized from 100 to 0 according to the formula listed below. (See Richard Nathan and Charles Adams, "Four Perspectives on Urban Hardship," *Political Science Quarterly* 104, 3 [1989]: 483–508.)

$X = (Y - Ymin)/(Ymax - Ymin)*100$
Where X = standardized values to be created
Y = values for different variables
$Ymax$ = maximum value of Y
$Ymin$ = minimum value of Y

38. These calculations are based on Type 3 data for both domestic and international assaults committed between 1998 and 2005.
39. See Valyev, "Urban Terrorism."

Notes to Chapter 2

1. For details, see the 9/11 Commission Report (2004) as well as the Federal Emergency Management Agency's *World Trade Center Building Performance Study* (2002).
2. For perspective on this, see Bruce Hoffman, "The Logic of Suicide Terrorism," and Hoffman (2003b) "Comment/Discussion" in *Terror in Jerusalem*, edited by Ami Pedhazuk and Gadi Paran (The Jerusalem Institute for Israeli Studies, June 30); and Jessica Stern, "The Protean Enemy," *Foreign Affairs* 82, 4 (2003): 27–40.
3. For a larger treatment of the subject see H.V. Savitch, with Gregg Ardashev, "Does Terror Have an Urban Future?" *Urban Studies* 38, 13 (2001a): 2515–2533; and Savitch, "Does 9–11 Portend a New Paradigm for Cities?" *Urban Affairs Review* 39, 1 (2003): 103–127.
4. The 9/11 Commission Report, *Terrorist Attacks Upon the United States*, pp. 71–72.
5. Unlike the Type 1 and Type 2 data used elsewhere in this study, these data take into account domestic terrorism for earlier decades going back to 1968. See BBC Report, 2005, http://news.bbc.co.uk/2/hi/uk news/4661753.stm; and Tony Blair, "Speech of the Prime Minister in the House of Commons," July 21, 2005, available at http://www.number-10.gov.uk/output/Page 7969.asp.
6. For details, see the National Memorial Institute for the Prevention of Terrorism (MIPT) Terrorism Knowledge Base at www.tkb.org.
7. The account is intended to provide the reader with an idea about the extent of terror and uses India's major cities to illustrate this. Pakistan too has substantial damage to life and property due to terrorism. Since 1968, Karachi has sustained 151 incidents and over 1,300 casualties. Islamabad incurred 39 incidents and over 1,700 casualties. RAND database at www.tkb.org. Type 1 data.
8. The author was the single exception. See Savitch, with Ardashev, "Does Terror Have an Urban Future?" Other papers include Brennan (1999); Cardia (2000); Ducci (2000); Mehta (1999); Renner (1998); Rogers, Bouhia, and Kalbermatten (2001); Rolnik (1999); Stren (1998); Voronin (1998); Wilheim (1999); and Yacoob and Kelly (1999).
9. Robert Fishman, "The American Metropolis at Century's End: Past and Future," *Housing Policy Debate*, 11, 1 (2000): 199–213.
10. United Nations, *World Urbanization Prospect* (2003): p. 77.

11. UN-Habitat, *The Challenge of Slums: Global Report on Human Settlement* (2003), available at http://www.unhabitat.org/ p. 2. See also the International School of Geneva, at http://www.geographyjim.org/ and http://www.geographyjim.org/ Documents/Urban%20Debate/Urbanisation%20Notes.doc.

12. Sassen, *Cities in a World Economy*, p. 27.

13. Figures will differ depending on the particular year used. For New York City, see State of the Cities Data Systems, Output for New York, NY, available at http://socds.huduser.org/Census/incpov.odb. Also see Corporation of London et al., *London–New York Study: The Economics of Two Great Cities at the New Millennium* (2000), Section 1, pp. 14, 26.

14. John Mollenkopf and Manuel Castells, eds., *Dual City: Restructuring New York* (New York: Russell Sage, 1991); and Susan Fainstein, Ian Gordon, and Michal Harloe, *Divided Cities: New York and London in the Contemporary World* (Cambridge, MA: Blackwell Publishers, 1992).

15. See Larry Johnson, "The Declining Terrorist Threat," *New York Times*, July 10, 2001, p. A19.

16. Stern, "Protean Enemy."

17. Excluding the 9/11 attack, casualties for 2001 would have come to just 8.5 per attack. While worthy of note, this is a purely moot question because 9/11 did happen.

18. Walter Enders and Todd Sandler, "Is Transnational Terrorism Becoming More Threatening? A Time-Series Investigation," *Journal of Conflict Resolution* 44, 3 (2000): 307–332.

19. Hoffman, "Comment/Discussion," Part II, 8.

20. For confirmation of this growing trend see Robert Pape's *Dying to Win* (New York: Random House, 2005). There are differing accounts of who first took up the idea of suicide as a method of guerrilla or terrorist attack. Some attribute the idea to the secularist Popular Front for the Liberation of Palestine, which first used it in 1974 against civilians (terror attack). Others say the Tamil Tigers perfected it against the army in Sri Lanka (guerrilla attack). Hezbollah seems to have employed suicide in guerrilla attacks at an early date and in dramatic fashion. Hezbollah used explosive-laden trucks to drive into military installations.

21. David Veness mentions a number of features that make cities especially desirable targets. See David Veness, "Low Intensity and High Impact Conflict," *Terrorism and Political Violence* 11, 4 (1989): 8–14.

22. Anthony Tu, *Chemical Terrorism: Horrors in Tokyo Subway and Matsumo to City* (Fort Collins, CO: Alaken, 2002).

23. John Friedmann and Goetz Wolff, "World City Formation: An Agenda for Research and Action," *International Journal of Urban and Regional Research*, 6, 3 (1982): 309–344.

24. Jon Coaffee, *Terrorism, Risk and the City* (Burlington, VT: Ashgate Publishing House, 2003).

25. Israeli National Federation of Trade, 2004.

26. Dame Eliza Manningham-Buller, Director General of the Security Service, "The International Terrorist Threat," Queen Mary's College, London, November 9, 2006.

27. Bruce Hoffman, *Inside Terrorism* (New York: Columbia University Press, 1998), p. 61.

28. See Noam Chomsky, *9–11, New York* (New York: Seven Stories Press, 2001); and Stephone Graham, ed., *Cities, War and Terrorism* (Oxford, UK: Blackwell Press, 2004).

29. Michael Radu, "London 7/7 and Its Impact," *Foreign Policy Research Institute* 6 (2005): 5.

30. For an elaboration of this idea see Savitch and Ardashev, "Does Terror Have an Urban Future?"

31. See Jonas Rabinovich, "Practical Approaches to Urban Poverty Reduction," statement at the International Forum on Urban Poverty, Governance, and Participation, November 10–13, 1997, Florence, Italy; and David Satterthwaite, "The Underestimation of Urban Poverty in Low and Moderate Income Nations" (working paper on Poverty Reduction in Urban Areas 14, 2005).

32. See a splendid essay on this subject by Walter Laquer, "Postmodern Terrorism," *Foreign Affairs* 75 (1996): 24.

Notes to Chapter 3

1. In the United States, National Public Ratio (NPR) most often uses the term "militant" to refer to suicide attackers in Israel, Russia, and other countries. However, there occurred a palpable shift in noun usage when New York and London were attacked. In these latter instances, NPR discovered "terror" and "terrorist" to describe the situation. Similarly, the BBC insisted on the noun "militant" whenever terrorists killed Israeli and Russian civilians, and at least briefly found the nouns "terror" and "terrorist" when passengers on London's transit systems were killed. See Alex Safian, "Terror Rules at NPR," *CAMERA* (March 10, 2003), as well as Tom Gross, "The BBC Discovers 'Terrorism,' Briefly," *Jerusalem Post*, July 11, 2005.

2. Reuters Editorial Policy, available at http://about.Reuters.com. Accessed October 2004.

3. British Broadcasting Corporation, "Editorial Guidelines," available at www. bbc.co.uk/guidelines/editorial guidelines/edguide/war/mandatoryreferr.shtmi.

4. Michael Getler, "The Language of Terrorism," *Washington Post*, September 21, 2003.

5. Ibid.

6. It is apparent from the content of the interview that Secretary Rice took pains to emphasize the dismantling of terrorist organizations. While there was a single quote from Rice mentioning terrorism, the newspaper's reporters or editors were equally determined to avoid the term. Strictly speaking, this might not be a distortion, though the usage of particular wording did give the interview a particular tilt. See Steven Weisman and Joel Brinkley, "Rice Urges Israel and Palestinians to Sustain Momentum," *New York Times*, August 18, 2005.

7. Christine Chinlund, "Who Should Wear the Terrorist Label?" *Boston Globe*, September 8, 2003.

8. Michale Shuster, *Talk of the Nation*, NPR, May 19, 2003.

9. Years later, the Italian foreign minister, Massimo D'Alema voiced a similar opinion. D'Alema, however, was careful to note that it was simplistic to describe Hezbollah as "*solely* a terrorist organization" (emphasis added). D'Alema may have been searching for a straw man because most commentators who viewed Hezbollah as terrorists also recognized it carried out other functions. As noted, recent history shows that terrorist organizations can be multifunctional because carrying out social services increases mass support. See Meron Rapoport, "Italian Foreign Minister: Harsh Approach to Mideast Has Failed," *Haaretz*, August 8, 2006, p. 1. Eventually the European Union did designate Hamas as a terrorist organization, joining the United

States and Canada. See Staff Report, "UK, France at Odds over Banning Hamas Political Wing," *Jerusalem Post*, January 16, 2003.

10. In an effort to portray individuals who strap explosives around their bodies intending to blow up themselves and others, media guidelines advise journalists to employ "bomber" or "suicide bomber." While the term is confusing, it does not fall outside the bounds of accuracy.

11. For all its other biases, *Le Monde* does not shy from using the terrorist nomenclature and fully accepts it as an accurate descriptive.

12. Consider here three examples of the word militant. One well-known feminist who aggressively campaigned against pornography quite easily describes herself as a "militant." See Andrea's Dworkin's *Heartbreak: The Political Memoir of a Feminist Militant* (New York: Basic Books, 2002). Also, union workers with a high propensity to go on strike have been described as "militant," and the term has also been used to mean "extensive goal setting, resistance and membership mobilization underpinned by an ideology of conflicting interests. . . ." See Gregor Gall, *The Meaning of Militancy: Postal Workers and Industrial Relations* (Burlington, VT: Ashgate Press, 2003). Finally, for an account of a legitimate though radical political party called Militant Tendency, see Peter Taffe's and Tony Mulhearn's *Liverpool—A City that Dared to Fight London* (London: Fortress Press, 1988).

13. "The Egyptian Tawhid Wal Jihad Issues a Statement," Search for International Terrorist Entities (SITE Institute), available at www.siteinstitute.com.

14. Maria Reese, "Jayash Islamiya Claims Jakarta Car Bombing," available at http://cnn.worldnews.printthis.clikability.com.

15. Arnon Regular, "Hamas: Foreigners Should Leave Country," *Haaretz*, June 13, 2003, and "Arafat Calls on Palestinians to 'Terrorize Your Enemy,'" *Haaretz*, May 15, 2004.

16. Public Broadcasting System, Osama bin Laden, Interview, *Frontline*, available at www.pbs.org.

17. ABC News, Shamil Basayev, Interview, *Nightline*, available at http://abcnews. go.com.

18. The political price sometimes consists of threats to a particular news outlet or disapproval by sympathizers. As discussed earlier, neither conventional nor guerrilla nor insurgent warfare fits the "terrorist" description.

19. See, for example, Serge Schemann, "Day of Terror," *New York Times*, September 12, 2001, p. 1, and N.R. Klienfield, "A Creeping Horror and Panicked Flight," *New York Times*, September 12, 2001. For its part, the BBC labeled the 7/7 attacks as "terrorist," but as time elapsed resorted to familiar euphemisms. For commentaries on this, see *Economist*, June 24, 2006, p. 65, and Independent Panel for the BBC Governors, "Impartiality of BBC Coverage of the Israeli-Palestinian Conflict," London, April 2006.

20. See Center for Strategic Studies, "Post Amman Attacks, Jordanian Public Opinion and Terrorism," Public Opinion Polling Unit, University of Jordan: January 2005.

21. Ibid.

22. For an outstanding treatment of this subject, see Charles Perrow, *Complex Organizations* (New York: Random House, 1972). For its application to cities, see Susan Clarke, "Local Governance and Homeland Security" (paper presented at the Thomas J. Anton/Frederick Lippitt Conference on "Homeland Security in Urban America," panel on "National Perspectives on Urban Homeland Security," Brown University, September 23–24, 2004).

23. See, for example, E. Glaeser and M. Shapiro, "Cities and Warfare: The Impact of Terrorism on Urban Form," *Journal of Urban Economics* 51 (March 2002): 205–224. See also H.V. Savitch, "An Anatomy of Urban Terror: Lessons from Jerusalem and Elsewhere," *Urban Studies* 42, 3 (2005): 361–395; and Savitch, "Does 9–11 Portend a New Paradigm for Cities?" *Urban Affairs Review* 39, 1 (2003): 103–127.

24. As an empirical detail, terrorists are often not "weak," and relative to their victims can be quite "strong." For example, the Ku Klux Klan terrorized blacks in America's South for nearly a century. The Klan was the dominant party, and for a time their strength through terror succeeded in disenfranchising blacks. Similarly, in this century in Sudan, Arab marauders constituting the "Janjaweed" are clearly the dominant group and terrorize African blacks by carrying out campaigns of mass murder. Also, in Afghanistan, the Taliban were able to intimidate unarmed civilians by using brute force. The Ku Klux Klan, the Janjaweed, and the Taliban were or are strong relative to their victims while at the same time being low-resource groups that rely or relied on primitive weapons.

25. Quoted in Rand Center for Risk Management Policy, *Trend in Terrorism* (Santa Monica, CA: RAND, 2005), p. 31.

26. See Anthony T. Tu, *Chemical Terrorism: Horrors in the Tokyo Subway and Matsumoto City* (Fort Collins, CO: Alaken, 2002).

27. See Graham Allison, *Nuclear Terrorism* (New York: Times Books, 2004).

28. Richard Lugar, "The Lugar Survey on Proliferation: Threats and Response," United States Senate, Washington, DC, 2005, available at http://lugar.senate.gov.

29. The extent of the disagreement is considerable. Some experts judge the likelihood of a successful biological or nuclear attack to be "very low" or "extremely low," and the possibility of a chemical attack to be "low." See Michael O'Hanlon, Ivo Daalder, David Gunter, Peter Orszag, I.M. Destler, Robert Litan, and James Sternberg, *Protecting the Homeland: A Preliminary Analysis* (Washington, DC: Brookings Institution Press, 2002), p. 6. See also John J. Kiefer, "Implementing Strategies to Mitigate the Impact of Terrorist Attacks against the Built Environment" (Ph.D. dissertation, Old Dominion University, Norfolk, VA, n.d.).

30. See Michael Reinemer and Chris Hoene, "Cities Taking on New Security Roles amid Economic Concerns," *Nation's Cities Weekly* 25, 36 (September 9, 2002): 1–2.

31. For a powerful essay on the subject, see Gene Weingarten, "Fear Itself," *Washington Post Magazine*, August 22, 2004, p. W-18.

32. For a not entirely fair comparison of Londoners' attitudes after 7/7 and during World War II, see Charles Glass, "The Last of England: Churchill Gave London Courage, Blair is Serving Fear," *Harpers Magazine*, 311, 1866 (November 2005): 43–49. For an account of the editorial cartoon, see Sarah Lyall, "Londoners Grappling with Pervasive New Foes: Fear and Suspicion," *New York Times*, July 26, 2005, p. A6.

33. *Economist*, July 30, 2005, p. 12.

34. Pew Research Center, September 5, 2002, "One Year Later New Yorkers More Troubled, Washingtonians More on Edge, The Personal Toll Persists, Policy Opinions Change," available at http://people-press.org/reports/print.php.

35. See Darrell West and Marion Orr, "Managing Citizen Fears: Public Attitudes toward Terrorism," *Urban Affairs Review* 41, 1 (2005): 93–105.

36. Soon after 9/11, only 12 percent of New Yorkers agreed that they felt safe in that city, while the national figure was 17 percent. Oklahoma City and Washington, DC, residents, however, came closer to the national level. "Worries about Terrorism Subside in Mid-America," The Pew Research Center, November 8, 2001, available at http://people-press.org/reports/print.php3.

37. Ibid.

38. The reader can compare the results in the *New York Times*/CBS News Poll, August 17–21, 2006, p. 9, and August 23–27, p. 6.

39. David Cohen, Brian Gerber, and Kendra Stewart, "State and Local Government Actions on Homeland Security: Explaining Variation in Preparedness Efforts" (paper prepared for the 2004 annual meeting of the Midwest Political Science Association, Chicago, April 2004).

40. Pew Research Center, September 5, 2002, "One Year Later New Yorkers More Troubled, Washingtonians More on Edge, The Personal Toll Persists, Policy Opinions Change."

41. Following are the responses and sources for Table 3.1.

Geographical Proximity

Response 1—Percentage of people feeling fear (stress, depression, worry) depending on proximity to crash sites. Areas include New York, Washington, DC, other major metropolitan areas, and in the remainder of the United States.
From William E. Schlenger et al., "Psychological Reactions to Terrorist Attacks," *Journal of the American Medical Association* 288, 5 (2002): 586.

Response 2—Percentage of people feeling fear (stress, depression, worry) depending on residential proximity. Areas include upper Manhattan and lower Manhattan.
From Sandro Galea et al., "Psychological Sequelae of the September 11 Terrorist Attacks in New York City," *New England Journal of Medicine* 346, 13 (2002): 982–987.

Social Proximity

Response 3—Percentage of people who directly witnessed events.
From Galea et al., "Psychological Sequelae."

Response 4—Percentage of people whose friends or relatives were killed.
From Galea et al., "Psychological Sequelae."

Response 5—Percentage of people whose acquaintances were killed or injured.
From Schlenger et al., "Psychological Reactions."

Chronological Proximity

Response 6—Percentage of people worried by greater chances of attack before and after September 11, 2001.
From "Two Years Later, the Fear Lingers," The Pew Research Center, September 17, 2003, http://people-press.org/reports/display.php3?ReportID=192.

Response 7—Percentage of people worried by greater chances of attack before and after July 7, 2005, attacks.
From CNN/*USA Today*/Gallup Poll, *USA Today*, July 12, 2005, http://www.usatoday.com/news/washington/2005-07-11-bush-poll.htm.

42. *New York Times*/CBS News Poll, August 23–27, 2006, p. 4.

43. Gabriel Ben-Dor, and Daphna Canetti-Nisim, *Psychologically Coping with the Intifada: Haifa University Survey Finds* (National Security Studies Center, 2004).

44. See, for example, Yaacov Garb and Hank V. Savitch, *Urban Trauma in Jerusalem: Impacts and Possibilities for Recovery* (The Floersheimer Institute for Policy Studies, 2005).

45. Ami Pedahzur and Daphna Canetti-Nisim, "The Impact of Terrorism on Political Attitudes: A Two-Edged Sword" (Presentation at the National Security Studies Center, University of Haifa, 2004).

46. Avraham B. Bleich, Marc Gelkopf, and Zahava Solomon, "Exposure to Terrorism, Stress-Related Mental Health Symptoms, and Coping Behaviors among a Nationally Representative Sample in Israel," *Journal of the American Medical Association* 290, 5 (2003): 612–620.

47. The idea was born in the National Interstate and Defense Highway Act of 1956. Policymakers actually believed Americans could escape a nuclear attack by dispersing into the hinterlands. President Dwight D. Eisenhower recounts the reasoning and inspiration behind the national highway system: "Our roads ought to be avenues for persons living in big cities threatened by aerial attack or natural disaster; but I knew that if such a crisis ever occurred, our obsolescent highways, too small for the flood of traffic of an entire city's population going one way, would turn into traps of death and destruction." See Dwight D. Eisenhower, *Mandate for Change* (New York: Doubleday, 1963), p. 548.

48. See, for example, Todd Swanstrom, "Are Fear and Urbanism at War?" *Urban Affairs Review* 38, 1 (2002): 135–140.

49. For an account of how this works in Belfast, see William Nell, "Marketing the Urban Experience: Reflections on the Place of Fear in the Promotional Strategies of Belfast, Detroit and Berlin," *Urban Studies* 38, 5–6 (2001): 815–828.

50. An excellent summary of these symptoms can be found in Raphel Yehuda, "Current Concepts: Post-Traumatic Stress Disorder," *New England Journal of Medicine* 346, 2 (2002): 108–114.

51. Following are the responses and sources for Table 3.2.

Spatial Response

Response 1—Percentage of people uneasy about crowded areas.
From "Changes since September 11," *New York Times*/CBS News Poll, *New York Times*, June 11, 2002.

Response 2—Percentage of people uneasy about traveling by subway.
From "Changes since September 11."

Response 3—Percentage of people uneasy about going into skyscrapers.
From "Changes since September 11."

Political Response

Response 4—Percentage of people willing to relinquish some liberties before and after September 11, 2001, attacks.
From Amitai Etzioni, "American Society in the Age of Terror," in *American Society*

in the Wake of Terrorism: Communitarian Perspectives, 2002.
http://www.gwu.edu/~ccps/news_american_society.html#n_1

Response 5—Percentage of people willing to require metal detector searches for office buildings.
From "On Security, Public Draws Blurred Lines," *USA Today*, August 3, 2005, http://www.usatoday.com/news/nation/2005–08–03-security-lines-public-opinion_x.htm?csp=N009.

Response 6—Percentage of people willing to require Arabs to undergo special checks at airports (including U.S. citizens).
From "On Security, Public Draws Blurred Lines."

Response 7—Percentage of people willing to require Arabs to carry special identification (including U.S. citizens).
From "On Security, Public Draws Blurred Lines."

Response 8—Percentage of people willing that government searches for borrowed library books.
From "Changes since September 11."

52. *New York Times*/CBS News Poll, September 2003, available at http://www.nytimes.com/packages/html.
53. After the September attack, 42 percent of New Yorkers reported feeling "nervous or edgy," and by August 2006 that percentage stood at 40 percent. *New York Times*/CBS News Poll, August 23–27, 2006, p. 7.
54. *Economist*, July 30, 2005, p. 49.
55. *Transatlantic Trends: Key Findings* (Washington, DC: The German Marshall Fund of the United States, 2006).
56. Ibid., p. 16. Nations with the highest percentages are Germany, 67 percent; Slovakia, 63 percent; Spain, 62 percent; and Italy, 62 percent.
57. Unlike Long's framework, the ecology of games for terrorists does not entail "systematic functional results" where actions felicitously mesh with each other. See Norton Long, "The Local Community as an Ecology of Games," *American Journal of Sociology* 64, 3 (November 1958): 251–261.
58. In rejecting talks with the Chechans, Putin declared, "You find it possible to set some limitation in your dealings with these bastards. So why should we talk to people who are child-killers?" Putin's view changed when it came to Hamas, and he readily demonstrated his willingness to meet with that organization, stating, "The Russian Foreign Ministry has never regarded Hamas as a terrorist organization. . . . We should sit down together and listen and hear what others say, and we should make concerted decisions." "Putin Rejects Child Killer Talks," BBC News, February 10, 2006, and "World Should Not Cut Off Aid to Palestinians—Putin," Mosnews, January 31, 2006.
59. For Livingstone's remarks, see BBC News, "Mayor Blames Middle East Policy," October 5, 2005, available at http://newsvote.bbc.co.uk/mpapps/pagetools/print/news.bbc.co.uk. See also Michael Radu, "London 7/7 and Its Impact," *Foreign Policy Research Institute* 6, 5 (July 2005): 1–8. Aside from numerous other reasons, Livingstone's cause and effect is faulty. Algeria, which has virtually no oil,

experienced the most severe terrorism in the Arab world and hundreds of thousands have been killed in that country. Afghanistan, which housed the most notorious terrorists within al Qaeda and the Taliban, has no oil. Neither does Livingstone's attribution explain rampant terrorism in Indonesia, Thailand, the Phillipines, and the Indian subcontinent. Livingstone might pick and choose whatever idiosyncrasies might be blamed on Western foreign policy, but this self-serving selection hardly establishes a case.

60. For Galloway, see his remarks in the House of Commons, available at http://www.publication.parliament.uk. The same faults for Livingstone equally pertain to Galloway. Galloway is particularly crude on the subject of global capitalism. While capitalism is supposed to have a worldwide impact, he does not explain why terrorism has not developed indigenous roots throughout East Europe, much of Latin America, or most of sub-Saharan Africa.

61. For a complimentary account of Giuliani's performance see Fred Siegel, *Prince of the City* (San Francisco: Encounter Books, 2005).

62. *New York Times*/CBS News Poll.

63. Jill Lawless, "London Tube Reopens Month after Bombings," *Seacoast Online*, September 9, 2005, available at www.seacoastonline.com.

Notes to Chapter 4

1. David Rapoport, "The Fourth Wave: September 11 in the History of Terrorism," *Current History* (December 2001): 419–424. Jessica Stern developed the notion of terror as a "protean enemy" in "The Protean Enemy," *Foreign Affairs* 82, 4 (July–August 2003): 27–40. See also Gabriel Sheffer, *Diaspora Politics: At Home and Abroad* (Cambridge, UK: Cambridge University Press, 2003).

2. It is difficult to generalize or determine about whether religion was put to the service of terrorism or terrorism enlisted for religious and/or political objectives. See Sheffer's cogent argument in *Diaspora Politics* that terrorism has been enlisted in the service of political-religious ideologies.

3. For an account of Aum Shinrikyo, see Anthony Tu's *Chemical Terrorism: Horrors in Tokyo Subway and Matsumoto City* (Fort Collins, CO: Alaken, 2002).

4. While recognizing that "certain users of terrorism form a class apart," Charles Tilly comes to the conclusion that terrorism is a strategy and should not be judged as an ideology. On this count I disagree with Tilly, and would argue that because most terrorists are often motivated by ideological extremism, and leaving the particulars of ideology aside, they can be evaluated by the commonalities that make up that extremism. See Charles Tilly, "Violence, Terror and Politics as Usual," *Boston Review* 27, 3–4 (Summer), p. 10. See also Jonathan Ariel, "A War without an Enemy," *Maariv*, August 9, 2004, p. 1.

5. Thus Hamas takes pains to distinguish itself from al Qaeda, and in some ways the two organizations are different. The most obvious difference is that Hamas purports to follow the path of local jihad whereas al Qaeda embraces a world jihad. At a minimum, both organizations believe in Islamic rule, both are willing to intentionally kill civilians in pursuit of their objectives, and both have used indoctrinated suicide attackers to carry out warfare.

6. See Eric Hoffer, *The True Believer* (New York: Harper and Row, 1951).

7. The long-term data will hold the longitudinal advantage of being able to collect more incidents over time with a narrow field of subjects. The recent, short-

term data will hold a broader field of subjects, but these are constricted by a more limited time frame. Used together they can confirm basic patterns. These databases cannot be used in comparison with each other, but rather to verify a set of independent propositions. These databases conform to the Type 2 and Type 3 data described in Chapter 1.

8. As distinguished from casualties, David Tucker develops a lethality index. See David Tucker, "What Is New about the New Terrorism and How Dangerous Is It?" *Terrorism and Political Violence* 13, 3 (Autumn 2001): 1–14.

9. *New York Times*, March 14, 2004, section 4, p. 1. C.J.M. Drake, *Terrorists' Target Selection* (London: Macmillan Press, 1998).

10. See Drake, *Terrorists' Target Selection*, 104.

11. The nationalist LTTE (Tamil Tigers) also used suicide terror, and while they have inflicted high casualties, their human toll is still much smaller than that of their Islamist counterparts. Thus, between 1968 and 2005, the Tamil Tigers were responsible for 134 attacks resulting in 3,060 casualties, or 22.83 casualties per attack. Compare this with Islamist terror for the same period resulting in over 200 incidents and more than 30,000 casualties, or 143.9 casualties per attack (Rand Corporation, Terrorist Knowledge Base, www.tkb.org). Any doubts about the use to which Islam has been put to rationalize terror should be resolved by consulting the film "Ask for Death. The Indoctrination of Palestinian Children to Seek Death for Allah–Shahada," Itamar Marcus, Director of Palestinian Media Watch, available at http://www.pmw.org.il/. The notion of martyrdom is very much an Islamic concept and used extensively to justify suicide attacks.

12. While some attribute the onset of suicide terrorism to the LTTE (Tamil Tigers) of Sri Lanka, the "model" for such attacks was furnished by Hezbollah in Lebanon. In October 1983, Hezbollah carried out suicide attacks that killed 241 American marines at the multinational force barracks in Beirut. Ehud Sprinzak argues that the Tamil Tigers made a strategic decision to adopt the method of suicide attack after observing its lethal effectiveness in the 1983 suicide bombings of the U.S. and French barracks in Beirut. The Tamil Tigers first began employing suicide operations in 1987 in their efforts to retard the movement of Sri Lankan troops into Jaffna City. These attacks involved driving explosives-laden trucks into Sri Lankan army positions. See Ehud Sprinzak, "Rational Fanatics," *Foreign Policy* 120 (September–October 2000): pp. 66–73.

13. See Roger Masters, "Pre-Emptive War, Iraq and Suicide Bombers," *Forum* 1, 2 (2002): pp. 1–3.

14. While the distinction between secular and religious terrorism is relatively clear, the line between religious and political terrorism often blurs. Religious terrorists like Hamas often have political goals. While Hamas can be considered to be a political and a religious organization, its objective lies in the ascendance to government by clerics or theocrats. See Sheffer, *Diaspora Politics*.

15. The United States still has a formidable array of neofascist/nationalist groups. The attack in Oklahoma City was carried out by Timothy McVeigh and Terry Nichols, who represent the extremes of this identity. South America's leading terrorists are members of leftist revolutionary organizations such as the Revolutionary Armed Force of Colombia (FARC) and Peru's Shining Path. With the exception of Sri Lanka's Tamil Tigers, the Indian subcontinent and Southeast Asia are dominated by Islamist /nationalist terrorism.

16. For the cost of the 9/11 attack, see the 9/11 Commission Report, *Terrorist*

Attacks upon the United States, p. 169. For the cost of 7/7, see House of Commons, *Report of the Official Account of the Bombings in London on 7 July, 2005* (London, the Stationery Office, May 2006). Where applicable, the amounts were converted to dollars using exchange rates that were current at the time. The exchange rate for the year 2005 was calculated at 1.8 dollars per British pound. Other writers have come up with lower cost estimates. See Michael Buchanan, "London Bombs Cost Just Hundreds," British Broadcast Corporation, available at http://newsvote.bbc.co.uk (accessed January 3, 2006).

17. Rapoport, *History of Terrorism.*

18. Marc Sageman's excellent work, *Understanding Terrorist Networks* (Philadelphia: University of Pennsylvania Press, 2004), makes a different point. He reveals that while Milan, Madrid, and Hamburg have harbored world jihadists, other cities like Barcelona, Berlin, Rome, and Paris have not done so (p. 143). I find this not to be the case for the Parisian area, especially if we are talking about Maghrebian terrorism. See Jean Chichizola "Une filière de braqueurs et d'islamistes démantelée," *Le Figaro*, December 13, 2005, pp. 1, 11.

19. *Le Monde*, December 25, 2004.

20. Reuters, October 4, 2004.

21. This section is drawn from Lorenzo Vidino, "Is Italy Next in Line after London?" *Terrorism Monitor* 3:18 (Washington, DC: The Jamestown Foundation, September 21, 2005).

22. "Al Qaeda's New Front," Public Broadcasting System Video, www.pbs.org.

23. Ibid., p. 5.

24. This section is drawn from Paul Tumelty, "An In-Depth Look at the London Bombers," *Terrorism Monitor* 3:15 (Washington, DC: The Jamestown Foundation, July 28, 2005).

25. Particulars on London's boroughs can be found in *London Key Statistical Tables*, Crown Copyright, 2001 (London: 2001), Table KS09 A and Table KS11A.

26. Police did raid a North London apartment belonging to members of Hamza's mosque and discovered small quantities of ricin.

27. Simon Freeman, "Abu Hamza Jailed for Seven Years for Inciting Murder," February 7, 2006, *Times On Line,* available at http://www.timesonline.co.uk.

28. See Jens Dangschat, "Economic Improvement Divides the City: The Case of Hamburg" (manuscript, Department of Sociology, University of Hamburg, n.d.).

29. In total, the cell had eight members consisting of Mohammed Atta, Marwan al-Shehhi, Ziad Jarrah, Ramzi Binalshibh, Said Bahaji, Zakariya Essabar, Mounir el Motassadeq, and Abdelghani Mzoudi. See the 9/11 Commission Report, *Terrorist Attacks upon the United States*, pp. 160–173.

30. Elena Lappin, "Portrait: Atta in Hamburg," *Prospect*, August 29, 2003, p. 2.

31. Audio and video tapes discovered by the police revealed an extensive record of sermons urging followers to attack unbelievers and "slit the throats of Christians and Jews." See Douglas Frantz and Desmond Butler, "Imam at German Mosque Preached Hate to 9/11 Pilots," *New York Times*, July 16, 2002, p. 2.

32. Peter Finn, "Hamburg's Cauldron of Terror," *Washington Post*, September 11, 2002, p. 6.

33. Lappin, "Portrait: Atta in Hamburg," p. 7.

34. Sageman, *Understanding Terrorist Networks*, p. 151.

35. Ibid., p. 151.

36. Radu, "London 7/7 and Its Impact."

37. Manningham-Buller, "The International Terrorist Threat."
38. Sageman, *Understanding Terrorist Networks*, pp. 139–158.
39. The 9/11 Commission Report, *Terrorist Attacks upon the United States*, pp. 215–241.
40. Public Broadcasting System, "Al Qaeda's New Front."
41. Sageman, *Understanding Terrorist Networks*, p. 159.

Notes to Chapter 5

1. Kevin Hetherington, "In Place of Geometry: The Materiality of Place," in *Ideas of Difference* (London: Blackwell, 1977), p. 184.
2. See H.V. Savitch, *Post Industrial Cities: Politics and Planning in New York, Paris and London* (Princeton, NJ: Princeton University Press, 1988).
3. Lewis Mumford, *The City in History* (New York: Harcourt Brace Janovich, 1960). Louis Wirth, "Urbanism as a Way of Life," *American Journal of Sociology* 44 (1938): 1–24. Consult Jake Jacobs, *The Economy of Cities* (New York: Random House, 1970) and *Cities and the Wealth of Nations* (New York: Random House, 1984).
4. A foremost proponent of this view was Joseph Schumpeter, *Capitalism, Socialism and Democracy* (New York: Harper and Row, 1950).
5. See, for example, the treatment of different cities in Michael Cohen, Blair Ruble, Joseph Tulchin, and Allison Garland, eds., *Preparing for the Urban Future* (Washington, DC: Woodrow Wilson Center Press, 1996); and Roland Fuchs, Ellen Brennan, Joseph Chamie, Fu Chen Lo, and Juha Uitto, eds., *Mega City Growth and the Future* (New York: United Nations University Press, 1994). See also Fulong Wu, "Globalization, Place Promotion and Urban Development in Shanghai," *Journal of Urban Affairs* 25, 1 (2003): 55–78.
6. For an account of the discretion afforded to cities, see H.V. Savitch and Paul Kantor, *Cities in the International Marketplace* (Princeton, NJ: Princeton University Press, 2002), especially Chapter 2. For an interesting discussion of how planners make space, see David Perry, "Making Space: Planning as a Mode of Thought," in *Spatial Practices*, ed. Helen Ligget and David Perry (Thousand Oaks, CA: Sage Publications, 1993).
7. Type 1 data is portrayed in the table and its results compared to Type 2 data. No significant differences were found.
8. Not all terrorism works with this kind of consistent precision, and some terrorists will attack the nearest target of opportunity. But the most efficient terrorist organizations do exercise impressive levels of tactical and strategic awareness. For the indiscriminate nature of terrorism, see Raymond Aron, *Peace and War* (London: Wiedenfeld and Nicolson, 1966).
9. An adolescent later explained, "I wanted to die as a hero and meet 70 virgins promised in paradise." Stephanie Le Bars, "Un Jeune Palestinien voulait se faire sauter á un barrage en Cisjordanie," *Le Monde*, March 25, 2004, p. 1. See also Amos Harel, "Tanzim Recruiting Minors for Attacks," *Haaretz*, April 15, 2004, p. 1; and Jerusalem Post Staff, "Woman Found with Grenade While Holding Baby," *Jerusalem Post*, October 22, 2005.
10. See the U.S. Department of Justice, *The Al Qaeda Training Manual*, available at http://www.usdoj.gov/ag/trainingmanual.htm.
11. For a thorough analysis, see D. Radlauer, "An Engineered Tragedy: Statistical Analysis of Casualties in the Palestinian-Israeli Conflict, September 2000–September

2002." International Policy Institute for Counter Terrorism, June 24, 2002. http://www.
ict.org.il/index.php?sid=119&lang=en&act=page&id=5305&str=Radlauer.

12. Tel Aviv's metropolitan area contains 2 million inhabitants, while Haifa's
metropolitan district includes 980,000. As opposed to the metropolitan area, the
municipal size of Tel Aviv and Haifa is considerably smaller than that of Jerusalem.
Tel Aviv's municipal population is 360,000 while Haifa stands at 270,000 (Israeli
Central Bureau of Statistics, Jerusalem, Israel, 2004).

13. The breakdown for terrorist means of attack is for the year 2002. See Jerusalem
Municipal Government Statistical Profiles, 2003, available at http://www.jerusalem.
muni.il.

14. See Ami Pedahzur and Gadi Paran, "Lessons from the Numerous Acts of Terror
and Violence against Civilians in Jerusalem"; and Hoffman, "The Logic of Suicide
Terrorism," *Atlantic Monthly*, June 2003.

15. Masters "Pre-Emptive War, Iraq, and Suicide Bombers," *Forum* 1, 2 (2002):
1–3.

16. Hoffman, "Comment/Discussion."

17. Rates of incidence and casualties rates will vary according to the time periods
selected. Thus, over a recent twenty-five-year period, this small area accounted for
65 percent of all casualties within the entire city. See International Policy Institute
for Counter-Terrorism, 2004, Database, Herzliya, Israel, available at http://www.ict.
org.il. See also Savitch, "An Anatomy of Urban Terror: Lessons from Jerusalem and
Elsewhere," *Urban Studies* 42, 3: 361–395.

18. S. Hazam and D. Felsenstein, "A Spatial Analysis of Terror in Jerusalem,"
(unpublished paper, Institute of Urban and Regional Studies, Hebrew University of
Jerusalem, 2004).

19. For a succinct account, see Y. Sheleg, "A Short History of Terror," *Haaretz*,
December 3, 2001.

20. See, for example, Ami Pedahzur and Gady Paran, *Terror in Jerusalem*, as well
as Paran, Pedahzur, and Arie Perliger, *Coping with Terrorism in Jerusalem: 1967–
2002* (The Jerusalem Institute of Israel Studies, 2005).

21. Arabs and Jews are served by different school systems, utility and bus
companies.

22. Avi Dichter, *Security Chief Names Iran as World N1 Terror State*; *Says Security
Fence Is Vital*, Israel Ministry of Foreign Affairs, 2003, available at www.israel-mfa.
gov.il/mfa/go.asp?MFAH002r0.

23. David Makovsky, "How to Build a Fence," *Foreign Affairs* (March–April,
2004): 50–64.

24. For an account of this episode, see Beverly Gage, "The First Wall Street Bomb,"
in Michael Sorkin and Sharon Zukin, eds., *After the World Trade Center: Rethinking
New York City* (New York: Routledge, 2002).

25. Ibid., p. 48.

26. The practice of "preemptive arrests" by local or national agencies tends to
exaggerate threats because suspects are intercepted as quickly as possible—often
before any real act is executed. The reality of these threats is then unclear, though it is
fair to assume that some of them would have materialized.

27. Information on this can be found in Federal Emergency Management Agency,
World Trade Center Building Performance Study, FEMA, Region II (New York, May
2002).

28. The 9/11 Tapes, City of New York, 2006.

29. The account is taken from Ron Susskind, *The One Percent Doctrine* (New York: Simon and Schuster, 2006).

30. Ibid., p. xx.

31. The gradual accretion of events over a longer period of thirty years has resulted in about 300 incidents, leaving 119 dead and 1,550 wounded. See Tony Blair, "Speech of the Prime Minister in the House of Commons," available at http://www.number-10.gov.uk/output/Page 7969.asp.

32. The factions of the Irish Republican Army (IRA) consist of the Provisional Irish Republican Army (PIRA) as well as the Real Irish Republican Army (RIRA). The PIRA splintered from the IRA during the 1970s. The RIRA is a dissident group responsible for the Omagh bombing in August 1998. It opposed cease-fires in 1994 and 1997.

33. See Jon Coaffee, *Terrorism, Risk and the City* (Burlington, VT: Ashgate Publishing House, 2003), p. 75.

34. *Seaggate*, Associated Press, July 7, 2005.

35. BBC reports, www.bbc.co.uk

36. Caoffee, *Terrorism, Risk and the City*, p. 75.

37. The Corporation of London, *London–New York Study*. See also Tubeprune, London Underground Statistics, available at www.trainweb.org/tubeprune/Statistics.htm.

38. Ibid.

39. During this period and afterward there were scattered attacks and attempts elsewhere in London. In November of 1992, a bomb was found and defused at Canary Wharf, and in 1996 a bomb was detonated in the Docklands area of London, killing two persons and wounding 100 others. In 2001, a car bomb exploded outside the BBC's main television facilities, causing slight property damage and no injuries. See Coaffee, *Terrorism, Risk and the City*, p. 76, and BBC Reports, www.bbc.co.uk.

40. MI5 is supposed to have confirmed this claim. Consult Andrew Dorman, "The British Experience with Terrorist Networks," (paper presented at the American Political Science Association, 102nd Annual Meeting, Philadelphia, August 31–September 3, 2006).

41. See, for example, Prime Minister Tony Blair's statement a year earlier on the imminence of a terror attack, Intelligence and Security Committee, *Report into the London Terrorist Attacks on 7 July 2005*, Whitehall, London, March 30, 2006.

42. Manningham-Buller, "International Terrorist Threat."

43. Greater London Authority, *Report of the 7 July Review Committee* (London, June 2006), p. 73.

44. Ibid., p. 27.

45. Ibid., p. 12.

46. Ibid., p. 26.

47. Ibid., p. 34.

48. For a revealing account of London and the rise of Islamic radicalism, see Melanie Phillips, *Londonistan* (New York: Encounter Books, 2006).

49. BBC News, "Profile, Jawad Akbar" May 1, 2007, available at http://.bbc.co.uk.

50. Manningham-Buller, "International Terrorist Threat."

51. As can be seen from the figure, the next most frequent target is in the nearby Old City, located just across the Golden Horn. Terrorists have also attacked the Old City's "Old Bazaar" (a main marketplace) as well as the renowned Blue Mosque and Haga Sofia Mosque.

52. BBC News, November 20, 2003.

Notes to Chapter 6

1. For a discussion, see Howard J. Nelson, "Walled Cities of the United States," *Annals of the Association of American Geographers* 51, 1 (March 1961): 1–22.

2. See Lewis Mumford, *The Culture of Cities* (New York: Harcourt Brace, 1938), p. 15.

3. Quoted in Nelson, "Walled Cities of the United States," p. 1.

4. Henri Pirenne, *Medieval Cities* (Garden City, NY: Doubleday, 1956), p. 49.

5. Concrete slabs are installed in congested urban areas where wider barriers are impractical or to prevent sniping by gunfire.

6. See H.V. Savitch and Yaakov Garb, "Terror, Barriers and the Re-topography of Jerusalem," *Journal of Planning Education and Research* (Winter 2006).

7. The reduction in terrorist attacks is particularly well documented for Jerusalem. Since the partial construction of the barrier, terrorist attacks in Jerusalem between 2002 and 2004 have been reduced by 90 percent and casualties reduced by more than 84 percent (International Policy Institute for Counter-Terrorism, 2004; Pedahzur and Canetti-Nisim, 2004; Rand Corporation, 2004). A substantial number of attempts have either been stopped or mitigated, and potential attackers have been caught while trying to circumvent the barrier. (See Israel Ministry of Defense, 2003, 2004, *The Security Fence,* available at www.securityfence.mod.gov.il.

8. See Karina Landman, "Alley-Gating and Neighborhood Gating: Are They Two Sides of the Same Face?" (paper presented at the conference on "Gated Communities: Building Social Division or Safer Communities?" Glasgow, UK, September 18–19, 2003).

9. The literature on this subject is extensive. For gated communities in the United States, see Edward Blakely and M.G. Snyder, *Fortress America: Gated Communities in the United States* (Washington, DC: Brookings Institution, 1997). See also Adri van de Wetering, "Enclosed Neighborhoods in Perspective" (research paper, University of Pretoria, 2000). For South Africa, see Karina Landman, "Gated Communities and Urban Sustainability: Taking a Closer Look at the Future" (paper presented at the Southern African Conference on Sustainable Development in a Built Environment, panel on "Strategies for a Sustainable Built Environment," Pretoria, South Africa, August 23–25, 2000), and "Gated Communities in South Africa: Building Bridges or Barriers?" (paper presented at the International Conference on "Private Urban Governance," Mainz, Germany, June 6–9, 2002). See also Derek Hook and Michele Vrdoljak, "Gated Communities, Heterotopia, and a 'Rights' of Privilege: A 'Heterotopology' of the South African Security-Park," *ITDP Geoforum* 33 (2002): 195–219.

10. See Surveillance Studies Network, *A Report on the Surveillance Society*, ed. David M. Wood (London, 2006).

11. Surveillance can be seen as a form of protection and as an instrument of abuse. The fact of the matter is that societies usually require a degree of surveillance in order to safeguard citizens, but surveillance is also subject to overuse. For classic examples of the abuses of surveillance see George Orwell, *1984* (New York: Bantam Books, 1932); and Aldous Huxley, *Brave New World* (New York: Bantam Books, 1932).

12. These classifications are modified and the general idea taken from Taner Oc and Steven Tiesdell, "Urban Design Approaches to Safer City Centers: The Fortress, the Panoptic, the Regulatory and the Animated," in *Landscapes of Defense*, ed. J.R. Gold and G. Revill (Upper Saddle River, NJ: Prentice Hall, 2000).

13. For a discussion of urban osmosis, see Oc and Tiesdell, "Urban Design Approaches to Safer City Centers," p. 200.

14. Jane Jacobs, *The Death and Life of Great American Cities* (New York: Random House, 1961), p. 48.

15. Oscar Newman, *Defensible Space* (New York: Macmillan, 1972).

16. See Jeremy Bentham, *The Panopticon Writings*, ed. Miran Bozovic (London: Verso, 1995).

17. Quoted in Nan Ellin, "Shelter from the Storm or Form Follows Fear and Vice Versa," in *Architecture of Fear*, ed. Nan Ellin (New York: Princeton Architectural Press, 1997), p. 16.

18. Surveillance Studies Network, *A Report on the Surveillance Society*, Section 9.52.

19. See Katherine S. Williams, Craig Johnstone, and Mark Goodwin, "CCTV Surveillance in Urban Britain: Beyond the Rhetoric of Crime Reduction," in *Landscapes of Defense*; and Eric Topfer, "The Rise of CCTV and the Transformation of Violent Conflict," (paper presented at the conference on "Cities as Strategic Site: Militarisation, Anti-Globalisation, Warfare," Manchester, UK, November 6–9, 2002).

20. See Jon Coaffee, "Rings of Steel, Rings of Concrete and Rings of Confidence: Designing Out Terrorism in Central London pre and post-September 11th," *International Journal of Urban and Regional Research*, 28, 1 (March 2004): 201–211. See also John Schwartz, "Cameras in Britain Record the Criminal and the Banal," *New York Times*, July 23, 2005, p. A8.

21. Williams, Johnstone, and Goodwin, "CCTV Surveillance in Urban Britain: Beyond the Rhetoric of Crime Reduction."

22. See Peter W. Huber and Mark P. Mills, "How Technology Will Defeat Terrorism," *City Journal* (Winter 2002).

23. Ibid., p. 2.

24. Eventually the plastic was converted into concrete stanchions and bollards, but this hardly made it a ring of steel. See Coaffee, *Terrorism, Risk and the City* (Burlington, VT: Ashgate, 2003), pp. 100, 114.

25. See H.V. Savitch, "An Anatomy of Urban Terror: Lessons from Jerusalem and Elsewhere," *Urban Studies* 42, 3 (2005): 361–395.

26. For the concept of an "edge city," see Joel Garreau, *Edge City: Life on the Urban Frontier* (New York: Doubleday, 1991).

27. There is some debate about the "defensible space" aspects of new neighborhoods. Some scholars will point out that this kind of architecture is indigenous to Jerusalem, and new neighborhoods would have been built in this style anyway. While these points are well taken, there is a distinct difference between new neighborhoods on the periphery and those closer to the center of the city (whose defensible space is relatively minimal).

28. Some of the spaces designated here are my own, inspired by the work of others. For insights on urban space I am indebted to Steven Flusty's "Building Paranoia" in *Architecture of Fear*, ed. Nan Ellin, pp. 47–59.

29. Contextual zones are communities with buildings, blocks, streets, and functions capable of being treated in like manner. This is supposed to ensure a certain consistency in applying different protective measures. The zones were identified as President's Park (White House and environs), Capitol Hill (House, Senate, Library of Congress), The Mall (Smithsonian, museums, and so forth), Federal Triangle (Ronald Reagan Building and vicinity), the West End (Department of State, Foggy Bottom),

and Downtown (commercial central business district). See U.S. National Capital Planning Commission, *Designing for Security in the Nation's Capital* (Washington, DC: October, 2001).

30. For prickly spaces see Flusty, "Building Paranoia."

31. Uri Shetreet, interview by author, May 26, 2004.

32. See Matthew Levitt, "The Political Economy of Middle East Terrorism," *Middle East Review of International Affairs* 6, 4 (December 2002).

33. U.S. House. Committee on Finance, Steven Emerson, speaking on the Fund Raising Methods and Procedures for International Terrorist Organizations to the Subcommittee on Oversight and Investigations (February 12, 2002).

34. Ibid.

35. Ibid.

36. U.S. Senate Committee, Undersecretary Alan Larson of Economic, Business, and Agricultural Affairs, speaking on the International Dimensions of Combating the Financing of Terrorism to the Committee on Finance (October 9, 2002).

37. See "Bank Data Sifted in Secret by U.S. to Block Terror," *New York Times*, June 23, 2006, available at http://bert.lib.indiana.edu:2310/iw-serch/we/InfoWeb/?p_ action.

38. Levitt, "The Political Economy of Middle East Terrorism."

39. See William Finnegan, "The Terrorism Beat," *New Yorker*, July 25, 2005, p. 58.

40. Raymond A. Kelly, interview by Charlie Rose, *The Charlie Rose Show*, PBS, August 8, 2006.

41. See, for example, Craig Horowitz, "The NYPD's War on Terror," 2005, available at www.NewYorkmetro.com.

42. Finnegan, "The Terrorism Beat," p. 23.

43. Kelly, interview by Charlie Rose.

44. David Lyon, *Surveillance after September 11* (Cambridge, UK: Polity Publications, 2003), p. 8.

45. The term "surveillance creep" is attributed to Gary Marx. See Gary Marx, "The Engineering of Social Control," in *Crime and Equality*, ed. J. Hagan and R. Peterson (Stanford, CA: Stanford University Press, 1995). For a discussion, see also David Wood, Eli Kronwitz, and Kirstie Ball, "The Constant State of Emergency: Surveillance after 9/11," in *The Intensification of Surveillance*, ed. Kirstie Ball and Frank Webster (Sterling, VA: Pluto Press, 2003), pp. 137–150.

46. Ibid.

47. For very critical attitudes toward surveillance—some of which recommend resistance to it, see Lyon, *Surveillance after September 11*, as well as Wood, Kronwitz, and Ball, "The Constant State of Emergency? Surveillance after 9/11."

48. See the U.S. German Marshall Fund, *Transatlantic Trends: Key Findings* (Washington, DC: 2006).

49. M. Lovall, interview by author, May 18, 2003. Anglo Saxon Real Estate, Jerusalem, Israel.

50. Ariel Shachar, interview by author, May 9, 2003. The Hebrew University of Jerusalem, Israel.

51. David Harvey, "Cracks in the Edifice of the Empire State," in *After the World Trade Center*, ed. Michael Sorkin and Sharon Zukin (New York: Routledge, 2002) pp. 57–68. For Harvey's quote, see p. 62.

52. Dearborn is misspelled in the article as "Dearbon" and is mistakenly identified as a neighborhood in Detroit rather than a separate city. See Stephen Graham, "Cities

and the War on Terror," *International Journal of Urban and Regional Planning* 30, 2 (2006): 255–276, p. 261.

53. Estimates vary by source, the time taken for judging incarcerations, and the population considered. None of the available sources suggests thousands of incarcerations of either American citizens or resident aliens—at least not within any reasonable period of time after 9/11. In the first eleven months after 9/11, the U.S. Department of Justice identified 762 aliens who were detained for various offenses, including visa overstays and illegal entry. According to this source, eighty-four of these aliens were held at a correctional facility during the eleven months after the attack. See U.S. Department of Justice, "Supplemental Report on September 11 Detainees' Allegations of Abuse at the Metropolitan Detention Center in Brooklyn, New York," (December 2003), available at http://www.usdoj.gov/oig/special/0312/chapter1.htm. Human Rights Watch (HRW) takes a different view and uses three categories to examine detentions—(1) noncitizens or aliens who were in the United States, (2) American citizens, and (3) captured enemy combatants. HRW identifies at least 1,200 noncitizens who were detained in connection with terrorist investigations. In the category of U.S. citizens are just two individuals. These figures do not include the third category of combatants who were captured in a foreign war in Afghanistan and imprisoned at Guantanamo Bay, Cuba, consisting of almost 600 detainees (more recent figures put this number well above 700). Normally, HRW closely monitors incarcerations and since its last report in 2003 appears not to have pursued the subject. See Human Rights World Report, *Country Report USA* (2003), available at http://www.hrw.org/wr2k3/pdf/us.pdf.

54. Graham, in "Cities and the War on Terror," relies on an article by Sally Howell and Andrew Shyrock to make the case for mass repression in the United States. These authors have used the 1,200 figure for alien detainees but cite no source for that figure. Also, contrary to U.S. Department of Justice statements, these authors claim the detainees were never named or charged with crimes. See Sally Howell and Andrew Shyrock, "Cracking Down on Diaspora: Arab Detroit and America's War on Terror," *Anthropological Quarterly*, 76 (2003): 443–462, p. 449. Mike Davis compounds the distortion by stating that "11,000-plus people have been arrested and detained in the course of the government's terrorism investigation." Davis cites a *New York Times,* editorial for the 11,000 figure. While anxious to use the inflated number, Davis either neglected or ignored a *New York Times* correction to the editorial stating that the figure was "about 1,100 not 11,000." The corrected figure is closer to that cited by Howell and Shyrock. See Mike Davis, "The Flames of New York," *New Left Review* 12 (November–December 2001), pp. 34–50, at p. 49; and compare it to *New York Times,* Editorial Desk, "Disappearing in America," November 10, 2001, p. 22.

55. Susan Clarke, Michael Pagano, and Gary Gaile, "Urban Scholarship after September 11, 2001," *Urban Affairs Review* 37, 3 (2002): 460–467.

56. Todd Swanstrom, "Are Fear and Urbanism at War?" *Urban Affairs Review* 38, 1 (2002): 135–140.

57. The controversy over the SWIFT program was carried in newspapers across the country. For an early breaking story see Etich Lichtblau and James Risen, "Bank Data is Sifted by U.S. in Secret to Block Terror," *New York Times*, June 23, 2006, p. 1. A different view of Operation SWIFT is taken by the Surveillance Studies Network in *A Report on Surveillance.* According to newspaper reports, hundreds of cases have been dropped, thrown out of court, or resulted in acquittals. See "Judge Throws Out Terror

Conviction," *Washington Post*, September 1, 2004, p. 1; and Maureen O'Hagan, "A Terrorism Case That Went Awry," *Seattle Times*, November 22, 2004, p. 1.

58. A number of American cities do receive large numbers of immigrants, and some have designated themselves "sanctuaries," indicating that their police would not enforce tightened immigration laws. The largest include New York, Houston, Portland, Los Angeles, San Diego, and San Francisco (New York has since repealed its "sanctuary status"). See Judith Garber, "Cities as Agents of Antiterrorist Policy" (paper presented at the Annual Meeting of the Urban Affairs Association, Washington, DC, March 31–April 3, 2003).

59. See Charles Lindblom, "The Science of "Muddling Through,"" *Public Administration Review* 19 (1959): 79–88; as well as "Still Muddling, Not Yet Through," *Public Administration Review* 39 (1979): 517–526.

60. For the local applications of "institutional thickness," see H.V. Savitch, "Global Challenge and Institutional Capacity: Or How We Can Refit Local Administration for the Next Century," *Administration and Society* 30, 3 (1998): 248–273.

Notes to Chapter 7

1. See Harold Lasswell, "The Garrison State," *American Journal of Urban Sociology* 46 (January 1941): 455–468.

2. Ibid., p. 455.

3. See Mike Davis, "The Flames of New York," *New Left Review* 12 (November–December 2001): 45.

4. Ibid., p. 44.

5. David Dixon, "Is Density Dangerous? The Architects' Obligations after the Towers Fell," in *Perspective on Preparedness*, Belfare Center for International Affairs and Taubman Center for State and Local Government, Harvard University (October 12, 2002): 1.

6. See Peter Marcuse, "Urban Form and Globalization after September 11: The View from New York," *International Journal of Urban and Regional Research* 23, 3 (September 2002): 596–606. For Marcuse's quote, see p. 596. Marcuse held much the same opinion in an earlier article. See Peter Marcuse, "Alternate Visions for New York City: By Whom, for Whom," *MetroPlanner* (January–February 2002), p. 3.

7. There appeared to be a uniformity of opinion in most of the published articles. See the *International Journal of Urban and Regional Research* 26 (September 2002): 589–590, and 27, 3 (2003): 649–698.

8. Michael Dudley, "Sprawl as Strategy: City Planners Face the Bomb," *Journal of Planning Education and Research* (Fall 2001): 52–63.

9. The idea actually began in the 1960s and was elaborated during the 1990s. See Melvin Weber, "Order in Diversity: Community without Propinquity," in *Cities and Space: The Future*, ed. Lowdon Wingo, Jr. (Baltimore, MD: Johns Hopkins University Press, 1963). For later and cruder versions, see Harry Richardson and Peter Gordon, "Market Planning: Oxymoron or Common Sense?" *Journal of the American Planning Association* 59 (Summer 1993): 59–77; and Peter Gordon and Harry Richardson, "Are Compact Cities a Desirable Planning Goal?" *Journal of the American Planning Association* 63 (Winter 1997): 95–107.

10. Quoted in Keith Schneider, "Sprawl Not an Antidote to Terror," *Elm Street Writers Group* (Michigan Land Institute, December 2001).

11. See Joel Kotkin, "The Declustering of America," *Wall Street Journal*, August

12, 2002, p. A12. For extended discussion, see Joel Kotkin, *The New Geography: How the Digital Landscape Is Reshaping the American Landscape* (New York: Random House, 2000).

12. Ibid.

13. James Kunstler and Nikos Slingaros attribute the term "urban hypertrophy" to Leon Krier. See Leon Krier, *Leon Krier: Houses, Palaces, Cities* (New York: St. Martin's Press, 1984). See James Kunstler and Nikos Slingaros, "The End of Tall Buildings," *Planetizen* (September 17, 2001), available at www.panetizen.com/oped/item.php.

14. Ibid.

15. See Edward Glaeser and Jesse Shapiro, "Cities and Warfare: The Impact of Terrorism on Urban Form," *Journal of Urban Economics* 51 (March 2002): 205–224; and Ronald R. Davis and Weinstein E. David, "Bones, Bombs and Breakpoint: The Geography of Economic Activity," *American Economic Review* 92 (December 2002): 1269–1289. See also Steven Brackman, Harry Garretsen, and Mark Schramm, "The Strategic Bombing of German Cities during World War II and Its Impact on City Growth," *Journal of Economic Geography* 42, 2 (2004): 201–208.

16. For varying interpretations of the war on terror, including the garrison state, see Kathe Callahan, Melvin Dubnick, and Dorothy Olshfski, "War Narratives: Framing Our Understanding of the War on Terror," *Public Administration Review* 66, 4 (July–August 2006): 554–568.

17. See Peter Eisinger, "The American City in an Age of Terror: A Preliminary Assessment of the Effects of September 11," *Urban Affairs Review* 40, 1 (2004): 115–130.

18. Ibid. Brackman, Garretsen, and Schramm, *Strategy Bombing*, do point out that cities in West Germany (FRG) incurred a temporary impact but fully recovered, while those in East Germany (GDR) did not and the Allied bombing had a permanent impact. While the authors do not venture into why the FRG cities would show a different recovery than GDR cities, a plausible reason might be that FRG cities were located in more dynamic, aggressive, and productive national economies. Those economies acted differently on their respective cities.

19. In distinguishing between conventional warfare and terrorism, we can talk about the unbounded friction of urban terror. This friction is akin to the experience of the Middle Ages, where plunder and siege lasted for 20, 30, or 100 years. In these instances, constant invasions and centuries of pillage caused many cities to wither or disappear (see Pirenne, *Medieval Cities*). The Thirty Years' War resulted in a radical depopulation of German cities in which Marburg and Augsburg lost more than half their inhabitants, never to regain their predominant status (C.V. Wedgewood, *The Thirty Years War* [Garden City, NY: Doubleday, 1961]). Another way of understanding how the friction of terror might affect cities is to examine the relationship between crime and urban settlement. Like terrorism, crime creates chronic apprehension and paralyzes normal life. Much as guards, gates, and surveillance are used to thwart terror, so too are they employed to prevent criminal aggression.

20. James Harrigan and Philippe Martin, "Terrorism and the Resilience of Cities," *Economic Policy Review* (November 2002): 97–116.

21. Robert Greenbaum and Andy Hultquist, "The Impact of Terrorism on Italian Employment and Business Activity" (unpublished manuscript, 2006).

22. For the Israeli case, see Zvi Eckstein and Daniel Tsiddon, "Macroeconomic Consequences of Terror: Theory and the Case of Israel" (paper presented at the conference on "Public Policy," Carnegie-Rochester, November 21–22, 2003); and

Daniel Felsenstein and Shlomie Hazam, "The Effect of Terror on Behavior in the Jerusalem Housing Market" (unpublished manuscript, Institute of Urban and Regional Studies, Hebrew University of Jerusalem, 2005). For the Basque case, see Alberto Abadie and Javier Gardeazabai, "The Economic Costs of Conflict: A Case Control Study for the Basque Country," National Bureau of Economic Research (Cambridge, MA, September 2001).

23. Resilience can also be complex, and Vale and Campanella adumbrate its processes beginning with the onset of disaster to rebuilding. The purpose here is simpler and involves narrowing down a condition to see whether the disruption endures, for how long, and whether there has been a restoration. See Lawrence Vale and Thomas Campanella, eds., *The Resilient City: How Modern Cities Recover from Disaster* (New York: Oxford University Press, 2005).

24. For an account of New York's economy after 9/11, see Edward Hill and Iryna Lendell, "Did 9/11 Change Manhattan and the New York Region as Places to Conduct Business?" in *Resilient City: The Economic Impact of 9/11*, ed. Howard Chernick (New York: Russell Sage, 2005), pp. 23–61.

25. Ibid., p. 35.

26. Gross city product is calculated differently from one country to another, and this may account for the London's lower figure. See Corporation of London, *London/New York: The Economies of Two Cities at the Millennium*, Executive Summary (London: Corporation of London, June 2000), p. 16.

27. Ibid., sec. 2, "Driving Forces of Change in London and New York Economies."

28. Jerusalem Institute for Israel Studies, 1999–2000, *The Jerusalem Yearbook*, available at www.jiis.org.il/shnaton.

29. U.S. Department of Labor, Bureau of Labor Statistics, *Current Employment Survey*, 2006. See also Eisinger, "The American City in an Age of Terror," *Urban Affairs Review* 40, 1: 115–130; and Hill and Lendell, "Did 9/11 Change Manhattan and the New York Region as Places to Conduct Business?" in Chernick, ed., *Resilient City*.

30. See Chernick, ed., *Resilient City*, for the period up through 2004, and James Parrot, *New York City's Labor Market Outlook with a Special Emphasis on Immigrant Workers,* New York: Fiscal Policy Institute, December 2005.

31. The year taken for the previous period is 1989 and the year taken for the cessation of terror is 1994. As of this writing, data on London were not available to assess the employment effects due to the attacks of July 2005. See City of London Corporation, *City Research Focus*, available at http://www.cityoflondon.gov.uk /Corporation/business_city/research_statistics/Research+periodicals.htm#focus, and *Annual Business Inquiry.*

32. See H.V. Savitch and Garb Yaacov, "Terror, Barriers and the Re-topography of Jerusalem," as well as Hank V. Savitch, "An Anatomy of Urban Terror."

33. Jerusalem Institute for Israel Studies, "Statistical Yearbook of Jerusalem 2001–2004."

34. The comparisons made are between the pre-attack year of 2000 and the post-attack years of 2002 and 2003. The tourist figures cited in this section deal with tourism from other nations, or "foreign tourists." New York statistics are obtainable on the New York City Official Tourism Website at http://www.nycvisit.com/content/index.cfm?pagePkey=57.

35. Visit London Corporate, *London Monthly Trends, Monthly Visitor Index* (London: Visit London, July–September 2005).

36. Ibid.

37. Franz Fuerst, "The Impact of 9/11 on the Manhattan Office Market," in *Resilient City*, ed. Howard Chernick (New York: Russell Sage, 2005) pp. 62–98.

38. Ibid. About 20 percent of firms chose to move out of the city.

39. Ibid., p. 81.

40. See Igal Charney, "Reflections on the Post-WTC Skyline: Manhattan and Elsewhere," *International Journal of Urban and Regional Research* 29 (March 2005): 172–179.

41. Ibid.

42. Ibid. The skyscraper in Dubai will rise to over 2,300 feet (705 meters). The antenna/spire of the World Trade Center was 1,731.9 feet (527.9 meters) and its roofline was 1,368 feet (417 meters).

43. Quoted in Edwin Mills, "Terrorism and U.S. Real Estate," *Journal of Urban Economics* 51 (2002): 198–204.

44. Quoted in "Special Report: The Skyscraper Boom," *Economist*, June 3, 2006, pp. 65–67.

45. Eisinger, "The American City in an Age of Terror," p. 126.

46. Savitch, "An Anatomy of Urban Terror," p. 388.

47. Ibid., p. 389.

48. Thomas Wolfe, *You Can't Go Home Again*, 2d ed. (New York: Harper Perennial Classic, 1998).

49. Jonathan Schwabish and Joshua Chang, "New York City and Terrorism Insurance in a Post 9/11 World," *Issue Brief* (Partnership for New York City, September 2004).

50. National Underwriter Company, *Property and Casualty/Risks and Benefits* (National Underwriter Company, November 2002).

51. Editorial, *London Times*, December 14, 2002. p. 1.

52. See Organization for Economic Cooperation and Development, *Terrorism Risk Insurance in OECD Countries* (Paris: Organization for Economic Cooperation and Development, 2005).

53. As disasters go, terrorism is generally less expensive than natural calamities. Most hurricanes cost upward of $3 billion, and Hurricane Katrina, which racked America's Gulf Coast, cost over $35 billion. The World Trade Center was unusual in this sense. It should also be noted that natural disasters cover a much larger geographic area than human-made disasters. Rawle King, "Hurricane Katrina: Insurance Losses and National Capacities for Financing Disaster Risk," a Congressional Research Service report prepared for the U.S. Congress, September 2005, p. 15.

54. Susan Clarke and Erica Chenoweth, "The Politics of Vulnerability: Constructing Local Performance Regimes for Homeland Security," *Review of Policy Research* 23, 1 (January 2006): 95–114.

55. German Marshal Fund, *Transatlantic Trends: Key Findings,* p. 7.

56. National League of Cities, "Cities Report Change in Financial Conditions," *State of American Cities Survey*. (Washington, DC: National League of Cities, 2001).

57. Ibid.

58. U.S. Senate, Undersecretary of Preparedness George Foresman, Department of Homeland Security, speaking "For the Record" to the Committee on Homeland Security (June 21, 2006), p. 3. This does not take account of other sources, and some have pegged the total amount at $28.9 billion. See Clarke and Chenoweth, "Politics of Vulnerability."

59. U.S. House Committee, Mayor Michael R. Bloomberg of New York City

and Mayor Anthony Williams of Washington, DC, speaking on "DHS Terrorism Preparedness Grants: Risk-Based or Guess Work?" to the Committee on Homeland Security (June 21, 2006).

60. Department of Homeland Security, *FY 2006 Urban Area Security Initiative (UASI) by Urban Areas* sec. 2 (Washington, DC, 2006).

61. For a discussion of this see Peter Eisinger, "Imperfect Federalism: The Intergovernmental Partnership for Homeland Security," *Public Administration Review*, (July/August 2006): 537–545.

62. This is a political logic that decades ago marked efforts to create full employment and model cities. See, for example, Charles Haar, *Between the Idea and the Reality* (Boston: Little, Brown, 1975).

63. See Theodore Lowi, "American Business, Public Policy, and Case Studies and Political Theory," *World Politics* 16: (1964): 677–715; and Paul Peterson, *City Limits* (Chicago: University of Chicago Press, 1981).

64. See Clarke and Chenoweth, "Politics of Vulnerability."

Notes to Chapter 8

1. See Jurgen Habermas and Jacques Derrida, *Philosophy in a Time of Terror*, Introduction and Comments by Giovanna Borradori (Chicago: University of Chicago Press, 2003), p. 94.

2. Ibid.

3. *The Politics of Aristotle*, ed. Earnest Barker (New York: Oxford University Press, 1962), especially consult Books I and III.

References

Abadie, A., and J. Gardeazabai. 2001. "The Economic Costs of Conflict: A Case Control Study for the Basque Country." National Bureau of Economic Research Cambridge, MA, September.

ABC News, "Chechen Guerilla Leader Calls Russians 'Terrorists'," July 29, 2005, http://abcnews.go.com/Nightline/story?id=989549&page=1.

Allison, G. 2004. *Nuclear Terrorism.* New York: Henry Holt.

Ariel, J. 2004. "A War without an Enemy." *Maariv*, August 9, p. 1.

Aron, R. 1966. *Peace and War: A Theory of International Relations.* London: Wiedenfeld and Nicolson.

Barker, E., ed. 1962. *The Politics of Aristotle.* New York: Oxford University Press.

BBC News. 2005. "Mayor Blames Middle East Policy." http://newsvote.bbc.co.uk /mpapps/pagetools/print/news.bbc.co.uk.

———. 2005. "Litany of Terror Attacks" http://news.bbc.co.uk/2/hi/uk_news /4661753.stm.

———. 2006. "Putin Rejects Child Killer Talks." February 10.

———. 2006. "Abu Hamza Jailed for Seven Years." http://news.bbc.co.uk/1/hi /uk/4690224.stm (accessed February 7).

———. 2007. "Profile Jawad Akbar" http://.bbc.co.uk (accessed May 1).

BBC Report. 2005. "Litany of Terror Attacks." http://news.bbc.co.uk/2/hi/uk news/4661753.stm.

BBC World Service. 2006. *Newshour 12:00 GMT.* February 14. http://www.bbc. co.uk/worldservice/programmes/newshour/.

Bell, D. 1995. "The Coming of Post Industrial Society." New York: Basic Books.

Ben-Dor, and Canetti-Nisim. 2004. *Psychologically Coping with the Intifada: Haifa University Survey Finds.* National Security Studies Center. Haifa University, Haifa, Israel.

Bentham, J. 1995. *The Panopticon Writings,* ed. Miran Bozovic. London: Verso.

Blair, T. 2005. "Speech of the Prime Minister in the House of Commons." July 21. Available at http://www.number-10.gov.uk/output/Page 7969.asp.

Blakely, E., and M.G. Snyder. 1997. *Fortress America: Gated Communities in the United States.* Washington, DC: Brookings Institution.

Bleich, A.B., M. Gelkopf, and Z. Solomon. 2003. "Exposure to Terrorism, Stress-Related Mental Health Symptoms, and Coping Behaviors among a Nationally Representative Sample in Israel." *Journal of the American Medical Association* 290, 5: 612–620.

Borradori, G. 2003. *Philosophy in a Time of Terror: Dialogues with Jurgen Habermas and Jacques Derrida.* Chicago: University of Chicago Press, 2003.

Brackman, S., H. Garretsen, and M. Schramm. 2004. "The Strategic Bombing of German Cities during World War II and Its Impact on City Growth," *Journal of Economic Geography* 42, 2: 201–208.

Brennan, E. 1999. *Population, Urbanization, Environment, and Security: A Summary of the Issues.* Comparative Urban Studies Occasional Series, 22. Washington, DC: Woodrow Wilson International Center for Scholars.

Buchanan, M. 2006. "London Bombs Cost Just Hundreds." British Broadcast Corporation. http://newsvote.bbc.co.uk (accessed January 3, 2006).

Callahan, K., M. Dubnick, and D. Olshfski. 2006. "War Narratives: Framing Our Understanding of the War on Terror." *Public Administration Review* 66, 4 (July/August): 554–568.

Cardia, N. 2000. *Urban Violence in São Paulo.* Comparative Urban Studies Occasional Series, 33. Washington, DC: Woodrow Wilson International Center for Scholars.

Center for Strategic Studies. 2005. "Post Amman Attacks, Jordanian Public Opinion and Terrorism." Public Opinion Polling Unit, University of Jordan. January.

Charlie Rose Show. 2006. Interview with Raymond Kelly. PBS. August 8.

Charney, I. 2005. "Reflections on the Post-WTC Skyline: Manhattan and Elsewhere." *International Journal of Urban and Regional Planning Research* 29 (March): 172–179.

Chichizola, J. 2005. "Une filière de braqueurs et d'islamistes démantelée." *Le Figaro*, December 13.

Chinlund, C. 2003. "Who Should Wear the Terrorist Label?" *Boston Globe.* September 8.

Chomsky, N. 2001. *9–11, New York.* New York: Seven Stories Press.

Clarke, S. 2004. "Local Governance and Homeland Security." Paper presented at the Thomas J. Anton/Frederick Lippitt Conference on "Homeland Security in Urban America," panel on "National Perspectives on Urban Homeland Security." Brown University. September 23–24.

Clarke, S., and E. Chenoweth. 2006. "The Politics of Vulnerability: Constructing Local Performance Regimes for Homeland Security." *Review of Policy Research* 23, 1 (January): 95–114.

Clarke, S., M. Pagano, and G. Gaile. 2002. "Urban Scholarship after September 11, 2001." *Urban Affairs Review* 37, 3: 460–467.

Clutterbuck, R. 1990. *Terrorism and Guerrilla Warfare.* London: Routledge Press.

Coaffee, J. 2003. *Terrorism, Risk and the City.* Burlington, VT: Ashgate Publishing House.

———. 2004. "Rings of Steel, Rings of Concrete and Rings of Confidence: Designing Out Terrorism in Central London pre and post-September 11th." *International Journal of Urban and Regional Research* 28, 1 (March): 201–211.

Cohen, D., B. Gerber, and K. Stewart. 2004. "State and Local Government Actions on Homeland Security: Explaining Variation in Preparedness Efforts." Paper prepared for the 2004 annual meeting of the Midwest Political Science Association, Chicago. April.

Cohen, M., B. Ruble, J. Tulchin, and A. Garland, eds. 1996. *Preparing for the Urban Future.* Washington, DC: Woodrow Wilson Center Press.

Corporation of London (COL). 2000. *London/New York: The Economies of Two Cities at the Millennium.* London: Corporation of London.

Crown Copyright. 2001. *London Key Statistical Tables.* London.

Dangschat, J. n.d. "Economic Improvement Divides the City: The Case of Hamburg" (manuscript). Department of Sociology, University of Hamburg.

Davis, M. 2001. "The Flames of New York." *New Left Review* 12 (November/December): 34–50.

Davis, R.R., and E.W. David. 2002. "Bones, Bombs and Breakpoint: The Geography of Economic Activity." *American Economic Review* 92 (December): 1269–1289.

Dichter, Avi. 2003. *Security Chief Names Iran as World N1 Terror State*; *Says Security Fence Is Vital.* Israel Ministry of Foreign Affairs. http://www.israel-mfa.gov.il/mfa/go.asp?MFAH002r0.

Dixon, D. 2002. "Is Density Dangerous? The Architects' Obligations after the Towers Fell." In *Perspective on Preparedness.* Belfare Center for International Affairs and Taubman Center for State and Local Government, Harvard University. October.

Dorman, A. 2006. "The British Experience with Terrorist Networks." Paper presented at the 102nd annual meeting of the American Political Science Association, Philadelphia. August 31–September 3.

Drake, C.J.M. 1998. *Terrorists' Target Selection.* London: Macmillan Press.

Ducci, M. 2000. *Governance, Urban Environment, and the Growing Role of Civil Society.* Comparative Urban Studies Occasional Series, 34. Washington, DC: Woodrow Wilson International Center for Scholars.

Dudley, M. 2001. "Sprawl as Strategy: City Planners Face the Bomb." *Journal of Planning Education and Research* (Fall): 52–63.

Dworkin, A. 2002. *Heartbreak: The Political Memoir of a Feminist Militant.* New York: Basic Books.

Eckstein, Z., and D. Tsiddon. 2003. "Macroeconomic Consequences of Terror: Theory and the Case of Israel." Paper presented at the conference on "Public Policy," Carnegie-Rochester. November 21–22.

Economist, 2006. Special Report: The Skyscraper Boom." Editorial, June 3–24.

Eisenhower, D. 1963. *Mandate for Change.* New York: Doubleday.

Eisinger, P. 2004. "The American City in an Age of Terror: A Preliminary Assessment of the Effects of September 11." *Urban Affairs Review* 40, 1: 115–130.

———. 2006. "Imperfect Federalism: The Intergovernmental Partnership for Homeland Security," *Public Administration Review*, July/August: 537–545.

Ellin, N. 1997. "Shelter from the Storm or Form Follows Fear and Vice Versa." In *Architecture of Fear*, ed. Nan Ellin. New York: Princeton Architectural Press.

Enders, W., and T. Sandler. 2000. "Is Transnational Terrorism Becoming More Threatening? A Time-Series Investigation." *Journal of Conflict Resolution* 44, 3: 307–332.

Etzioni, A. 2002. "American Society in the Age of Terror." In *American Society in the Wake of Terrorism: Communitarian Perspectives.* Available at http://www.gwu.edu/~ccps/news_american_society.html#n_1.

European Union. 2002. "Framework Decision on Combating Terrorism 2002." http://www.statewatch.org/news/2002/jul/frameterr622en00030007.pdf.

Fainstein, S., I. Gordon, and M. Harloe. 1992. *Divided Cities: New York and London in the Contemporary World.* Cambridge, MA: Blackwell Publishers.

Federal Emergency Management Agency. 2002. *World Trade Center Building Performance Study.* FEMA, Region II, New York, N.Y.

Felsenstein, D., and S. Hazam. 2005. "The Effect of Terror on Behavior in the Jerusalem Housing Market" (manuscript). Institute of Urban and Regional Studies, Hebrew University of Jerusalem.

Finn, P. 2002. "Hamburg's Cauldron of Terror." *Washington Post*, September 11.

Finnegan, W. 2005. "The Terrorism Beat." *New Yorker*, July 25, p. 58.

Fishman, R. 2000. "The American Metropolis at Century's End: Past and Future." *Housing Policy Debate* 11, 1: 199–213.

Florida, R. 2002. *The Rise of the Creative Class.* New York: Basic Books.

———. 2005. *Cities and the Creative Class.* New York: Routledge.

Flusty, S. 1997. "Building Paranoia." In *Architecture of Fear*, ed. Nan Ellin. New York: Princeton Architectural Press.

Forrester, J. 1969. *Urban Dynamic*. Cambridge, MA: MIT Press.

Frantz, D., and D. Butler. 2002. "Imam at German Mosque Preached Hate to 9/11 Pilots." *New York Times*, July 16, p. 2.

Freeman, S. 2006. "Abu Hamza Jailed for Seven Years for Inciting Murder." *Times On Line* (February 7). http://www.timesonline.co.uk.

Friedmann, J., and G. Wolff. 1982. "World City Formation: An Agenda for Research and Action." *International Journal of Urban and Regional Research* 6, 3: 309–344.

Frontline. Interview with Osama bin Laden. http://www.pbs.org/wgbh/pages/frontline/ shows/binladen/who/interview.html John Miller, May 1998.

Fuchs, R., E. Brennan, J. Chamie, C.L. Fu, and J. Uitto, eds. 1994. *Mega City Growth and the Future*. New York: United Nations University Press.

Fuerst, F. 2005. "The Impact of 9/11 on the Manhattan Office Market." In *Resilient City: The Economic Impact of 9/11*, ed. Howard Chernick. New York: Russell Sage.

Gage, B. 2002. "The First Wall Street Bomb." In *After the World Trade Center: Rethinking New York City*, ed. Michael Sorkin and Sharon Zukin. New York: Routledge.

Galea, S., J. Ahern, H. Resnick, D. Kilpatrick, M. Bucavalas, J. Gold, and D. Vlahov. 2002. "Psychological Sequelae of the September 11 Terrorist Attacks in New York City." *New England Journal of Medicine* 346, 13: 982–987.

Gall, G. 2003. *The Meaning of Militancy: Postal Workers and Industrial Relations*. Burlington, VT: Ashgate Press.

Garb, Y., and H.V. Savitch. 2005. *Urban Trauma in Jerusalem: Impacts and Possibilities for Recovery*. The Floersheimer Institute for Policy Studies.

Garber, J. 2003. "Cities as Agents of Antiterrorist Policy." Paper presented at the annual meeting of the Urban Affairs Association, Washington, DC. March 31–April 3.

Getler, M. 2003. "The Language of Terrorism." *Washington Post*, September 21.

Glaeser, E., and M. Shapiro. 2002. "Cities and Warfare: The Impact of Terrorism on Urban Form." *Journal of Urban Economics* 51 (March): 205–224.

Glass, C. 2005. "The Last of England: Churchill Gave London Courage, Blair Is Serving Fear." *Harpers Magazine*, 311, 1866 (November): 43–49.

Goldberg, J. 2001. "The Martyr Strategy." *New Yorker*, July 9, pp. 34–39.

Gordon, P., and H. Richardson. 1997. "Are Compact Cities a Desirable Planning Goal?" *Journal of the American Planning Association* 63 (Winter): 95–107.

Graham, S., ed. 2004. *Cities, War and Terrorism*. Oxford, UK: Blackwell Press.

———. 2006. "Cities and the War on Terror." *International Journal of Urban and Regional Planning* 30, 2: 255–276.

Greenbaum, R., and A. Hultquist. 2006. "The Impact of Terrorism on Italian Employment and Business Activity." Manuscript.

Gross, T. 2005. "The BBC Discovers 'Terrorism,' Briefly." *Jerusalem Post*, July 11.

Haar, C. 1975. *Between the Idea and the Reality: A Study in the Origin, Fate, and Legacy of the Model Cities Program*. Boston: Little, Brown.

Hall, P. 1998. *Cities in Civilization*. New York: Random House.

Harel, A. 2004. "Tanzim Recruiting Minors for Attacks." *Haaretz*, April 15, 2004.

———. 2005. "Mastermind of 2002 Passover Bombing Also Planned Mass Poisoning of Israelis." *Haaretz*, November 11.

Harrigan, J., and P. Martin. 2002. "Terorism and the Resilience of Cities." *Economic Policy Review* (November): 97–116.

Harvey, D. 2002. "Cracks in the Edifice of the Empire State." In *After the World Trade Center*, ed. Michael Sorkin and Sharon Zukin. New York: Routledge.

Hazam, S., and D. Felsenstein. 2004. "A Spatial Analysis of Terror in Jerusalem." Unpublished Paper. Institute of Urban and Regional Studies. Hebrew University of Jerusalem.

Hetherington, K. 1977. "In Place of Geometry: The Materiality of Place." In *Ideas of Difference*. London: Blackwell.

Hill, E., and I. Lendell. 2005. "Did 9/11 Change Manhattan and the New York Region as Places to Conduct Business?" In *Resilient City: The Economic Impact of 9/11*, ed. Howard Chernick. New York: Russell Sage, 2005, pp. 23–61.

Hobbes, T. 1950. *Leviathan*, Introduction by A.D. Lindsay. New York: Dutton.

Hoffer, E. 1951. *The True Believer.* New York: Harper and Row.

Hoffman, B. 1998. *Inside Terrorism.* New York: Columbia University Press.

———. 2003a. "The Logic of Suicide Terrorism." *Atlantic Monthly*, June.

———.2003b. "Comment/Discussion" in *Terror in Jerusalem,"* ed. by Ami Pedhazur and Gadi Paran. Jerusalem Institute for Israeli Studies, June 30.

Hook, D., and M. Vrdoljak. 2002. "Gated Communities, Heterotopia and a 'Rights' of Privilege: A 'Heterotopology' of the South African Security-Park." *Institute for Transportation and Development Policy Geoforum* 33: 195–219.

Horowitz, C. 2005. "The NYPD's War on Terror." http://www.NewYorkmetro. com.

House of Commons. 2006. *Report of the Official Account of the Bombings in London on 7th July, 2005.* London: The Stationery Office, May.

Howell, S., and A. Shyrock. 2003. "Cracking Down on Diaspora: Arab Detroit and America's War on Terror." *Anthropological Quarterly* 76: 443–462.

Huber, P.W., and M.P. Mills. 2002. "How Technology Will Defeat Terrorism." *City Journal*, Vol. 12, no. 1 (Winter) pp. 24–33.

Human Rights World Report. 2003. *Country Report USA.* http://www.hrw.org/wr2k3 /pdf/us.pdf.

Huxley, A. 1932. *Brave New World.* New York: Bantam Books.

Independent Panel for the BBC Governors. 2006. "Impartiality of BBC Coverage of the Israeli-Palestinian Conflict." April.

Intelligence and Security Committee. 2006. *Report into the London Terrorist Attacks on 7 July 2005.* Whitehall: London, March 30.

International Policy Institute for Counter-Terrorism. 2004. Database, Herzliya, Israel. http://www.ict.org.il.

Israel Ministry of Defense, 2003, 2004. *The Security Fence.* Available at www. securityfence.mod.gov.il.

Jacobs, J. 1961. *The Death and Life of Great American Cities.* New York: Random House.

———. 1970. *The Economy of Cities.* New York: Random House.

———. 1984. *Cities and the Wealth of Nations.* New York: Random House.

Jerusalem Institute for Israel Studies. 2000. *The Jerusalem Yearbook 1999–2000.* http://www.jiis.org.il/content.asp?englishArticleID=3.

———. *Statistical Yearbook of Jerusalem 2001–2004.* http://www.jiis.org.il/content. asp?englishArticleID=3.

Jerusalem Municipal Government Statistical Profiles. 2003. http://www.jerusalem.muni.il.

Jerusalem Post. 2003. "UK, France at Odds over Banning Hamas Political Wing." January 16.

———. 2005. "Woman Found with Grenade While Holding Baby." October 22.

Johnson, L. 2001. "The Declining Terrorist Threat." *New York Times*, July 10, p. A19.

Josephus, F. 1959. *The Jewish War*. Baltimore, MD: Penquin Books.

Kiefer, J.J. n.d. "Implementing Strategies to Mitigate the Impact of Terrorist Attacks against the Built Environment." Ph.D. dissertation. Old Dominion University, Norfolk, VA.

King, R. 2005. "Hurricane Katrina: Insurance Losses and National Capacities for Financing Disaster Risk." A Congressional Research Service report prepared for the U.S. Congress. September.

Klienfield, N.R. 2001. "A Creeping Horror and Panicked Flight." *New York Times*, September 12.

Kotkin J. 2000. *The New Geography: How the Digital Landscape Is Reshaping the American Landscape*. New York: Random House.

———. 2002. "The Declustering of America." *Wall Street Journal*, August 12.

Kunstler, J., and N. Salingaros. 2001. "The End of Tall Buildings." *Planetizen*, September 17. http://www.panetizen.com/oped/item.php (accessed July 29, 2002).

Kydd, Andrew, and Barbara Walter. 2006. "The Strategies of Terrorism." *International Security* 31, 1.

Labi, N. 2006. "Jihad 2.0." *The Atlantic Monthly*, July–August.

Landman, K. 2000. "Gated Communities and Urban Sustainability: Taking a Closer Look at the Future." Paper presented at the Southern African Conference on "Sustainable Development in a Built Environment," panel on "Strategies for a Sustainable Built Environment," Pretoria, South Africa. August 23–25.

———. 2002. "Gated Communities in South Africa: Building Bridges or Barriers?" Paper presented at the International Conference on "Private Urban Governance," Mainz, Germany. June 6–9.

———. 2003. "Alley-Gating and Neighborhood Gating: Are They Two Sides of the Same Face?" Paper presented at the conference on "Gated Communities: Building Social Division or Safer Communities?" Glasgow, UK. September 18–19.

Lappin, E. 2003. "Portrait: Atta in Hamburg." *Prospect*, August 29, p. 2.

Laquer, W. 1977. *Terrorism*. London: Weidenfeld & Nicolson.

———. 1986. "Reflections on Terrorism." *Foreign Affairs* 65: 1.

———. 1987. *The Age of Terrorism*. Boston: Little, Brown.

———. 1996. "Postmodern Terrorism." *Foreign Affairs* 75: 24.

Lasswell, H. 1941. "The Garrison State." *American Journal of Urban Sociology* 46 (January): 445–468.

Lawless, J. 2005. "London Tube Reopens Month after Bombings." *Seacoast Online.* September 9. http://www.seacoastonline.com.

Le Bars, S. 2004. "Un jeune Palestinien voulait se faire sauter à un barrage en Cisjordanie." *Le Monde*, March 25, p. 1.

Lefebvre, Henri. 1970. *La Revolution urbaine*. Paris: Gallimard.

Lelyveld, J. 2001. "All Suicide Bombers Are Not Alike." *New York Times Magazine*, October 28.

Levitt, M. 2002. "The Political Economy of Middle East Terrorism." *Middle East Review of International Affairs* 6, 4 (December).

Lindblom, C. 1959. "The Science of Muddling Through." *Public Administration Review* 19: 79–88.

————. 1979. "Still Muddling, Not Yet Through." *Public Administration Review* 39: 517–526.

Long, N. 1958. "The Local Community as an Ecology of Games." *American Journal of Sociology* 64, 3 (November): 251–261.

Lowi, T. 1964. "American Business, Public Policy and Case Studies and Political Theory." *World Politics* 16: 677–715.

Lugar, R. 2005. "The Lugar Survey on Proliferation: Threats and Response." United States Senate, Washington, DC. http://lugar.senate.gov.

Lyall, S. 2005. "Londoners Grappling with Pervasive New Foes: Fear and Suspicion." *New York Times*, July 26, p. A6.

Lyon, D. 2003. *Surveillance after September 11.* Cambridge, UK: Polity Publications.

Makovsky, D. 2004. "How to Build a Fence." *Foreign Affairs* (March–April): 50–64.

The Manhattan Engineer District. 1946. *The Atomic Bombings of Hiroshima and Nagasaki.* http://www.cddc.vt.edu/host/atomic/hiroshim/hiro_med.pdf.

Manningham-Buller, E. 2006. "The International Terrorist Threat." Paper read at Queen Mary's College, London. November 9.

Marcuse, P. 2002a. "Urban Form and Globalization after September 11: The View from New York." *International Journal of Urban and Regional Planning Research* 23, 3: (September): 596–606.

————. 2002b. "Alternate Visions for New York City: By Whom for Whom?" *MetroPlanner* (January/ February).

Marx, G. 1995. "The Engineering of Social Control." In *Crime and Equality*, ed. J. Hagan and R. Peterson. Stanford, CA: Stanford University Press.

Masters, R. 2002. "Pre-Emptive War, Iraq and Suicide Bombers." *Forum* 1, 2: 1–3.

Mehta, D. 1999. *Participatory Urban Environmental Management: The Case of Ahmedabad, India.* Comparative Urban Studies Occasional Series, 20. Washington, DC: Woodrow Wilson International Center for Scholars.

Mills, E. 2002. "Terrorism and U.S. Real Estate." *Journal of Urban Economics* 51: 198–204.

Mollenkopf, J., and M. Castells, eds. 1991. *Dual City: Restructuring New York.* New York: Russell Sage.

Mosnews. 2006. "World Should Not Cut Off Aid to Palestinians—Putin." January 31.

Mueller, J. 2006. "Is There Still a Terrorist Threat?" *Foreign Affairs* 85, 4: 1–8.

Mumford, L. 1938. *The Culture of Cities.* New York: Harcourt Brace.

————. 1960. *The City in History.* New York: Harcourt Brace Janovich.

Murphy, P. 2004. *The Wolves of Islam.* Dulles, VA: Brassey.

Nacos, B.L. 2002. *Mass-Mediated Terrorism.* Lanham, MD: Rowman & Littlefield.

Nathan, R., and C. Adams. 1989. "Four Perspectives on Urban Hardship." *Political Science Quarterly* 104, 3: 483–508.

National League of Cities (NLC). 2001. *State of American Cities Survey.* Washington, DC: National League of Cities.

————. 2005. *State of American Cities 2005.* Washington, DC: National League of Cities.

National Underwriter Company (NUC). 2002. *Property and Casualty/Risks and Benefits.* National Underwriter Company. November.

Nell, W. 2001 "Marketing the Urban Experience: Reflections on the Place of Fear in the Promotional Strategies of Belfast, Detroit and Berlin." *Urban Studies* 38, 5–6: 815–828.

Nelson, H.J. 1961. "Walled Cities of the United States." *Annals of the Association of American Geographers* 51, 1 (March): 1–22.

Newman, O. 1972. *Defensible Space*. New York: Macmillan.

New York Times. 2004. Editorial, March 14. Section IV, p. 1.

———. 2002. Editorial, December 14.

———. 2001. "Disappearing in America." Editorial, November 10, p. 22.

———. 2002. Changes since September 11: *New York Times*/CBS News Poll. June 11.

———. 2006. *New York Times*/CBS News Poll. August 17–27.

———. 2006. Editorial, June 23.

9/11 Commission, The. 2004. *Final Report of the National Commission on Terrorist Attacks Upon the United States*. New York: W.W. Norton.

Oc, T., and S. Tiesdell. 2000. "Urban Design Approaches to Safer City Centers: The Fortress, the Panoptic, the Regulatory and the Animated." In *Landscapes of Defense*. ed. J.R. Gold and G. Revill. Upper Saddle River, NJ: Prentice Hall.

O'Hagan, M., "A Terrorism Case that Went Awry," *Seattle Times*, November 22, 2004, p. 1.

O'Hanlon, E.M., I. Daalder, D. Gunter, P. Orszag, I.M. Destler, R. Litan, and J. Sternberg. 2002. *Protecting the Homeland: A Preliminary Analysis*. Washington, DC: Brookings Institution Press.

Organization for Economic Cooperation and Development (OECD). 2005. *Terrorism Risk Insurance in OECD Countries*. Paris: Organization for Economic Cooperation and Development.

Pape, R. 2003. "The Logic of Suicide Terrorism." *American Political Science Review* 97, 3: 343–361.

———. 2005. *Dying to Win*. New York: Random House.

Paran, G., A. Pedahzur, and A. Perliger. 2005. *Coping with Terrorism in Jerusalem: 1967–2002*. The Jerusalem Institute for Israel Studies.

Parrot, J. 2005. *New York City's Labor Market Outlook with a Special Emphasis on Immigrant Workers*. New York: Fiscal Policy Institute.

Pedahzur, A., and D. Canetti-Nisim. 2004. "The Impact of Terrorism on Political Attitudes: A Two-Edged Sword." Presentation at the National Security Studies Center, University of Haifa.

Pedahzur, A., and G. Paran. 2003. *Terror in Jerusalem*. Jerusalem Institute for Israeli Studies, June 30.

Peterson, P. 1981. *City Limits*. Chicago: University of Chicago Press.

Perry, D. 1993. "Making Space: Planning as a Mode of Thought." In *Spatial Practices*. ed. Helen Ligget and David Perry. Thousand Oaks, CA: Sage Publications.

Perrow, C. 1972. *Complex Organizations*. New York: Random House.

Pew Research Center for the People and the Press. 2001. "Worries about Terrorism Subside in Mid-America." November 8. http://people-press.org/reports/print. php3.

———. 2002. "One Year Later: New Yorkers More Troubled, Washingtonians More on Edge: The Personal Toll Persists, Policy Opinions Change." September 5. http://people-press.org/reports/print.php.

———. 2003. "Two Years Later, the Fear Lingers." September 17. http://people-press.org/reports/display.php3?ReportID=192.

Phillips, M. 2006. *Londonistan*. New York: Encounter Books.

Pirenne, H. 1956. *Medieval Cities*. Garden City, NY: Doubleday.

Rabinovich, J. 1997. "Practical Approaches to Urban Poverty Reduction." Statement at the International Forum on Urban Poverty, Governance and Participation, Florence, Italy. November 10–13.

Radlauer, D. 2002. "An Engineered Tragedy: Statistical Analysis of Casualties in the Palestinian-Israeli Conflict, September 2000–September 2002," International Policy Institute for CounterTerrorism, June 24, 2002. http://www.ict.org.il/index.php?sid=119&lang=en&act=page&id=5305&str=Radlauer.

Radu, M. 2005. "London 7/7 and Its Impact." *Foreign Policy Research Institute* 6, 5: 1–8.

Rapoport, D. 2001. "The Fourth Wave: September 11 in the History of Terrorism." *Current History* (December): 419–424.

Rapoport, M. 2006. "Italian Foreign Minister: Harsh Approach to Mideast Has Failed." *Haaretz*, August 25, p. 1.

Regular, A. 2003. "Hamas: Foreigners Should Leave Country." *Haaretz*, June 13.

———. 2004. "Arafat Calls on Palestinians to 'Terrorize Your Enemy.'" *Haaret*, May 15.

Reinemer, M., and C. Hoene. 2002. "Cities Taking on New Security Roles amid Economic Concerns." *Nation's Cities Weekly* 25, 36 (September 9): 1–2.

Renner, M. 1998. *Environmental and Social Stress Factors, Governance, and Small Arms Availability: The Potential for Conflict in Urban Areas.* Comparative Urban Studies Occasional Series, 15. Washington, DC: Woodrow Wilson International Center for Scholars.

Reuters. October 4, 2004. Editorial Policy.

Richardson, H., and P. Gordon. 1993. "Market Planning: Oxymoron or Common Sense?" *Journal of the American Planning Association* 59 (Summer): 59–77.

Richardson, L. 1998. "Global Rebels." *Harvard International Review* 20: 52.

Rogers, P., H. Bouhia, and J.M. Kalbermatten. 2001. *Water for Big Cities: Big Problems, Easy Solutions?* Comparative Urban Studies Occasional Series, 35. Washington, DC: Woodrow Wilson International Center for Scholars.

Rolnik, R. 1999. *Territorial Exclusion and Violence: The Case of São Paulo, Brazil.* Comparative Urban Studies Occasional Series, 26. Washington, DC: Woodrow Wilson International Center for Scholars.

Rosenberg, M. 1968. *The Logic of Survey Analysis.* New York: Basic Books.

Rubin, B., and J.C. Rubin, eds. 2001. "Al Qaeda Statement, October 10, 2001." In *Anti-American Terrorism and the Middle East.* Oxford: Oxford University Press.

Safian, A. 2003. "Terror Rules at NPR." *CAMERA* (Committee for Accuracy in Middle East Reporting in America). March 10. http://www.camera.org/index.asp?x_context=4&x_outlet=28&x_article=430.

Sageman, M. 2004. *Understanding Terrorist Networks.* Philadelphia: University of Pennsylvania Press.

Sassen, S. 2000. *Cities in a World Economy.* London: Pine Forge Press.

Satterthwaite, D. 2005. "The Underestimation of Urban Poverty in Low and Moderate Income Nations." Working Paper on Poverty Reduction in Urban Areas 14. http://www.iied.org/docs/urban/urbpov_wp14.pdf.

Savitch, H.V. 1998. "Global Challenge and Institutional Capacity: Or How We Can Refit Local Administration for the Next Century." *Administration and Society* 30, 3: 248–273.

———. 1988. *Post Industrial Cities: Politics and Planning in New York, Paris and London.* Princeton, NJ: Princeton University Press.

————. 2003. "Does 9–11 Portend a New Paradigm for Cities?" *Urban Affairs Review* 39, 1: 103–127.

————. 2005. "An Anatomy of Urban Terror: Lessons from Jerusalem and Elsewhere." *Urban Studies* 42, 3: 361–395.

Savitch, H.V. with G. Ardashev. 2001a. "Does Terror Have an Urban Future?" *Urban Studies* 38, 13: 2515–2533.

————. 2001b. *Cities and Security: A Risk Factor Approach*. Comparative Urban Studies Occasional Series, 36. Washington, DC: Woodrow Wilson International Center for Scholars.

Savitch, H.V., and P. Kantor. 2002. *Cities in the International Marketplace*. Princeton, NJ: Princeton University Press.

Savitch, H.V., and Y. Garb. 2006. "Terror, Barriers and the Re-topography of Jerusalem." *Journal of Planning Education and Research* (Winter).

Schwabish, J., and J. Chang. 2004. "New York City and Terorism Insurance in a Post 9/11 World." *Issue Brief.* Partnership for New York City. September.

Schwartz, J. 2005. "Cameras in Britain Record the Criminal and the Banal." *New York Times*, July 23, p. A8.

Schemann, S. 2001. "Day of Terror." *New York Times*, September 12, p. 1.

Schlenger, W.E., J. Caddell, L. Ebert, B.K. Jordan, K.M. Rourke, D. Wilson, L. Thalji, J.M. Dennis, J.A. Fairbank, R.A. Kulka. 2002. "Psychological Reactions to Terrorist Attacks: Findings from the National Study of Americans' Reactions to September 11." *Journal of American Medical Association* 288, 5: 586.

Schmidt, A., and A. Jongman. 1988. *Political Terrorism*. New Brunswick, NJ: Transaction Books.

Schneider, K. 2001. "Sprawl Not an Antidote to Terror." *Elm Street Writers Group*. Michigan Land Institute. December.

Seattle Times. 2004. Editorial. November 22.

Sheffer, G. 2003. *Diaspora Politics: At Home and Abroad*. Cambridge, UK: Cambridge University Press.

Sheleg, Y. 2001. "A Short History of Terror." *Haaretz*, December 3.

Shetreet, U. 2004. Interview by author. May 26.

Short, J.R. 2004. *Global Metropolitan: Globalizing Cities in a Capitalist World*. London: Routledge.

Shuster, M. 2003. *Talk of the Nation*. National Public Radio. May 19.

Siegel, F. 2005. *Prince of the City*. San Francisco: Encounter Books.

Sprinzak, E. 2000. "Rational Fanatics." *Foreign Policy* 120 (September/October): 66–73.

Stern, J. 1999. *The Ultimate Terrorist*. Cambridge, MA: Harvard University Press.

————. 2003. "The Protean Enemy." *Foreign Affairs* 82, 4: 27–40.

Stren, R. 1998. *Urban Research in the Developing World: From Governance to Security*. Comparative Urban Studies Occasional Series, 16. Washington, DC: Woodrow Wilson International Center for Scholars.

Surveillance Studies Network. 2006. *A Report on the Surveillance Society*, ed. David M. Wood. London.

Susskind, R. 2006. *The One Percent Doctrine*. New York: Simon and Schuster.

Swanstrom, T. 2002. "Are Fear and Urbanism at War?" *Urban Affairs Review* 38, 1: 135–140.

Taffe, P., and T. Mulhearn. 1988. *Liverpool—A City That Dared to Fight London*. London: Fortress Press.

Taylor, P.T. 2004. *World City Network: A Global Urban Analysis*. London: Routledge.

Tilly, C. 2002. "Violence, Terror and Politics as Usual." *Boston Review* 27, 3–4 (Summer).

Topfer, E. 2002. "The Rise of CCTV and the Transformation of Violent Conflict." Presented at the conference on "Cities as Strategic Site: Militarisation, Anti-Globalisation, Warfare," Manchester, UK. November 6–9.

Tu, A. 2002. *Chemical Terrorism: Horrors in Tokyo Subway and Matsumo to City.* Fort Collins, CO: Alaken.

Tubeprune. London Underground Statistics. http://www.trainweb.org/tuberprune /Statistics.htm.

Tucker, D. 2001. "What Is New About the New Terrorism and How Dangerous Is It?" *Terrorism and Political Violence* 13, 3 (Autumn): 1–14.

Tumelty, P. 2005. "An In-Depth Look at the London Bombers." *Terrorism Monitor* (July 28), 3:15. Washington, DC: The Jamestown Foundation.

Turk, A.T. 1982. "Social Dynamics of Terrorism." *Annals of the American Academy of Political and Social Science* 463: 119–128.

UN-Habitat. 2003. *The Challenge of Slums: Global Report on Human Settlement.* http://www.unhabitat.org/.

United Nations. 2003. *World Urbanization Prospect.* New York: United Nations Department of Economic and Social Affairs/Population Division.

USA Today. 2005. "On Security, Public Draws Blurred Lines." August 3. http: //www.usatoday.com/news/nation/2005–08–03-security-lines-public-opinion_ x.htm?csp=N009.

———. 2005. "CNN/*USA Today*/Gallup Poll: Percentage of People Worried by Greater Chances of Attack before and after July 7, 2005 Attacks." July 12. http: //www.usatoday.com/news/washington/2005–07–11-bush-poll.htm.

U.S. Department of Defense, n.d. http://www.usip.org/class/guides/terrorism.pdf.

U.S. Department of Homeland Security. 2006. *FY 2006 Urban Area Security Initiative (UASI) by Urban Areas.* Washington, DC.

U.S. Department of Justice. n.d. *The Al Qaeda Training Manual.* http://www.usdoj. gov/ag/trainingmanual.htm.

———. 2003. *Supplemental Report on September 11 Detainee's Allegations of Abuse at the Metropolitan Detention Center in Brooklyn, New York* (December). http: //www.usdoj.gov/oig/special/0312/chapter1.htm.

U.S. Department of Labor. Bureau of Labor Statistics. 2006. *Current Employment Survey.* Washington, DC.

U.S. Department of State. 1990. *Patterns of Global Terrorism 1990.* Washington, DC: U.S. Government Printing Office. http://www.state.gov/s/ct/rls/pgtrpt/.

———. 2002. *Patterns of Global Terrorism 1993–2001.* Released by the Office of the Coordinator for Counterterrorism 1994–2002, Washington, DC.

———. n.d. *U.S. CODE.* Title 22, Section 2656 (f).

U.S. Federal Emergency Management Agency. 2002. *World Trade Center Building Performance Study: Data Collection, Preliminary Observations, and Recommendations.* Washington, DC: Federal Insurance and Mitigation Administration.

U.S. German Marshall Fund. 2006. *Transatlantic Trends: Key Findings.* Prepared by the German Marshall Fund, Washington, DC.

U.S. House of Representatives. 2002. Committee on Finance. *Fund Raising Methods and Procedures for International Terrorist Organizations: Hearing before the Subcommittee on Oversight and Investigations*, February 12.

———. 2006. Committee on Homeland Security. "DHS Terrorism Preparedness Grants: Risk-Based or Guess Work?" Hearing before the Committee on Homeland Security, June 21.

U.S. National Capital Planning Commission. 2001. *Designing for Security in the Nation's Capital*. Washington, DC. October.

U.S. Senate. 2002. Committee on Finance. *The International Dimension of Combating the Financing of Terrorism: Hearing before the Committee on Finance*. October 9.

———. 2006. Committee on Homeland Security. *Statement for the Record: Hearing before the Committee on Homeland Security*. June 21.

Vale, L., and T. Campanella, eds. 2005. *The Resilient City: How Modern Cities Recover from Disaster*. New York: Oxford University Press.

Valyev, A. 2007. *The Evolution of Urban Terror: Changing Tactics, Strategy and Targets*. Unpublished Ph.D. dissertation, University of Louisville.

Van de Wetering, A. 2000. "Enclosed Neighborhoods in Perspective." Bachelor's paper, University of Pretoria.

Veness, D. 1989. "Low Intensity and High Impact Conflict." *Terrorism and Political Violence* 11, 4: 8–14.

Vidino, L. 2005. "Is Italy Next in Line after London?" *Terrorist Monitor* (September 21) 3:18. Washington, DC: The Jamestown Foundation.

Visit London Corporate (VLC). 2005. *London Monthly Trends, Monthly Visitor Index*. London: Visit London Corporate.

Voronin, Y. 1998. *Organized Crime: Its Influence on International Security and Urban Community Life in the Industrial Cities of the Urals*. Comparative Urban Studies Occasional Series, 17. Washington, DC: Woodrow Wilson International Center for Scholars.

Washington Post. 2004. Editorial. September 1.

Weber, M. 1947. *Theory of Economics and Social Organizations*, ed. Talcott Parsons. New York: Oxford University Press.

———. 1963. "Order in Diversity: Community without Propinquity." In *Cities and Space: The Future*, ed. Lowdon Wingo, Jr. Baltimore, MD: Johns Hopkins University Press.

Wedgewood, C.V. 1961. *The Thirty Years War*. Garden City, NY: Doubleday.

Weingarten, G. 2004. "Fear Itself." *The Washington Post Magazine*, August 22, p. W 18.

Weisman, S., and J. Brinkley. 2005. "Rice Urges Israel and Palestinians to Sustain Momentum." *New York Times*, August 18, A8.

West, D., and M. Orr. 2005. "Managing Citizen Fears: Public Attitudes toward Terrorism." *Urban Affairs Review* 41, 1: 93–105.

Wilheim, J. 1999. *Overcoming the Trauma of Transition: Trends and Changes on the Threshold of the 21st Century*. Comparative Urban Studies Occasional Series, 23. Washington, DC: Woodrow Wilson International Center for Scholars.

Williams, K.S., C. Johnstone, and M. Goodwin. 2000. "CCTV Surveillance in Urban Britain: Beyond the Rhetoric of Crime Reduction." In *Landscapes of Defense*, ed. J.R. Gold and G. Revill. Upper Saddle River, NJ: Prentice Hall.

Wirth, L. 1938. "Urbanism as a Way of Life." *American Journal of Sociology* 44, 1–24.

Wolfe, T. 1998. *You Can't Go Home Again.* 1st ed. New York: Harper Perennial Classic.

Wood, D., E. Kronvitz, and K. Ball. 2003. "The Constant State of Emergency? Surveillance after 9/11." In *The Intensification of Surveillance*, ed. Kirstie Ball and Frank Webster. Sterling, VA: Pluto Press.

Wu, F. 2003. "Globalization, Place Promotion and Urban Development in Shanghai." *Journal of Urban Affairs* 25, 1: 55–78.

Yacoob, M., and M. Kelly. 1999. *Secondary Cities in West Africa: The Challenge for Environmental Health and Prevention.* Comparative Urban Studies Occasional Series, 21. Washington, DC: Woodrow Wilson International Center for Scholars.

Yehuda, R. 2002. "Current Concepts: Post-Traumatic Stress Disorder." *New England Journal of Medicine* 346, 2: 108–114.

Index

About the Author

H.V. Savitch is the Brown and Williamson Distinguished Research Professor at the University of Louisville. He has published ten books and monographs. His co-authored work with Paul Kantor, *Cities in the International Marketplace*, was named Best Book in the urban field by the American Political Science Association. Professor Savitch has authored more than seventy scholarly articles and has received numerous awards for teaching and scholarship. He has been a Fulbright Scholar (France), a Lady Davis Fellow (Israel), and is a former president of the Urban Politics Section, American Political Science Association. He also served as a consultant to former mayor of New York City David Dinkins, the U.S. Department of Housing and Urban Development, the Mayors' Urban Summit, and the Organization for Economic Cooperation and Development.